Under
REVIEW

Marla Matrice Murphy

FIRST EDITION

ISBNs:
Paperback: 979-8-9936157-9-0
Hardcover: 979-8-9936157-0-7
Deluxe Case Laminate Edition: 979-8-9936157-8-3
eBook: 979-8-9936157-7-6

Trigger Warning

This book contains depictions of abuse, domestic violence, mental health crises, loss, and other situations that may be distressing or triggering for some readers. Please take care while reading.

If you have experienced or are currently experiencing abuse or violence, consider reaching out for help or support. In the United States, you can contact **the National Domestic Violence Hotline at 1-800-799-SAFE (7233)** or visit **www.thehotline.org** for confidential, 24-hour assistance.

Your well-being matters. Read at your own pace, and take breaks if you need to.

To my little heathens,

who kept me going.

To my therapist,

who kept me grounded.

And to Ms. Felicia,

who kept me covered in the word of God.

And to everyone else who came into my life,

whether for a season, to keep me believin',

through moments of grievin', to push me toward achievin',

or ended up deceivin',

whatever the reason,

thank y'all too.

CHAPTER 1

Through Her Eyes

"We don't see things as they are, we see them as we are."

— Anaïs Nin

Do you remember that 8 Mile rap battle, where Em was talking about Clarence's parents having a real good marriage? Well, that was her. Her parents had a real good marriage.

With seven kids, the house ran on more than noise. Respect wasn't a choice, it was a rule. Loyalty wasn't spoken, it was lived. And love held it all together, their foundation solid as stone.

But even stone can crack when the right pressure hits.

Or when the right man does.

For her, that man was Howard.

The first time she saw him, he was posted at the jukebox in the Blue Light Tavern. His parents owned the place, but the way he carried himself made it feel like it all belonged to him. Laughter softened, voices dropped, and the air itself seemed to pause around him.

Howard wasn't a tall man, but height didn't matter. He had a presence that was impossible to ignore. His skin the color of chocolate, his afro worn like the crown of a king. His suit sharp enough to draw blood and his smile burned so bright you needed sunglasses just to look his way.

When he walked into a room, eyes followed him, as if he carried gravity itself.

This wasn't just any man. He was the man. Trouble wrapped in charm.

Aunt Loretta still speaks of him with a kind of reverence, as if his name alone deserves respect. "Smooth like butter, swift as silk," she would say, dragging the words out with a grin, certain that no one else would ever measure up. The way she remembered him, you'd think she was a little smitten, maybe even spellbound herself.

But her? She never stood a chance. Even now, her face softens when she talks about him. Her eyes glow, her smile widens, and without fail, she repeats the same line she has said all my life.

"The finest man in Racine, Wisconsin." A title that, in her eyes, would always belong to him.

It's in those moments her mind drifts back. She can still see the way he drove hours to see her at her college dorm, his Cadillac gleaming, his suit pressed, his confidence so large it made the world stop and notice.

She was a single mother, juggling textbooks and car seats, and suddenly here was this man, larger than life, making her feel as if out of everyone in the world, she was the one he had chosen.

It wasn't just him who made her feel that way. His family did too. She laughed through meals with his parents. She spent afternoons with his sisters.

They shared the kind of closeness that made it seem she had always been part of their world. She felt safe. She felt seen. She felt loved.

But not Howard. Not his sisters. Not even his parents told her the truth.

And to understand mine, we have to first walk through hers.

My mother's.

CHAPTER 2

Everything but the Truth

"The cruelest lies are often told in silence."

— Robert Louis Stevenson

Once my mother found out Howard had a wife. Kids. A whole life she knew nothing about, it didn't just hit her. It knocked the bejeesus out of her. She was devastated. She didn't know who she was, what day it was, what time it was, or even where she was.

She had given him everything. Her trust. Her love. Her time. Every piece of herself she could spare.

It was more than heartbreak.

It was betrayal.

Humiliation.

Rage.

All of it crashed into her at once. A lie so carefully crafted, she couldn't even tell if there'd been any truth at all.

She questioned everything. Every whispered promise. Every night she spent believing she was his. Every look that made her feel like she was the center of his world.

But Howard didn't let those questions linger for long. He had explanations ready, words sweet enough to make betrayal sound like devotion. Reducing his wife and kids to nothing more than a technicality.

He pressed back in with visits, calls, and the right words at the right time, telling her she was the one who mattered. What they had was different, that nothing and no one else compared. He softened her anger with charm, blurred her doubts with so many promises, that the questions that once haunted her felt like they never mattered at all.

And against every brutal fact, against all reason, she clung to the belief that it had been real. That she was more than a stolen moment in his story. Not just a measly chapter to be skimmed. She was the book itself.

Plus, belief wasn't the only thing she carried. She carried his child. She told herself what they had was worth fighting for. She swallowed the hurt, pushed down the doubt, and they fought. He fought for her, she fought for them, and together they fought for their baby.

Slowly, the laughter returned. Phone calls started lasting so long she drifted off to sleep with the phone still against her cheek. He showed up with tenderness, with love, with the kind of gestures that made her remember why she had fallen in love in the first place.

The day their daughter Melody was born, the room filled with euphoria. Joy surged through every breath, every heartbeat, spilling out in laughter and tears. It was the kind of happiness that made the world outside disappear, leaving only her, him, and the tiny life they had brought into it.

In that moment, she hadn't just given Howard another child. She had given him something no one else had. A daughter. His only girl.

The complex was pristine. Well-kept lawns. Regular spraying for pests. Spotless hallways. Fresh paint on the walls. Management took pride in every detail, and she let herself believe in that perfection too. It was proof that dreams could come true.

That dream included her other children, Maverick and Makayla. Their laughter filled the home. But Melody was different. She was Howard's daughter. His joy. His treasure. His Everything.

She was different to my mom too. While Melody was Howard's pride, to my mom she was proof. Proof that the love she held onto had been worth it. Proof that she was going to have everything she had dreamed of. Proof that it was all going to work.

After all, Howard did his part. Even while splitting his time between two families, he made sure they felt his presence. He took care of her, of Maverick, of Makayla, of his Melody. More importantly, he provided love.

But no amount of love, no matter how strong, could protect her.

Not from what came next.

Marla Matrice Murphy

CHAPTER 3

Something in the Air

"What's invisible to you is often the most dangerous."

— Joyce Carol Oates

Melody was tiny, but her laugh could fill the whole apartment. She was curious, playful, always reaching for her brother. No one could have guessed that something as simple as the air around her would turn against her.

It began with a cough. Just a small one at first, the kind you almost ignore. A cold, maybe. Something that would pass.

But soon my mom was trying warm baths, medicine, sleepless nights holding her close, whispering promises that she would be okay.

It didn't pass. The cough only grew worse, rattling through her tiny lungs until every breath sounded like a struggle.
One night, scared and desperate, she rushed Melody to the hospital.

The doctors tried. They gave her treatments, tested different options, but nothing worked. Finally, they said there was only one way to help her breathe. A small opening in her throat.

A trach, they called it. Terrifying, but they explained it would keep her airway open. With it, she could breathe safely, and they could clear her lungs when she couldn't do it on her own. They promised it was temporary. Just until her body was stronger. Just until she could handle it herself.

The surgery was done, and for the first time in days Melody could breathe without the rattle. Relief came, but it was tangled with fear.

The tube in her throat was foreign, frightening. My mother had to learn everything from the start. How to comfort her. How to speak to her. How to hide her own tears so Melody would only see strength.

And somehow, she did.

My mother poured her heart into being there for Melody, learning sign language so they could still communicate. She'd sit for hours, fingers moving gently as she signed, watching her daughter's eyes light up with understanding. Howard came after work, his face lined with the exhaustion of a man stretched between two worlds, but he was there.

Eventually, Melody was stable enough to go home. The trach went with her, and so did the nurses, rotating in and out of the apartment to help. But my mother did most of it herself. She learned how to clean the tube, how to suction it, how to respond when something seemed wrong. It was terrifying, but it was also progress.

They were on the road to recovery.

They were home.

Life slowly started to feel normal again. The apartment felt alive again. Not like before, but better than the hospital. There was sound again. Laughter. Music. Hope. Melody.

Even after the hospital stay, the surgeries, the trach, Melody was still Maverick's playful little sister. She learned how to laugh around it, how to babble and squeal with excitement even when her voice came out softer than before. The trach didn't take away her spirit.

She still stood up waiting for him.
She still reached for him.

She was still his Melody.

One morning, like always, Maverick went in to wake her up. It was their routine. His little sister was his built-in best friend, always ready for him, to climb into his lap, to laugh at whatever silly game he had planned.

But that morning, something was wrong.

She wasn't standing up in her crib waiting for him. She wasn't standing at all.

He called her name. Reached out and nudged her. Gave her a gentle shake.

Nothing.

The playfulness in him vanished. He tried again, his voice louder, his small hands desperate, pressing against her arms, her cheeks.

But Melody didn't move. She didn't giggle. Didn't light up the way she always did when she saw him. Didn't reach for him, ready to play.

She was still.

Maverick screamed, bringing my mother running, her confusion giving way to horror the moment she saw.

Her baby.

Lying there.

Lifeless.

Gone.

Stolen by something invisible.

Something in the air.

A "safe" spray meant to kill pest.

Not their Melody.

CHAPTER 4

Man Down

"The past is never gone. It's not even past."

— William Faulkner

Howard was present. Gentle in his own quiet way. He wasn't the kind of man who spoke his love, he showed it. When he was there, he held Melody like she was the most fragile thing in the world, because to him, she was.

He learned to care for her like a nurse would. When he could, he cleaned her trach, managed her feedings, and poured himself into her care. Even after long shifts, he came home and showed up.

That version of him did not survive her.

He tried to forget, but the empty room where Melody once slept refused to let him.

The crib still stood against the wall, waiting for a child who would never climb back in. The toys sat frozen in place. He still sank into the chair where he used to rock her to sleep. In that stillness he swore he could hear her. A laugh. A squeal. A soft cry.

Forgetting was impossible.

So he did the next best thing. He worked. He would leave before dawn and come home long after dark, if he came home at all. It was the only thing that made sense. Keep moving. Keep doing. Anything to avoid sitting alone with his thoughts.

He was carrying more than he should have, both on the job and in his mind, and something gave. Maybe he got distracted. Maybe he was careless. Maybe the weight of everything he had been holding just became too much. Whatever it was, in that moment, he pushed his body past its limit. He lifted wrong, his back tearing under the pressure. Pain shot through him so suddenly it dropped him to his knees.

He landed in the hospital, excruciating pain keeping him down, his once-powerful body nothing but a distant memory.

Even his father looked shaken as he stood beside the hospital bed, staring at his son's face, tight with pain. He could not bear to see him suffer like that. So he did what, in that moment, felt like mercy.

He brought him something stronger.
Not a prescription.
Not a doctor's order.
Just something to make the pain stop.

Cocaine.

He delivered the shot into his son's arm, hoping it would be enough to take the pain away, even for a little bit.

The moment the needle emptied, it was a flood of relief. The pain faded. The grief dulled. The memories softened at the edges. It all slipped away in that single, euphoric moment, replaced by a feeling he hadn't known he needed so badly. For the first time since Melody passed, Howard felt peace. He could close his eyes and let his body relax.

But that peace came with a price. That first high was not just relief. It was an invitation. A way out of pain he didn't realize he would come to depend on. What started as survival became habit, and soon habit became the only road he knew.

The drugs changed him. The man who once worked hard and cared for his family slowly disappeared. In his place was someone angry, lost, unpredictable, abusive, and impossible to live with.

My mother, already broken from her own loss, was left to live through his unraveling on top of her own.

Maybe she stayed because it felt easier than leaving. Maybe she believed things could go back to how they once were. Or maybe she just didn't have the strength to start over with a heart that hadn't finished breaking. Grief has a way of keeping people stuck in places they never thought they'd stay.

Plus, while Howard was collapsing inside himself, she was pregnant with me. I don't know what it felt like to carry one child while mourning another. But I do know that by the time I came into the world, three months early and barely hanging on, whatever love lived between them had passed with my sister.

CHAPTER 5

A Mother's Love

"To feel that you aren't important to your mother leaves a hole. Most often it is felt as a hole in the heart. It's the hole where Mother was supposed to be."

— Jasmin Lee Cori

I don't remember birthday parties or bedtime stories or anyone caring for my scraped knees. No warmth. Just darkness. And the few memories I do have are ones I've spent my whole life wishing away.

The first begins with me trapped in a closet, forced to endure what no child should. My sister was downstairs the whole time, but she never came.

The other ends with me bleeding on the pavement, alone with a bicycle.

I was five. Howard had been teaching me to ride a bright orange bike. That day felt like everything. I remember the rush. The pedals pressed beneath my feet. The wind stung my face. The world blurred around me as I pushed forward, trying to stay upright.

He sent me around the block, and I don't know what I expected. Maybe that he would be there if I fell. Maybe he would come running, cheering, proud.

But when I fell off, he wasn't there. No outstretched hand. No familiar voice calling my name. Just me, sprawled on the concrete, skin burning, chest tight with shallow breaths.

I picked myself up and walked the bike home, sobbing with every step. And when I got there, he wasn't outside waiting. He hadn't been watching.

He was gone.

Maybe that's why the rest is a blur. Because the memories I do have are ones I wish I didn't. Just like I wish I didn't remember growing up without her love.

My own mother. She didn't look at me the way other mothers looked at their children. She looked at me like something she was stuck with.

In her eyes, I was the problem child. Reckless. Disruptive. Defiant. Always talking back. Always getting on her nerves. I was the one who embarrassed her. The one who ruined everything. The one she wanted to shut up and sit down. The one she wished would disappear.

She never even tried to hide it. She'd mutter about me while I was in the room, calling me difficult, stupid, worthless. Like everything about me was wrong.

And maybe I could have lived with all of that. If I hadn't seen what she was capable of.

She knew how to be a good mother. I watched her do it.

Not just to Maverick and Makayla, but to her foster kids. She treated them like they were everything she wanted me to be. She smiled at them. Took pictures. Posted them on the fridge. Bragged about their grades and their talents like they were her own.

She gave them warmth. Patience. Praise. Love.

Strangers' children got the mother I used to dream would show up for me.

Then she had the audacity to act surprised when I started acting out. To this day, she tells people I was crazy. She says I used to draw pictures of tombstones with "RIP" written on them for her and my siblings.

I did.

I was a child abused in every sense of the word. Sexually. Emotionally. Physically. Mentally.

She called me names. Mocked the way I dressed. Criticized everything I did. She hit me when I cried and ignored me when I didn't. She told stories about me to anyone who would listen. She told me I was nothing and made sure I believed it.

And when I started to act like it, she turned my response into her reasoning and my despair into their diagnosis.

She went looking for professionals to back her up. One doctor's visit at a time. One story at a time. And each time we went, the story changed. With every appointment, my life was under review, reshaped to match whatever version of me she needed them to see. Talking under my breath became talking to myself. Talking to myself became talking to people who weren't there. Then it became seeing people no one else could see and hearing voices no one else could hear.

I was dangerous. A threat. A problem she couldn't handle. But she never mentioned the part where I was reacting to the way she antagonized me. Never talked about the jewelry boxes she threw at my head, the belts and extension cords she beat me with, the threats, the humiliation, the coldness. She left out me being told I would never be anything. Being wished dead.

In front of the doctors, she was calm. Measured. Concerned. The mother doing everything she could for her disturbed, troubled child.

By the time she was done dragging me to appointment after appointment, I probably had every diagnosis in the book. Bipolar. Schizophrenic. Mood disorder with transient psychotic symptoms. The labels shifted with whatever story she decided to tell. And once she said it, that became the truth I had to live with.

She turned normal reactions to abuse into clinical symptoms. And when she wanted me gone, all she had to do was pick up the phone and say I was having a psychotic break. That I needed to be hospitalized.

If I argued back, that was a psychotic break. If I cried too loud, that was a psychotic break. If I tried to defend myself, a hospitalization was coming.

In those institutions, they didn't see me. They saw her version of me. They nodded, took notes, adjusted my "treatment plan," and pumped me with so much medication I started to feel numb.

After a while, it got hard to tell what was real and what wasn't.

By the time she was done spinning her stories, I was labeled a danger to myself and everyone around me. I was Homicidal. Suicidal. That I'd tried to hang myself. That I shoved a knife down my throat.

A knife.

Even as a kid, I knew how ridiculous that sounded.

But no one ever questioned it. No one asked what she did after I supposedly jammed a knife down my throat.

Did she take me to the ER? Did anyone check to see if my throat was torn or bruised?
No one asked. No one checked.

They just nodded, took their notes, and kept writing prescriptions like every word she said was gospel.

18

And of course it was to them.

She wasn't just some concerned parent. She was one of them. A family therapist. A foster mother. Someone who had built a whole career around helping children.

Why would they question her when she said her own daughter was disturbed?

It took me years to understand the truth.

That I wasn't the one who needed help.

She was.

She fabricated, manipulated, isolated, tormented, humiliated, and violated.

All for attention and sympathy, for people to believe the struggle was harder than it really was, and to admire the strength it supposedly took to survive it.

Even though it meant destroying her own child.

I later learned there's a name for that kind of cruelty.

Munchausen by proxy.

CHAPTER 6

A Walk in the Dark

"A lion is not afraid of walking alone, even if the whole jungle is pursuing it."

— Matshona Dhliwayo

I stopped trying to tell them I was fine. It didn't matter. No one was listening anyway.

The hospital had become a strange kind of refuge. Not because it was good, but because it was better than home. There were rules. Structure. People who checked in. People who listened. They treated me like I mattered. They didn't know what was real and what wasn't, but they tried. That was more than I'd ever had before. I didn't have to prove anything to survive. I just had to be there. After a while, I started acting out just to get sent back. Because, as backwards as it sounds, I felt more normal in there than I ever did at home.

And when she didn't feel like bothering with the hospital, she found another solution to get rid of me. She threw me out.

I was about ten the first time she kicked me out the house. No shoes. No coat. No place to go. Just out. I wandered the neighborhood, feeling every crack in the pavement under my feet.

Eventually, I made my way to Aunt Viv's. She was my mother's closest sister, and the only person I could think to turn to. I didn't know what she'd believe, but I hoped she'd at least let me stay for the night.

She opened the door, looked me over, and let me inside. I told her what had just happened. My voice shook as I tried to explain what it was like at home, she didn't say much. Just listened. Nodded. Her face stayed neutral, like she was trying to work it all out in her head.

At one point, she asked me to sit on the porch. "Hold still," she said, gathering her sketch pad and pencil. Aunt Viv was an artist. She painted and drew portraits. That day, she drew mine. I sat there in silence while she studied my face, pausing only to shift the angle of the page or wipe her hand.

She didn't say it, but I think that was her way of showing me something. That I mattered. That I was worth seeing. No one had ever taken the time to look at me like that before. Not to scold me. Not to accuse me. Just to look. Just to capture who I was.

For a moment, I thought maybe it meant something. Maybe she'd let me stay. Maybe someone finally saw me and wouldn't let me go back to where I had just escaped from.

But as the sun started to set, she told me it was time for me to go. She said it gently, like she thought my mother would never actually leave me out overnight. Like this was just a misunderstanding. A family thing that would blow over by morning. She didn't understand. Or maybe she did and just couldn't bring herself to intervene.

I begged her. I stood in her doorway, hoping that something in her would change. That something in me would be enough.

But it wasn't. And I walked away, barefoot.

I started heading toward Emma's house, hoping her family would take me in for the night. Emma was a classmate that lived right across the street from us. We went to the same elementary school. On mornings I missed the bus, her family would give me a ride to school without a second thought.

I believed that maybe this time, someone would care enough to keep me safe. I thought about the mornings Emma's family had taken me to school, how they'd show me these little kindnesses that felt like more than just rides. They felt like glimpses of a different kind of life. A better one. Even though I could barely stand to put weight on my bare feet, I was sure that if I could just make it to their door, everything would be okay.

But to get to Emma's, I had to pass the gas station at the corner. The kind of place that never felt safe. The overhead lights flickered, barely cutting through the dark. The air was thick with the smell of gasoline, cigarettes, and urine. Men lingered outside, hands in their pockets, their movements slow and deliberate. They exchanged quiet words and quick glances.

I kept my head down, heart pounding, hoping to pass unnoticed. But as I stood at the intersection, waiting for the light to change, a man walked up to me.

His voice cut through the hum of passing cars.

"Hey, little lady, why you out here with no shoes on?" he asked, his voice gentle, as if he was talking to a friend. "Where you headed?"

I looked at him. He was older, with a grin that didn't reach his eyes, but something about the way he spoke made me feel like he wanted to help. I didn't know any better; I was just ten, spilling my story to a stranger, trusting that he'd understand. He nodded, listening with a look of concern that seemed real, even comforting.

"They call me Cat Daddy," he said, like it was a name that held some kind of power. His gaze drifted over my dirty shirt, probably still sticky from the popsicle I'd had earlier at Aunt Viv's. "Looks like you could use a little freshening up. Come on, I'll help you get cleaned up and changed."

I was too young, too trusting to question his intentions. I followed him, hoping that he'd keep his promise and take me somewhere safe. He led me a few blocks to a beauty salon, a quiet place that seemed almost forgotten. I could feel a chill creeping up my spine as we stepped inside, but I tried to push it down, telling myself he was just helping me.

"Take off those dirty clothes," he said, his voice steady, a command disguised as a suggestion. I didn't know any better; I obeyed, pulling off my shirt, then my pants, until I was standing there, vulnerable and exposed, waiting for him to keep his word.

"Lay down on the table over there," he directed, nodding toward a cold, hard surface at the back of the salon. I climbed onto it, feeling the chill of the metal seep into my skin, making me shiver. I lay there, confused, trying to understand why he'd brought me here, what he was about to do. I was too innocent to know the danger I was in.

He moved closer, positioning himself between my legs, his body pressing down on mine. His face hovered inches above me, his breath warm and heavy in the stillness, filling the air in a way that felt thick, almost suffocating. I didn't know what he was doing, didn't understand the way his hands lingered on my body, touching places that felt wrong.

All I knew was that I was scared, my heart pounding so loud it echoed in my ears, and I wanted him to stop.

Then he leaned into me, pressing down harder, and I felt something foreign, something hard, trying to push its way into me. I didn't know what it was, only that the pressure was intense, terrifying, and it sent a wave of panic through my entire body. Every part of me wanted it to stop. I wanted to move, to get away, but his weight pressed down on me. I was frozen, paralyzed with fear. My whole body started to shake, trembling uncontrollably, my mind spinning as I tried to make sense of the horror happening to me. I didn't know how to scream. I didn't even know if I could.

All I could do was lie there, my small frame quivering, every nerve screaming for him to stop.

Maybe he saw the terror in my eyes, saw how my body was reacting, or maybe he realized in that moment that he was hurting a child, that he was about to cross a line he couldn't come back from. Whatever it was, it made him pull away, his face a mixture of guilt, shame, or maybe just frustration. Whatever he felt, it kept him from going any further, from doing the unthinkable. From taking the innocence of a little girl. He looked down at me for a long, quiet moment, like he was finally seeing me as a person, not just an object in his hands.

Without a word, he helped me back into my clothes, his touch strangely careful now, as though he was trying to erase the horror of what he had just tried to do. He led me out of the salon, guiding me through the darkness and sent me back toward Emma's house, alone.

When I finally reached Emma's, I was numb, too stunned to grasp the violation I had just escaped. I stood on her doorstep, hoping someone would let me in, my mind trying to block out the memory, pushing it down deep where I wouldn't have to face it. Emma's family took me in without question, offering me a bed to sleep in and a brief moment of peace. For a few days, I stayed there, surrounded by a kindness that felt foreign and almost too good to be true. I clung to the small comforts of their home: the warmth, the laughter, the sense of safety that seemed to wrap around me.

It felt like maybe I could disappear into their world and leave mine behind.

But it didn't last. My mom needed to cover her tracks. If anyone questioned her, she needed to show she had taken action.
When the police showed up at Emma's, the small sense of safety I had clung to dissolved. They said my mother had reported me as a runaway.

But I wasn't a runaway. She had put me out. I was ten years old, with no shoes, no coat, and nowhere to go. She knew exactly where I was.

She just needed to cover herself. Reporting me as a runaway made it look like she cared, like she was doing everything she could to find her "troubled" daughter. But it was never about finding me. It was about controlling the narrative and keeping people from seeing the truth.

Of course, I had no other choice, but to go back. But the moment I stepped through the door I regretted it. She didn't ask if I was okay. She didn't look relieved or even annoyed. She barely looked at me at all. No hug. No questions. No trace of concern in her eyes. It was like I hadn't been gone at all. Like nothing had happened. Like I didn't matter.

And in that quiet, empty silence, I remember wondering if she would have cared if something had happened to me. If I hadn't made it back. If I had simply disappeared. Would she have cared at all?

On paper, she did. In the version she presented to the world, she was the devoted mother struggling to help her broken child. She cared so much about her poor daughter, she filed a CHIPS petition.

She told the court I was unstable, dangerous, in need of protection. She made it sound like she was fighting for me. Child in Need of Protective Services.

But none of it was true.

I wasn't unstable.

I wasn't dangerous.

And I didn't run away.

She put me out. No shoes. No coat. Nowhere to go. It wasn't a choice. I was thrown away.

Now it wasn't just the doctors and hospitals who believed her. The courts bought into her story too.

With the CHIPS petition, she had the legal system on her side. She convinced them I was crazy. That I needed monitoring, treatment, control. And in return, they gave her permission to do whatever she wanted to me and call it help.

If I didn't comply, I would go bye-bye. Locked up. Shipped off. Handed over like property.

The CHIPS petition didn't protect me. It protected her. There was no way out. No one to tell. And no one would've believed me anyway.

While she stood in court pretending to be a struggling, concerned mother, convincing the judge that I needed protective services, my father, Howard, was either in jail or somewhere getting drunk or high. If he hadn't been lost in his addiction, maybe he could have stepped in. Maybe he could have given me the protection I needed.

Protection from her.

CHAPTER 7

Gone with no Goodbye

"They say that abandonment is a wound that never heals. I say only that an abandoned child never forgets."

— Mario Balotelli

It felt like any other car ride. Quiet. Long.

My mom didn't say much, just that we were going to see a new school. I didn't understand why I needed a new school, but I went along with it.

I was twelve, and I still believed in dreams and miracles. Maybe this school would be different. Maybe I'd get to go on field trips like the other kids. Maybe I'd be in school long enough to make a friend instead of being pulled out for another hospital stay.

I stared out the window and held onto that hope with everything I had, thinking maybe this would be the start of something good.

When we arrived, a woman with a polite smile met us at the door. The place looked a little like a school, but not the kind where kids laughed or ran through the corridors. It was too quiet, too structured, too still. Maybe it was for gifted students. The kind of place where silence mattered so it wouldn't mess with their concentration.

I followed behind, studying the rooms and wondering what this place really was. When the tour ended, my mom told me to sit in one of the classrooms to see how I liked it. She said she would be back after talking to the woman.

I watched her leave, expecting her to return any minute. I stayed in my seat, patient and obedient, just like she told me. But the minutes stretched on, then blurred into hours. I started watching the door like a hawk, eyes locked on it every time it opened. Each time, it was someone else. Never her.

My stomach twisted with worry, but I kept lying to myself. She must be coming back. She said she would. She had to.

Eventually, I asked one of the staff where my mom was. The woman looked at me with sympathy and said, "You'll be staying here for a little while."

She wasn't coming back. My mom had packed a suitcase and dropped me off like luggage. Left without a word. Not even a goodbye. I had no idea what this place even was. I was twelve, and had just been abandoned. Again.

Benet Lake looked like a school, but it wasn't. It was where they sent the kids nobody knew what to do with. It was a treatment center.

Not just to the staff, but to everyone. I held everything inside. The hurt. The disbelief. The rage. Where was I going to put it? I'd been left with strangers, abandoned with people I didn't even know. The moment I let it out, they'd see every bit of crazy she had already made me out to be.

So, I kept it in, and silence became the only thing I had left. Silence wasn't new to me. It was armor. I had learned how to disappear in plain sight.

I didn't speak in group, open up in therapy, cry, ask questions, or lash out. I just existed, doing what I was told without a word. I didn't even look anyone in the eye.

I wasn't there to heal or make friends. I was there because I'd been dumped. And since everything I did was under review, I chose to give them nothing.

Some staff gave up quickly. Others hovered, trying to coax me into speaking. They thought I was shy or scared. But I wasn't. I was done.

Everyone assumed my silence meant I had shut down. But I hadn't. I knew exactly what I was doing. I had seen enough to know exactly who I could count on.

No one.

So, I stayed quiet. It was the only thing no one could take from me.

They could lock the doors, control my schedule, decide when I ate, when I slept, but they couldn't force me to speak.

So, I didn't.

And honestly, I wasn't sure I had anything left to say.

Eventually, a counselor named Monee was assigned to me. The other residents warned me about her, saying she was tough, that I should avoid her if I could. But she was my counselor, so staying away wasn't an option. I'd sit across from her, arms crossed, barely looking up, and no matter how hard I tried to ignore her, she never stopped talking.

She would sit there, filling the silence with her voice, telling me over and over that she wasn't going anywhere, that I could trust her. At first, I didn't believe her. I figured she'd give up eventually, that she'd move on and let me sit in silence. But week after week, session after session, month after month she kept showing up and kept talking.

Then one day, something shifted. I don't know what made me speak, but for the first time, I responded. Just a few words. Barely a sentence. But it was the first time I let my voice meet hers.

She didn't act surprised. She just kept talking, like she always had, as if my words were a natural part of the conversation.

Little by little, I opened up. Monee had become my person. The one who never let me down. The one who didn't flinch when I threw my silence at her like a weapon. She absorbed every piece of anger, every ounce of skepticism, and gave me consistency in return. She saw past what I showed and kept choosing to stay.

She made me feel like I could actually trust someone. I had never had that before.

Once, she even took me to get my hair done. I didn't ask for it, didn't hint at it. It was the first time in a long time that I felt like someone cared because they wanted to, not because they were supposed to.

But Benet Lake wasn't built to replace family. It was built to reconnect you to it.

No matter how safe I felt with Monee, the program still required family therapy. Which meant facing my mother. Sitting across from the same woman who had driven me to that building, told me to wait, and never came back.

I didn't want to be in those sessions. I didn't want to sit on that couch and pretend like we had something to work through. As far as I was concerned, there was nothing left to fix.

The therapist would start the sessions with questions. "How are you feeling?" "What would you like to say to your mom today?"

But I had nothing to say. At least, nothing that felt safe to say out loud. I answered in shrugs or silence. I let my mother do the talking, because she was good at it. She knew how to make herself sound like the victim. Like she didn't have a choice. Like this was hard for her too.

Monee told me I didn't have to say anything until I was ready. That just showing up was enough. So that's what I did. I showed up. Sat in that chair. Stared at the floor. Waited for the clock to run out.

After six months, the home visits began.

The staff treated it like a milestone. Progress. Healing. But the minute they told me, my stomach tightened. I tried to act unbothered, told myself I could handle it, but the truth was already bubbling under the surface. The closer it got, the more the anger crept back in. The same anger I had finally learned to put down.

They thought I was nervous. That I was anxious to go home.
But I wasn't anxious. I was bracing for the coldness I knew would be waiting.

That Friday afternoon, my mother pulled up like it was just another day. Like she hadn't dropped me off without a goodbye. I climbed in the car, quiet, tense, trying to hold myself together.

But it didn't take long before we were at it again. The words between us sharp and fast, like old wounds being ripped open. Somewhere along the ride, she jerked the car to the side of the road, told me to get out, and drove off without hesitation.

No pause. No second thought. Just gone.

I stood there, watching the taillights disappear, too stunned to move. Then I walked. For hours. Each step cutting into my skin.

My thighs burned, raw by the time I finally made it back. And when I walked through that door, there was no apology. No acknowledgment. Like it hadn't even happened.

After that, each visit was just another reminder. I didn't belong there. Not in that house. Not in her world. The walls were cold. The air was heavy. And the silence between us louder than anything I'd ever known.

Then, one weekend, I noticed she had a boyfriend.

At first, I didn't pay much attention. I had trained myself not to care about the people in her life. But this one felt different. He introduced himself as Junior, and immediately, I noticed the contrast. He didn't carry her sharpness. He didn't ignore me or pretend I wasn't there. He smiled like it mattered. His laughter came easily and filled the room in a way that felt genuine.

He was big, round in the belly, full of energy and warmth. The kind of man who made people feel at ease just by being around. I couldn't understand what he saw in her, but I liked him. He made jokes, asked me how I was doing, and looked me in the eye when he spoke.

It was strange to feel kindness in that house. Strange to feel visible.

But I knew even his kindness couldn't shield me from her wrath. The warmth he brought felt borrowed. Temporary. And when I went back to Benet Lake, I didn't miss the house. I didn't miss her. I didn't even miss him.

I had Monee.

She was still there, still showing up. Still reminding me that I mattered. I trusted her in a way I hadn't trusted anyone in a long time. Maybe ever.

But that trust didn't last either. I was sitting in my room, brushing my hair, being a bit of a sassy teenager, when she came in with a look I hadn't seen before. It was serious, almost sad, and it stopped me in my tracks. I pretended not to care, but I could tell something was wrong. I looked at her, waiting for her to speak, hoping whatever it was, wouldn't be as bad as it seemed.

She sat down and told me that she had been transferred, that she'd be leaving soon and wouldn't be there anymore.

Her words knocked the air out of me. My chest burned, my throat tightened. I didn't understand. She had promised. She wasn't supposed to be like the others. She told me she wasn't going anywhere. That she would be there for me no matter what.

But now, she was leaving, just like my mother.

I felt betrayed. Lied to. I yelled at her. Called her a liar. Told her I never wanted to see her again. All the trust we'd built, all the safety I had finally started to feel, crumbled right there in that room.

She was just another person who left. Another person who promised and didn't keep it.

From the moment Monee told me she was leaving, something in me hardened. I stopped trying. I still showed up to sessions, followed the rules, and checked all the boxes, but I wasn't really there. Not anymore.

And I stayed like that for months. The closer it got to discharge, the worse it became. My attitude shifted even more. I was short-tempered, restless, always one wrong word away from snapping.

One counselor finally asked, "Do you not want to go home? Is that why you're acting this way?"

I stared at her, thought Duuuuuhhhhh, but didn't bother saying it out loud. What was the point?

I wasn't being sent home because I was healed. I was being discarded. Just like before. I was only being sent home because my insurance was running out.

It wasn't because I was ready. It wasn't because I felt safe.

It was because I was expensive.

Marla Matrice Murphy

CHAPTER 8

Love Beyond Blood

"Family isn't always blood, it's the people in your life who want you in theirs: the ones who accept you for who you are, the ones who would do anything to see you smile and who love you no matter what."

Maya Angelou

Coming home didn't feel like a return. It felt like being dropped back into a house that had no place for me. The walls didn't care. The rooms didn't care. It was colder, quieter, like I had never mattered there at all.

My siblings, Maverick and Makayla, slipped past me in the hall like I was just another shadow in the house. They laughed with her, joked with her, trusted her. I watched them from a distance and wondered if we had grown up in the same home.

Even at school, I felt like a ghost. I stopped going most days. The teachers didn't ask where I'd been. They just moved me to the next grade. My age mattered more than my effort.

When I did show up, they wished I hadn't. I picked fights, skipped class, and shut people out before they ever had the chance to leave me behind.

The only person who didn't leave was Junior. And part of me kept waiting for him to.

He had been there even before I came home, visiting during my time away. But it wasn't until I returned that I started to see him. Not just as my mother's boyfriend, but as someone who kept showing up. Even when the rest of the world didn't.

His own kids didn't like that he was with my mother, but that never stopped him from trying to build something with us. Junior was a mechanic at the Chrysler plant. He worked long shifts and came home covered in sweat and grease, but somehow still found the energy to be present. He paid bills. He brought groceries. And when the house quieted for the night, he sat at the table and asked how my day had been.

No one had ever asked and waited for the answer.

My mother was always physically there, but it never felt like she saw me. She didn't ask questions. She didn't listen. She didn't seem to notice when I disappeared inside myself. But Junior noticed. He didn't push. He didn't pry. He just kept showing up, offering consistency in a world where everything else felt temporary.

I wanted to believe he was different. But I had believed that once before.

Monee had looked at me like I mattered. She gave me her time, her warmth, her trust. And just like that, she was gone. So even as Junior stood steady in my life, I braced for the moment it would fall apart. I held back. Guarded myself. Because love always came with an expiration date.

But Junior didn't leave. Not even when I tried to push him away.

Over time, I stopped questioning why he remembered the small things I said. One night, I called him Daddy. I didn't plan to. The word just slipped out. I froze, waiting for the silence to swallow us. But it didn't. He just smiled, and from that night on, the name stayed.

My mother hated it. She hated our closeness. She didn't come right out and say it, but I felt it in the way she looked at us, like I had stolen something that belonged to her. If Junior paid attention to me, she suddenly had something to say. If he and I laughed, she went quiet.

She wanted me to feel the distance. She wanted him to notice it too. But no matter what, Junior kept showing up.

When the Chrysler plant shut down and he was transferred to Detroit, everything changed. The house felt colder without him walking through the door every night. I missed him, I missed the way he made space for me when no one else did. Even though he still came back on weekends, it wasn't the same.

He still provided. He made sure we were taken care of. Most of his paycheck came right back to the house. Groceries. Bills. Whatever she needed.

My mom didn't deserve that kind of loyalty, considering the circumstances.

Watching it all happen made me sick.

I loved Junior. He was a good man, one of the few people in my life who showed me what love really looked like. He worked hard, sacrificed his time and his money, and even though he didn't have to, he chose to be there for us.

I knew he loved me too, that he cared in ways most didn't, and I couldn't stand the thought of him being betrayed, used like some fool. My mom might have seen him as someone she could take advantage of, a man to fill the space and pay the bills, but to me, he was everything. He was my dad in every way that mattered.

Yet, as much as I wanted to protect him, this decision wasn't easy. My mom was still my mother. Not someone I trusted or felt close to, but still my mother. She didn't like me. She made that clear every chance she got. After everything she had done, I didn't like her much either. Still, a part of me felt disloyal for even thinking about exposing her. It felt like I was crossing some invisible line. I was stuck between betraying my mother and the truth that Junior, my dad, deserved better. I loved him, and in my heart, I knew I couldn't keep quiet.

My turmoil only deepened knowing that Junior's own sister, who lived right across the street, saw what was going on and didn't say a word. She and my mom were friends, and she never even thought to warn him or give him a heads-up. It felt wrong, seeing the people around him keep him in the dark like that, letting him believe a lie while he kept giving us his all.

And my mom, she knew what it felt like to be betrayed. Howard had done the same thing to her, living a double life and leaving her heartbroken. How could she turn around and do the same thing to someone else? She was repeating the cycle, and I could not let Junior stay blind.

I asked him to come back for a surprise visit one weekend. I didn't come right out and say what was happening, but I gave him just enough to make him curious. A quiet suggestion. A shift in my tone. He could tell something wasn't right. I told him not to let her know he was coming and that I'd leave the spare key under the little ceramic duck on the porch. I had hoped that when he got there, he'd see for himself.

I didn't know if he'd actually come. But when he did, everything changed.

The night he came, I woke to noise loud enough to rip me out of my sleep and set my heart pounding. Groggy but alert, I made my way to my mother's doorway to see what was happening. There, right in front of me, was Junior, straddling a man his hands locked around his wrists, both of them fighting for control over something in the man's hand. As I squinted, I realized with horror… it was a gun.

I stood there, frozen, as the struggle intensified. Junior was trying with every bit of strength he had to keep the weapon pointed away, to control it, but in the chaos, it twisted in his grip, the barrel shifting until it was pointed directly at me. His head snapped up then, eyes meeting mine in a flash of raw fear and fierce protectiveness.

40

"Move!" he shouted, his voice laced with desperation. I'd never heard him like that before, his words sharp and urgent, pleading with me to get out of harm's way. I couldn't move, my feet cemented to the spot, heart pounding as he shouted again, even more desperate. His whole focus was on me, his need to shield me greater than concern for himself.

Then, with one final surge of strength, Junior managed to wrench the gun away from the man's grip. He didn't waste a second; he took the gun and left the house, carrying it far from us. I stood there, shaken, trying to process what I'd just seen, feeling a strange mix of relief and guilt settle over me. I wanted him to know the truth, to see things as they really were, but I never imagined it would come to this.

Part of me thought he wouldn't come back. But the next day, he was back, holding my mother as she fake cried. Her tears weren't for what had happened, or the danger we'd narrowly escaped. She was crying over the embarrassment, over what others would say. Her pride and reputation were all that mattered to her.

And there he was, comforting her, standing by her side despite everything, forgiving in a way that I could hardly understand. In that moment, I felt the weight of my decision. I'd wanted to protect him, to open his eyes, but I hadn't realized the price he'd pay. All I'd done was bring pain to the only person who had ever shown me love without condition. He deserved so much better.

Seeing his forgiveness, his willingness to stay even after all that, was mind-boggling to me. It was a kind of love I couldn't fully understand, but it made me want to find it for myself. Something real. Something unshakable.

At first, I didn't know where to look. But then I thought about my mother. Despite everything she had done to me, I still loved her. Somewhere deep down, I believed a child would feel the same about me. That no matter what, they would love me. And I would love them. A child wouldn't leave. A child would give me the bond I had never felt. The kind of love that didn't walk away. The kind of love Junior gave my mother. The kind I had always longed for.

CHAPTER 9

She Was My Answer

"Before you were conceived, I wanted you. Before you were born, I loved you."
— Maureen Hawkins

During those early months, I felt a joy I had never known before. Most mornings, I woke up smiling, excited for the day. I had just turned fourteen when I found out I was going to have a baby. It was a dream come true. I sang to my baby, making up lullabies as I went. I talked to my belly, telling them everything I hoped for us. I shared dreams I had never dared to say out loud. I was so happy, I'd dance around the room. My body wasn't just mine anymore. It was a safe place. A home.

And for once, someone would belong to me.

Someone I would never walk away from. Never throw out into the cold at ten years old without so much as a pair of shoes. I would protect my baby the way I should have been protected.

Even my mom seemed to soften. It was like we had reached a truce, a mutual understanding. She'd come with me to doctor's appointments, watching the baby's growth alongside me, and every so often, she'd hand me her credit card, saying, "Get something nice for the baby."

Tiana and Candi had been my closest friends since ninth grade, people I never had to pretend with. When I wanted company for baby shopping, they were the ones I called. We turned the baby aisles into our own little world, choosing pastel onesies, soft blankets, tiny socks, and board books with bright pictures. One day we found the perfect snowsuit, thick and soft, just right for the cold months ahead.

Tiana helped me tuck everything away neatly in the drawers we'd cleared out. The tiny clothes, the blankets, the baby wash. I'd open them sometimes just to feel the fabric in my hands, to remind myself that she was almost here.

The night before my daughter was born, I went out looking for the perfect birthday gift for my mother. November 20. We had been getting along better than we had in a long time, and I wanted to get her something that showed I noticed, that I cared.

Blue was her favorite color, and she had a soft spot for knickknacks, the kind that didn't really do anything but made a space feel like home. I wandered the aisles slowly, picking things up and turning them over in my hands, trying to imagine what would make her smile.

I finally settled on a blue and yellow porcelain doll, something I hoped she'd keep on her dresser. The next morning, before heading out for school, I placed the wrapped box on her bed. She usually went to a bingo bash on her birthday, and I didn't want her to miss it. I left it there quietly, no note, just a small gift from her daughter. Then I walked out the door and headed to school.

I didn't even make it through second period before I knew something was wrong.

It started as a dull ache that slowly spread through my belly, pressing against me from the inside. At first, I tried to ignore it. I didn't want to make a scene or get sent to the nurse over something small. But the ache didn't go away. It stretched and wrapped around my sides until it was all I could focus on. A student noticed I wasn't okay and got the teacher. She didn't panic. She just quietly walked me home, her arm on my back, like she somehow understood this wasn't ordinary.

We only lived a few doors down from the school, but the walk felt endless. My legs were heavy, my thoughts scattered. By the time I reached the house, my whole body was tight with pain, and deep down, I knew this was it. My baby was coming. I had waited for this moment. I'd pictured it in my head more times than I could count. But now that it was here, I was scared.

Once at the hospital, the nurses moved quickly. Paperwork. Questions. Monitors strapped to my belly. I kept asking if the baby was okay. They said she was. That everything looked good. That she'd be here soon.

I remember the firm grip of Aunt Loretta's hand. She stood by me, her eyes steady. Her warmth gave me strength. Aunt Loretta wasn't just my aunt. She was the one person who would go against my mother if it meant protecting me. She had always been like that. Fierce. Loyal. She showed up when it mattered, and that day, her being there mattered.

The pain got worse. It was sharp and deep and rolled over me in waves I didn't know how to survive. The room blurred. I gripped the sides of the bed. I screamed. I begged. And then, just when I thought I couldn't take anymore, she came.

It felt like the world paused. She cried, and that tiny sound filled the room, piercing through years of loneliness and hurt.

They wrapped her in a blanket and placed her in my arms, and in that moment, nothing else mattered. She was tiny. Brown skin. Soft curls. Her eyes opened just enough to find mine before closing again. She didn't look like pain. She didn't look like fear. She looked like hope. Like everything I had ever wanted.

I named her Rayna. A name I had whispered to her for months. She was mine. And for the first time in my life, I felt like I belonged to someone too.

CHAPTER 10

A Child Left Behind

"The child who is not embraced by the village will burn it down to feel its warmth."

— African Proverb

In the weeks that followed, my mom and my sister fell in love with Rayna. Every little sound, every yawn, every stretch of her fingers seemed to pull them in deeper.

My mom, who had been so guarded when she first found out I was pregnant, softened in ways I hadn't expected. She started doing the things I had imagined I'd be doing like feeding her, changing her, picking out her clothes. It didn't feel like she was trying to push me aside. At least I didn't think she was. It just seemed like she got swept up in the excitement of having a baby around.

I did want to be the one doing it all, to prove I could be a good mother, but watching my mom take to her with such love, the way she held my daughter, the way her face lit up, made me feel like, for once, we were a family sharing something special. It was a quiet, unspoken harmony I'd never felt with her before. It wasn't perfect, but it was peaceful. And I needed that peace.

But that sense of peace didn't last.

My mom's foster daughters had been with us for a while, two sisters named Julissa and Amanda. Julissa was the older one, outgoing and bold, always talking, always in the middle of something. Amanda was younger, quieter, the type to sit in a corner and watch without saying much. At first they just blended into the background. But after my daughter was born, something changed.

Julissa still talked and played like nothing had changed. But Amanda... Amanda stayed quiet. She'd sit just outside the circle and stare. My daughter would be in my arms or lying next to me, and I could feel Amanda's eyes on her the whole time. Not once did she try to hold her, not once did she smile at her. She just watched, quiet and distant.

I just knew something about Amanda wasn't sitting right.

Then the fire happened.

I don't remember who shouted first or how the alarm was raised. What I remember is the smoke curling out of that upstairs closet, the smell of burning fabric, and the cold realization that my baby could have died in that house.

That little girl tried to kill my child.

Amanda was seven or eight, old enough to know what fire does. She didn't cry. She didn't panic. She just stood there like she hadn't just tried to burn down the house with my baby still inside it. Like this wasn't attempted murder.

I waited for the outrage. For someone to raise their voice, to send her away, to treat it like the crisis it was. But my mother said nothing. Did nothing.

She didn't even send Amanda back.

No phone call to the state. No report. No meeting. Nothing.

She let Amanda stay like it was some ordinary mistake.

If I had done anything close to that, my mother would've had the entire system at our door before the smoke cleared. But Amanda lit a fire with the intent to kill, and my mom acted like it was just a misunderstanding.

No consequences. No accountability.

My daughter and I didn't get protection. We didn't get space. We didn't even get to feel safe. What we got was a hotel room.

One room. Me, my mom, my baby, Amanda, and Julissa. There was barely enough space for the bed, let alone five people. We were stacked on top of each other, breathing the same stale air, pretending everything was fine.

It was suffocating.

Every time I looked at Amanda, I felt heat crawl up my spine. I hated her. I didn't care how young she was. I didn't care what she had been through. She tried to kill my child. I wanted her gone. And more than that, I wanted her to suffer. I wished she had burned in that fire instead of the drywall.

Amanda walked around that motel like nothing happened. Laughing. Eating snacks. Watching TV. Sleeping without fear. Meanwhile, I stayed curled around my daughter, afraid to blink too long. I didn't trust the silence. And I sure as hell didn't trust Amanda.

People love to talk about the tenderness of a mother's love.
Mine wasn't soft. Mine was rage.

It was the kind of love that made my hands clench and my jaw tighten every time Amanda breathed too close. I wanted to grab her. I wanted her to feel every bit of the fear, the fury, and the threat she had brought into our lives.

And still, I had to pretend. Every single day, I had to act like I didn't see her. Like I didn't hear her. Like my skin didn't crawl every time her shadow moved across the wall.

But it was eating me alive. I couldn't breathe in that room anymore. The walls felt smaller every day, like they were closing in around me. I just needed one moment where I could feel something other than fear and fury.

So, I called Tiana.

She came over just to keep me company. I needed someone normal in that room, even if just for a little while. At some point, she noticed one of my mom's wine coolers in the fridge. We took one small sip, just to see what it tasted like.

That was it.

But even that was too much.

When my mother noticed that tiny bit missing, she went ballistic.

One minute we were sitting there, and the next she was screaming like she lost her mind. Her face twisted. Her voice cracked. Loud, hateful, spitting every insult she could think of.

She yelled at us to get out. Screamed at me for disrespecting her. Called me every name in the book. Accused us of being fast, of being sluts, of not caring about my daughter.

And yet she was the one trying to throw a three-month-old baby out in the middle of a blizzard.

A baby she claimed to love so much.

She knew we didn't have a car. She knew we didn't have anywhere to go. But none of that mattered. She was insistent that we leave, and that I take my baby with me. There was no concern for how cold it was, no thought of what might happen once we stepped outside. She wanted us gone.

Thankfully, in the midst of her rage, Junior showed up. It felt like God himself had sent him because his timing was impeccable.

He walked in as she was in the middle of going off. He felt the tension. Saw the fear on my face, the baby in my arms, Tiana standing frozen beside me, and he acted.

He told us to get our things. He stayed calm, like he always did. That made my mother even angrier.

She turned her rage on him, yelling at him for interfering, accusing him of things that made no sense. Accused him of being the father of my child. Of sleeping with me.

She hurled bottle after bottle of Similac at him. Formula hit the walls, milk spraying across the floor as she kept screaming.

I stood there frozen in shock. This was Junior. The man who bought me shoes. Who listened. Who showed up. Who I called Daddy. And now he was being accused of the most disgusting thing my mother could conjure.

She knew it wasn't true. She knew who my child's father was. But none of that mattered. She was enraged that someone had dared to help me. That someone cared.

Junior didn't flinch. He stood his ground, let her scream, and then turned his back to her and opened the hotel door. He put his body between hers and mine. Shielded me and Tiana and the baby like it was nothing.

And we left.

He drove us through the snow in silence, the heater on full blast, my daughter tucked in my lap while Tiana stared out the window. The silence in that car said everything. No one asked questions. No one needed to.

When we pulled up to Tiana's house, I didn't want to move. I didn't want to get out of that car. I didn't want to leave him behind to deal with her, not after everything she just did. But what was I supposed to do? I couldn't stop her. I couldn't protect him.

She had always been cruel. But this was something else. Something feral.

That night confirmed what I had always felt deep down.

It didn't matter how much I loved her.

It didn't matter that she was my mother.

She would never feel the same.

CHAPTER 11

An Unlikely Ally

"Sometimes people surprise you, and the most unlikely ones have the most to give."

— Glennon Doyle, "Untamed"

I didn't have many options. Maybe I didn't have any at all. But somehow, I ended up at Gracie's door. Gracie was Junior's ex-wife. She welcomed me and my baby without hesitation. She offered us peace, calm, and care. Something she didn't have to do, especially considering I was the daughter of the woman who had taken her husband. But she didn't bring any of that up. She just opened the door and let us in. No questions. No resentment. And in contrast to what I had just come from, it felt like everything.

Most of my dad's family welcomed me, but Jeff, his son, stood out. He didn't have to care. He had no obligation to me. But he did. One day, after a fight broke out between me and another girl from the neighborhood, I found myself completely outnumbered. She brought nearly everyone on the block into it, and before I knew it, I was curled up under a car, trying to shield myself from kicks and punches coming from every direction.

I tasted metal. Gravel cut into my knees and palms. Shoes kept finding my ribs and hips, quick and mean, like they were trying to stomp me out. Someone yanked my hair and my cheek hit the curb. I heard the same two words over and over.

Get her.

The world narrowed to noise and pressure. I could not tell who was swinging. I only knew the weight of bodies and the hot sting in my throat. I tucked my chin and counted breaths so I didn't panic. One. Two. Three.

Then Jeff's voice cut through the shouting. "Move. Back up. Now." His hands were on me, solid and certain, and the kicks stopped. He pulled me up and wrapped himself around me, shielding me from any more blows.

That day, he didn't hesitate. He got me out of there, and I'll never forget it. Not that he would ever let me. Every time I see him, he brings it up like it's his favorite story. It's so annoying, but I can't complain too much. He did save me.

When word got back to my mother, she was livid. She did what she did best. She called the police and reported me missing. I wondered for a second if she called the police because she cared, but deep down, I knew better. Once she placed all her anger on Gracie, it was clear this wasn't about bringing me home. It was about revenge.

She blamed Gracie. The same woman who had taken me in when I had nowhere else to go. The same woman who showed me more care in a few days than my mother had in years. My mother accused her of harboring me and claimed she was responsible for the fight. It didn't matter that I was finally in a safe place. My mother needed someone to punish, and she chose the only person who had dared to be kind.

She also turned around and used the incident as ammunition to file for custody of Rayna.

Not to protect her.

Not because she cared.

Because I stayed with Gracie.

Because someone else stepped in when she wouldn't.

Taking my daughter wasn't about protection. It was punishment.

She wasn't trying to keep her safe. She was trying to get even.

She had begun building her case before we were even returned to her. She pulled from everything she could find. Old medical records. A history of forced hospitalizations. Poor grades. Days of missed school. Anything that could be twisted into proof. She stacked it piece by piece until she had all the evidence she needed to show I was reckless, and unfit.

She crafted a version of me that erased everything I had done to protect my daughter and replaced it with a story that made her look like the savior and me the serpent.

This was the same woman who had thrown us out in the middle of a blizzard. Who stood in the doorway and screamed for me to leave with a three-month-old baby, no car, no money, and nowhere to go. And now she was sitting in court, telling the judge that I was the one who put my daughter in danger. That I was unstable. That I was too young and too incompetent to raise her.

And of course, the court listened. I didn't stand a chance in there. They handed my daughter over to the one person who had made my life miserable. The one person she would need protection from the most.

Even though we still lived under the same roof, the custody ruling changed everything. My mother made every decision. I was still physically present, but completely shut out.

CHAPTER 12

Sharper Than Words

"Handle them carefully, for words have more power than atom bombs."

— Pearl Strachan Hurd

I hated her. No, hate wasn't a strong enough word to hold what I felt. I resented her with every fiber of my being. Every glance, every word, every calculated move she made felt like another brick added to the wall she built around me.

She had taken everything from me. She painted me as unstable, convinced everyone I wasn't fit to care for my own child, and used that narrative to take custody of my daughter, robbing me of the one thing in my life that brought me joy.

I lived under her roof because I had no choice. My daughter was there, and I was only fifteen with nowhere else to go.

But every day was a battle. She would whisper on the phone just loud enough for me to hear. "She don't know what she's doing with that baby." "I don't know how she thought she was gonna take care of a child when she can barely take care of herself." Every word was meant to wound. And if she wasn't whispering behind my back, she was hissing it straight to my face. "You're nothing but a failure," she'd sneer. "Unfit to be a mother. I told you that from the start."

The house was a war zone. I was always on edge, waiting for the next explosion. Her anger found me no matter where I hid. I hated the way she looked at me, the way her voice dripped with contempt, the way she could cut me down without lifting a finger.

The rage inside me simmered. I stayed quiet to keep the peace, to survive. But the slaps, the stares, the sideways comments chipped away at what little strength I had left.

I held it in as long as I could. But there were moments when it slipped. Like that night in my room. The night everything changed.

That night I sat there on the edge of my bed, fists clenched, staring at the floor, trying to block her out. But the words got in anyway. I wanted to scream at her to stop, to tell her to shut up, that she didn't know me.

"You think you're grown now, don't you? Walking around here with your head in the clouds like you're somebody." Every word was a knife.

And slowly, I started to believe her. Maybe I wasn't good enough.

Maybe I was as unfit and crazy as she said.

But there was still a spark in me, a stubborn little piece that refused to die.

That spark was my daughter.

I'd look at her tiny face and remind myself that no matter what my mother said, I had something worth fighting for.

But even that spark wasn't enough to stop what happened next. The tension had been building for too many years, and that night, it finally reached its breaking point. My mother stormed into my room, her voice sharp and full of disdain. I don't even remember what she was yelling about. I could barely hear her words, but I felt every bit of her anger, every ounce of her judgment.

As she ranted, her voice rising with each insult, a memory clawed its way to the surface. It was one that still made my stomach churn with shame and fury. I was back in my room, feeding my daughter while finishing up homework. She had drifted off, her tiny hands relaxed, her bottle barely clinging to her lips. I laid her down gently and propped the bottle with a blanket, letting her finish the last bit of Similac while I focused on my schoolwork.

The door creaked open, and there she was, my mother, standing silently in the doorway. I could feel her eyes on me, on my daughter. I didn't look up, hoping she would leave, but she didn't. She crossed the room then, like a whip, her hand flew across my face. The slap came out of nowhere, leaving my cheek stinging and my head spinning as it hit the wall behind me.

"What the hell is this?" she spat, yanking the bottle from my daughter's mouth like it was poison. "You trying to kill her?" she hissed. "What kind of mother are you?"

I couldn't get a word in, couldn't explain. She didn't care about explanations. All I could do was sit there, stunned, as she picked up my daughter and cradled her like she was saving her from some monster.

She whispered softly to her, as though reassuring her that she was safe now, safe from me. And then she walked out, leaving me alone with the searing humiliation and the quiet ache of my daughter's absence.

That night played on a loop in my mind, a wound that refused to close. A reminder of how powerless I was under her roof. It was what made tonight different. It wasn't just the slaps, the whispers, the never-ending taunts that brought me to this breaking point.

It was everything. Years of being made to feel small, inadequate, worthless. And this time, I wasn't sure how much longer I could keep it together.

But here she was, in my room uninvited, as always, the one place that was supposed to be mine, where I could shut the door and pretend for a little while that I was anywhere but there, her words dripping with the same venom that had poisoned so many nights before. But this time, I wasn't the girl in the memory. I wasn't the girl sitting in silence, taking it. This time, something inside me snapped.

59

Her voice was louder than the pounding in my chest, sharp and taunting as she screamed something at me while I sat on the bed. My hands trembled. My breath came in jagged bursts, each one harder to catch than the last. I tried to block it out, to focus on anything else, but every word was another wound ripped open. I gripped the edge of the bed, chest tight, like my heart couldn't decide whether to break or explode. It wasn't just her words. It was the way she said them, like she reveled in my pain, like she thrived on tearing me apart.

Her words were like gasoline, and the years of anger and humiliation inside me were the match.

Before I even realized what I was doing, my hand was under the pillow, gripping the handle of the butcher knife I kept there.

"I'm done!" I screamed holding the knife against her throat. My hand was shaking, but my voice carried every ounce of the rage I'd bottled up. "Leave me alone, or I swear to God, I'll cut your damn throat!"

She froze, her eyes wide, her mouth opening and closing like she couldn't believe what she was hearing. For a moment, the room was silent except for the pounding of my heart in my ears. And then, just as quickly, she snapped out of it, stumbling backward toward the door.

"You're crazy!" she screamed. "You've lost your damn mind!" "They're gonna lock your crazy ass up," she hissed.
She ran out, and moments later, I heard her frantic voice on the phone. This time, it wasn't her friends or sisters on the other end. It was the police. "She's lost it!" she cried. "She's threatening me with a knife! Come quick!"

When they arrived, I was still sitting on the edge of my bed, the knife dangling from my hand. They didn't ask questions. They didn't care about what led up to that moment. All they saw was what she wanted them to see: a crazy, dangerous, out-of-control teenager with a knife and a mother who seemed scared for her life. They asked no questions before cuffing me and pulling me out of the house, the cold metal around my wrists the only thing I could feel.

My mother stood by the doorway looking on. Her arms were crossed, her face an unreadable mask. For once, she didn't yell, didn't call me crazy, didn't hurl insults. She just watched as they cuffed me and led me to the car.

I sat in the back of the police car, staring out at the darkened street, trying to process what had just happened. The flashing lights from the cop cars made the house look almost haunted, like a crime scene from one of those TV shows. Except this wasn't fiction. It was my life.

Regret sat heavy on my chest, mingling with the residual anger that still coursed through my veins. Pulling that knife on her had been instinctual, a culmination of years of pain and mistreatment exploding all at once. But now, in the quiet aftermath, all I could think was how close I'd come to doing something irreversible. What if she hadn't walked away? What if the rage had taken over completely?

I wasn't even sure who I was in that moment. The girl who had been pushed too far? The daughter who had snapped trying to survive her for too long? Or the reflection of everything she had always accused me of being? The questions buzzed in my mind, loud and unrelenting, but I had no answers. I wasn't even sure I wanted them.

CHAPTER 13

It Wasn't Me

"When one person makes an accusation, check to be sure he himself is not the guilty one."

— Piers Anthony

When we arrived at the hospital, the nurses and doctors looked at me like I was fragile, like I might shatter if they said the wrong thing. The police had treated me as a threat, someone to be subdued and controlled. But here, it felt like I was finally being seen as a person again. Maybe it was the exhaustion etched on my face or the tears that wouldn't stop falling, but their eyes weren't filled with judgment. They were filled with concern.

A social worker sat across from me in a small, sterile room, her voice soft but probing. She asked questions, trying to piece together the events that had led me here. At first, I gave her nothing. I was too drained to talk, too overwhelmed to even think. But then she asked the one question that broke through my walls.

"Do you feel safe at home?"

The words hung in the air like a lifeline. Safe? I didn't even know what that word meant anymore. My mind raced through years of memories. Slaps. Belts. Cords. Screams. Nights spent hiding under my blankets, hoping she wouldn't come storming in. And then there was tonight.

The knife. The shouting. The raw fear in her eyes as she backed away.

No, I didn't feel safe. I had never felt safe.

For the first time, I opened up. Hesitantly at first, then with more urgency as the floodgates burst. I told her about the years of mistreatment, the constant put-downs, how much my mother hated me, and how she made up stories about me being crazy. I told her about my daughter and how my mother had taken her from me.

The social worker nodded, her face calm but empathetic, as if she'd heard stories like mine before. She didn't interrupt. She didn't try to fix it. She just listened.

I don't know if she said anything to anyone. Maybe she did. Or maybe the staff finally started paying attention.

I had been sent to these facilities repeatedly. I was evaluated and monitored. They put my every action under review. The staff waited for the episodes she described, but they never came. Slowly, the cracks in her story began to show. The truth that I wasn't who she said I was started to surface.

They began to question her claims, piecing together a different version of me, one that didn't align with the monster she had described. They saw I wasn't aggressive without cause. I wasn't dangerous or crazy. I was just a girl who had been through too much and was trying to survive in a world that had never been safe to me. And the more they saw, the clearer it became that the problem wasn't me. It was her.

The mother who had spent years crafting a narrative that cast herself as the victim and me as the villain.

I had lived with that truth for years, but now they were finally starting to see it too.

The system stepped in and called it protection. But what they thought was helping only made everything worse. It felt like punishment. Like exile.
They would have been better off just leaving me alone. Leaving me with her. Because putting me in foster care didn't just mean walking

away from the house where I had endured so much pain. It meant leaving my daughter.

Even though my mother had custody, at least when we lived under the same roof, I could see her, hold her, and be part of her life, even if it wasn't in the way I wanted. I still had small, precious moments.

Checking on her while she slept. Hearing her laugh. Whispering to her that I loved her. Those moments were everything to me, little shards of light in a world that felt endlessly dark.

But now, foster care was taking me away completely.

The heartbreak was unbearable. It wasn't just separation, it was a complete erasure of the little bit of motherhood I had left. I couldn't imagine waking up in a stranger's home, knowing my daughter wouldn't be there to greet me with her tiny, sleepy smile. I couldn't fathom falling asleep without hearing her soft breaths nearby, the sound that had anchored me through so many restless nights.

As I packed my things, the weight of it all crushed me. What would happen to her without me? Would she even remember me if I was gone too long? Would she think I had abandoned her?

She was all I had.

The system decided I would be better off not staying with my mother, but no one stopped to consider what that would cost me. What it would cost my daughter. They didn't just remove me from harm. They took me from the only person I loved.

What they did was worse than anything my mother had ever done. I didn't even know when I would see my daughter again. I didn't know if I would. It wasn't just the pain of leaving her behind. It was knowing that, for now, I would have to face the world without her.

And for the first time, I wasn't sure if I wanted to keep facing the world at all.

CHAPTER 14

Not Without Her

"Making the decision to have a child is momentous. It is to decide forever to have your heart go walking around outside your body."

— Elizabeth Stone

I was furious. Not just because they took me from my daughter, but because they had the nerve to act like they were saving me.

From the very beginning, my life had been under review, doctors, social workers, the court systems, and nothing ever got better. For years they believed every word she said. They didn't ask questions. They didn't look closer. They just listened to her.

And now they wanted to help?! Now they wanted to care all of a sudden?! And not even in a way that made sense. Not in a way that felt like care. They were just placing me somewhere else, like that could undo everything they had ignored.

The first one they tried to place me in was with the James, a brown family. "We think this environment will be good for you," one of the social workers said, her voice full of optimism.

The moment the car pulled up to their house, my stomach turned. I couldn't do it. I wouldn't do it. Everything about them reminded me of the family I had just escaped from, and I wasn't going through that again.

The house had a well-manicured lawn and flowerbeds that seemed to promise safety and stability. But I couldn't see any of that. All I saw was my own family: my mother, her sisters, the screaming, the manipulation, the betrayal. I couldn't trust brown families. Not after what I had been through.

The James' looked warm. Kind. The type who probably smiled at the neighbors and said grace before dinner. My mother looked like that too when certain people were around. I wasn't getting out of that car.

Mrs. James came to the window, trying to coax me out with a gentle voice. "Come on, sweetheart. I'll make you a sammich."

A sammich? I'd never heard the word before and didn't know what it meant. All I could think was that it didn't sound like anything I wanted. Her words didn't comfort me. They made it worse." I shook my head violently, sinking further into my seat. I'd rather sit in that car forever than walk into another house where I wasn't safe.

The social worker tried coaxing me out of the car, her tone alternating between gentle encouragement and thinly veiled frustration. "They're good people," she said, as if that was enough to erase the fear gripping my chest. But I didn't budge. I sat there, arms crossed, shaking my head so fiercely it was as if the motion alone could make the situation disappear.

After what felt like hours, they gave up. "She's not ready," the social worker murmured to herself, shutting the car door and leaving me to stew in my silence. The truth was I wasn't just scared. I was terrified. Terrified that the cycle of pain I'd lived with my own family would repeat itself, that I'd trade one hell for another. And if I had to live without my daughter, it sure as hell wouldn't be in a place that felt like the one that tore us apart.

Eventually, they placed me with the Hamptons. They were an older white couple with a house so big it felt like I'd stepped into another world. The walls were lined with photos of children, dozens of them, each smiling brightly, each carefully framed. "These are all the foster kids we've had over the years," Mrs. Hampton said as she gave me the tour, her voice warm and inviting. There was pride in her tone, not in a boastful way, but in a way that made it clear how much she cared for each child who'd passed through her home.

I hadn't expected kindness. I hadn't expected warmth. Not after everything I'd been through with my mother. But the Hamptons weren't cold or guarded. They actually asked what I liked, what I needed, how to make me feel comfortable. It was nothing like I thought a foster home would be.

Their house was enormous, with enough space for the quiet moments I craved and the security I so desperately needed. There were multiple bedrooms, a cozy living room with an old but comfortable couch, and a kitchen that always smelled like freshly baked bread or cookies. For the first time in a long time, I didn't feel suffocated.

Mrs. Hampton's cooking was a surprise. I wasn't used to real meals. My mother's idea of cooking consisted of boiling seasonings to make it smell like she was cooking when the state came around. But if they had lifted the lid, they'd have seen it was nothing but seasoned water.

So when I saw Mrs. Hampton in the kitchen one night, peeling an actual potato with quiet focus, I just watched. At first, I didn't understand what she was doing. Back home, potatoes came from a box, whipped into flaky powder with water. But here she was, pulling the skin off an actual potato, boiling it, then mashing it by hand until it turned creamy. I couldn't help but ask, "Why not just use the box?"

She looked at me with a small smile, her Southern drawl warm and teasing. "We don't half ass cook around here, honey." The mashed potatoes tasted better than anything I'd ever had, and to this day, I can't bring myself to make them from flakes. The memory of that moment is etched into every bite I take now.

But not everything about their meals felt familiar or welcoming. Steak was a staple in their home, often grilled and served pink and bloody. I stared at the plate, horrified. I politely pushed my plate aside, mumbling something about not being hungry, but really, I couldn't fathom eating something that looked raw.

Even in that environment of the Hamptons with their welcoming nature, and nightly meals, the emptiness I felt still lingered. No amount of kindness could fill the void left by being separated from my daughter.

The Hamptons tried, though. They really did. They encouraged me to talk, to open up, to let them in. And while I appreciated their efforts, I wasn't ready.

The weight of Rayna's absence was unbearable, and no matter how many times I told myself that this was better than where I'd come from, the ache in my chest didn't lessen. The Hamptons gave me a house, but it wasn't a home.

Not without her.

CHAPTER 15

I Wasn't Supposed to Be Here

"And when the world failed you, you became your own rescue mission."

— Nikita Gill

The weight of her absence bore down on me like an unrelenting storm, and no amount of kind words or structured routines could pierce through it. I wasn't just lonely. I was broken. My daughter was my everything, and now we were separated.

Her laugh, her tiny hands clutching at mine, the way her eyes lit up when I walked into a room all felt like a distant memory, a life I was no longer allowed to be part of. I went through the motions, but my heart was somewhere else. It was back at my mother's house with the child I had created, carried, and could no longer hold.

I couldn't let go. I couldn't accept being apart from her. So, I left. Quietly. Carefully. I knew her nap schedule by heart, just as I knew my mom's work schedule. My sister, Makayla, was Rayna's caretaker during the day, and I knew that once Makayla laid Rayna down, she'd catch up on whatever else needed to be done. That was my window. I'd let myself in through the back door, using the key I still had.

When the foster home was busy, I'd wait for the right moment to slip away unnoticed. My heart raced as I walked to my mother's house, a mix of excitement and dread coursing through me. By the time I reached the back door, I'd be holding my breath, praying everything would go as planned. I'd let myself in, moving quickly and quietly, and head straight to her crib.

For those stolen moments, I could breathe again. I watched her, held her, and whispered that one day we'd be together. She didn't know it, but those moments were my lifeline. I never stayed long, just long enough to remind myself that I was still her mother, and she was still my baby. Then I'd slip back out, lock the door behind me, and make my way back to the foster home before anyone noticed I was gone.

For a while, no one did. It was my secret, a fragile thread keeping me connected to my daughter.

Then came the day it all fell apart. The world had a way of reminding me I wasn't allowed peace. I had gone to see her like usual, confident no one would notice. Makayla was there. She saw me this time, but she didn't say anything. She didn't stop me. She didn't warn me. She just let it happen. For a second, I let myself believe she was on my side. I thought, maybe she understood.

That she'd let me have those few precious minutes with my child. But she didn't. While I was with my daughter, the foster family realized I was gone. They called Makayla to ask if I was there and told her they were going to call the police. That was probably the only reason she even noticed I was there this time. And still, she said nothing. She didn't warn me. She didn't tell me to leave. She just stayed quiet, watching as the minutes ticked by, knowing exactly what was coming.

I was blindsided when the police showed up. I didn't resist. I couldn't. The cops didn't care why I was there. To them, I was just another delinquent, a runaway who didn't know how to follow the rules. They arrested me on the spot, dragging me away from my daughter as she stirred in her crib, her tiny hand reaching for someone who couldn't be there.

Makayla stood in the doorway, silent as I was hauled off. I don't know why I expected anything different. She was my mother's pet, her shadow, her mouthpiece. If my mother said the sky was green, my sister would swear she saw it too. Still, watching her just stand there, saying nothing, made her betrayal cut deeper than the handcuffs digging into my wrists. Even my Uncle Bob, who was at the house, questioned why she hadn't said anything. He couldn't understand it. And neither could I.

The police didn't take me back to the foster home. They took me to the juvenile detention center, a place meant for troubled kids but filled with more cruelty than most prisons. Being arrested for wanting to see my daughter felt like the cruelest irony. I wasn't a criminal. I wasn't dangerous. I was a mother, desperate for a few stolen moments with her child.

But they didn't treat me like a child who'd lost her way. They treated me like an animal. I had just gotten my hair done, long gorgeous braids. But they took that from me too, forcing me to take them out. They didn't give me anything to redo my hair, leaving me looking and feeling as broken on the outside as I did on the inside.

The staff at the detention center didn't care who we were or what we'd been through. They barked orders, threatened us with pepper spray, and punished the smallest missteps.

Most of the girls there were just as bad. They didn't trust anyone. They were tough, hardened by lives even more difficult than mine.

Fights broke out over everything and nothing. Every glance, every word felt like a challenge, and before I knew it, I was swinging, fighting just to survive. The anger I carried inside me, the betrayal and heartbreak, it all spilled out in those moments. But no fight could distract me from the real pain.

Nothing could numb the ache of being separated from my daughter, not when I replayed my sister's silence over and over in my mind.

I had stopped expecting good news. I had stopped expecting anything at all. So, when they told me I had a doctor's appointment, I felt something unfamiliar. Relief. A chance to step outside, to feel fresh air on my skin, to wear real clothes instead of the constant reminder of confinement. Maybe, just for a little while, I could feel normal again.

But then they handed me the orange jumpsuit.

Whatever hope I had vanished in an instant. They weren't letting me go outside to feel human. They were dragging me out into the world to be paraded like a criminal. Shackles tightened around my wrists and ankles, heavy and cold, a reminder that even in public, I wasn't free. I was something to be judged, something to be put on display.

I asked for something, anything, to fix my hair. To look like someone, anyone, other than the girl they were forcing into that degrading uniform. They didn't even respond. Just turned away like I hadn't said a word. Defeated, I put on the jumpsuit. It swallowed me whole, hanging awkwardly on my frame, one more insult stacked on top of everything else.

By the time we got to the doctor's office, the shame had already settled in my chest. I couldn't do it. I couldn't let people see me like this. Humiliated. Caged.

The van door swung open.

"Get out," one of the male guards barked, his hand already resting on his pepper spray, like he was daring me to resist.

"No," I whispered, my voice trembling but defiant. "I'm not going in there like this."

"You don't have a choice," the other guard snapped, his tone colder. "Get out now, or I'll make you."
"I'm not going," I said again. There was nothing they could do that would make me walk into that building looking like this.

That's when he pulled out the pepper spray and looked me straight in the eye. "Do you wanna get pepper sprayed?"

He said it like a question, but it wasn't one.

I froze. The sharp reality of their threat sank in. Two men, larger and more powerful than me, holding all the control. My defiance faltered, and I stepped out of the van, my chains clinking loudly against the pavement. The fight in me was gone.

The walk from the van to the clinic felt endless. Every step dragged, my chains rattling with a rhythm that made my humiliation louder. I kept my head down, but I could still feel their eyes.

Heads turned the moment I entered. Adults looked on with disdain, their judgment radiating off them like heat, and children clung to their parents, eyes wide with fear. I wanted to scream that I wasn't a monster, that I wasn't what they thought I was. But the shame was so heavy it swallowed every word before it could form.

When we got to the examination room, the guards tried to follow me in, insisting they needed to stay. I braced myself for the violation. But the doctor, a woman I'll never forget, stood her ground.

They argued, insisting that I couldn't be left alone. But she didn't budge.

"Where is she going to go?" she shot back, crossing her arms. "I'm locking the door. She's not a threat to me, and it's a violation for you to be in here."

Reluctantly, they left, grumbling as the door clicked shut behind them. And in that moment, something in me cracked. The doctor turned to me, her face softening, and asked, "Are you okay?" Her voice was kind, free of the judgment I had grown so used to.

I couldn't hold it in anymore. The tears came fast and hard, my shoulders shaking as I sobbed. She didn't try to stop me or tell me it would be okay. She just let me cry. She saw me. Not as a criminal. Not as a failure. As a human being.

CHAPTER 16

A Quiet Surrender

"Sometimes even to live is an act of courage."

— Seneca

When I got out of the juvenile detention center, they sent me back to the Hamptons' house. Same place, same people, but everything felt different. I wasn't who I was before. Being locked up, betrayed, dragged out in chains changed something in me. I came back with a heaviness I couldn't explain, like something had settled into me and wasn't going to leave.

They acted like nothing had happened. Same polite voices, same tight smiles. But I remembered. They were the ones who called the police. They followed protocol, not because they cared, but because the rules told them to. And the worst part? She knew exactly where I had gone.

She knew I was just trying to see my daughter. There was no danger, no emergency, no reason to involve the police. But she did it anyway. I didn't matter. The rules did.

I was spiraling. Sinking deeper into something I couldn't pull myself out of. Nobody cared that I was just a girl, not even sixteen, trying to survive a life I never asked for.

One morning, as I sat silently at the kitchen table, staring at a bowl of cereal I couldn't bring myself to eat, the words slipped out before I could stop them.

"I can't do this anymore."

My voice was barely above a whisper, but it carried the weight of everything I'd been holding in.

Capri, my foster sister, froze mid-bite. She looked at me, her fork hovering in the air. "What do you mean?" she asked cautiously.

"I mean… I can't," I said, my voice cracking. "I can't do this. I can't live like this. I can't live without her."

She didn't say anything else. Instead, she stood up and opened one of the kitchen drawers, pulling out a small screwdriver. She handed it to me and nodded toward the medicine cabinet. It was mounted on the wall above the counter, locked with a small padlock.

That wasn't unusual.

With so many kids in the house, all with different prescriptions, she kept the medication secured. But that morning, it became something else entirely.

Together, we worked to pry the padlock open. The screwdriver slipped and scraped against the metal, but eventually, the lock gave way with a sharp snap. The cabinet creaked open, revealing rows of prescription bottles.

Capri stepped back, her face caught between worry and something quieter, like resignation. I don't know if she fully understood what I was about to do, but she didn't try to stop me.

I grabbed a handful of bottles and sat back down at the kitchen table. My hands didn't shake. There were no tears. Just a numb resolve.

I twisted off the caps and swallowed pill after pill, washing them down with water from a glass that had been left on the counter. I didn't count them. I didn't care. I just wanted the pain to stop. I wanted to fall asleep and never wake up, to escape the ache that had taken over everything.

After I finished swallowing the last of the pills, Capri silently reached for my arm. She helped me back to bed without a word.

She pulled the blanket over me and stood there for a moment, her eyes locked on mine.

There was pity in them. Maybe guilt. Maybe fear. Then she reached out and gently rubbed my arm, her touch light and unsure, like she didn't know whether it would help or hurt.

A moment later, she turned and walked out to catch the bus, leaving me alone with what I had done.
As the pills took hold, the world started to blur. My body felt light, like I was floating just above the bed. I slipped into the quiet, into the darkness. It felt like peace was finally coming.

But peace didn't come.

Instead, there were flashes. Voices shouting. A door slamming. The cold press of metal under my body. I was on a gurney. Someone was yelling. Then the burning jolt of paddles hitting my chest. My body arched and slammed back down.

Everything inside me screamed even as I tried to let go.

 "We've got a pulse!"

The voices rushed around me, urgent and unfamiliar, but I didn't want to come back. I wanted it to be over. I wanted silence.

But I didn't get silence. And I didn't wake up either. I slipped into something in between.

I was in a coma for days. I couldn't move. I couldn't open my eyes. I couldn't speak.

But I could hear them. I could feel the people around me, calling my name, trying to bring me back.

Some voices reached me more than others. Most faded in and out, hard to hold onto. But Jamie's cut through everything.

"Wake up, Baby Girl."

He didn't sound scared. He sounded sure. Like he knew I was still in there.

And then there was my mother.

Even in the depths of unconsciousness, I could feel her there. That presence I could never escape. Always watching. Always waiting.

When I finally came to, there she was.

For a second, I thought it was still part of the dream. Part of the coma. That maybe my mind was playing tricks on me. But as my eyes adjusted to the room, I realized it was real. She was really sitting beside me like she belonged there.

Her face was the last thing I wanted to see. It made me angry. Confused. Hurt. Betrayed. All of it came rushing in at once. I wanted to scream. I wanted to tell her to leave. To ask how she could sit there like she hadn't played a part in me ending up in that hospital bed.

But I couldn't.

Her presence filled the room like a shadow, dense and suffocating. Beneath all the bitterness, something inside me leaned toward her. Not trust. Not forgiveness. Just something tired and small that wanted to be held, even if it was by the same hands that had pushed me to the edge.

I hated that part of me. Hated that her nearness could still feel like safety when it should've felt like danger.

She even looked softer than I remembered. Her usual sharpness was gone, replaced by something I couldn't quite recognize. Guilt maybe. Or concern. I couldn't tell.

She didn't say much. And when she did, her voice was low. Careful. Almost gentle. Like she thought even a whisper might unravel what little I had left holding me together. The softness didn't feel like her. It felt like something she was trying on, something she didn't know how to wear. I couldn't tell if it was real or just another performance.

The nurses sure believed it was real. I heard them whisper to each other about how devoted she was, how she hadn't left my side since I'd been brought in. They said I was lucky. Lucky to have a mother who cared that much. The word sat bitter in my mouth, sharp and cruel. They didn't know the truth. They didn't know that the same woman smoothing the blanket over my legs was the reason I ended up there in the first place.

I wondered if she was there out of love or guilt, if she wanted me to live or if some small, dark part of her had hoped I wouldn't wake up. I can't say if her presence at my bedside was a sign of love or just another way to remind me that no matter how far I tried to go, I'd never really escape her.

Everyone. The nurses, the doctors, the system that thought survival was enough. I was angry. Angry at her for showing up now, angry at the staff for pretending this was care, angry at the world for dragging me back into it without ever asking if I wanted to stay.

They told themselves they were doing something good, like keeping me alive meant they'd accomplished something. As if forcing someone to keep breathing, to sit in pain they couldn't fix, was some kind of noble act. They weren't trying to understand me. They just needed to say they did their part. That they checked the right boxes. That they kept another broken girl alive long enough to say they saved her.

Like I was supposed to be grateful to be breathing. But I wasn't.

I was angry. Angry that they dragged me back into a life I never asked for. I couldn't even decide whether I lived or died. Every day felt like punishment, a pain I couldn't escape.

But here I was. Still breathing. Still moving. Still alive. Not because I wanted to be, but because, like everything else in my life, it was a decision made by someone else.

CHAPTER 17

Back to Life

"Our greatest glory is not in never falling, but in rising every time we fall."

— Confucius

When I was released from the hospital, I was sent back to the Hamptons. They greeted me with warmth, soft words, and careful eyes. They saw how fragile I had become. The way they spoke to me, the way they watched me, it was like they thought I might fall apart at any moment.

No one said a word about what had happened or why I'd ended up there. Not one mention of what led to it. Just quiet glances and uneasy smiles.

I know they thought they were doing the right thing. Maybe they were scared. Maybe they didn't know what else to do. But that decision changed everything. In that moment, I went from being a girl who needed to be heard to a problem that needed to be handled. And once that label was attached to me, it followed me everywhere.

To their credit, they understood how much my daughter meant to me. They helped get biweekly visits arranged. Those visits were everything. I could hold her, rock her, breathe her in. I could remember what it felt like to have a purpose. Letting go hurt every time, but I lived for those visits. Even if it was only a few hours, something was better than nothing. They reminded me of who I was and what I was still fighting for.

In addition to the visits, the courts insisted I return to school. The Hamptons encouraged me gently, and deep down, I knew they were right. If I wanted a future with my daughter, education was the first step.

School had never been my refuge. Even before my world turned upside down, it had always been a place where I struggled. My grades made it clear. Mostly F's, if I even showed up at all. I was either suspended for fighting, talking back to teachers, or skipping altogether.

I only passed because I was too old to be held back.
My mother had spent so much time painting me as unstable that eventually they gave her the brush.

That's how I ended up with an IEP.

An IEP was supposed to mean oversight. My education was supposed to be under review, with teachers checking progress, adjusting plans, and making sure I didn't fall through the cracks.

Instead, they pushed me straight into the cracks. There wasn't any oversight. No one sought progress. No one sought potential. No one even sought my struggles so they could help me with what I truly needed. There wasn't no sight at all.

My entire education was treated like an open book test with no review necessary. My mother had already written the answers for them. They copied those answers word for word. Didn't change the font, didn't add a single note, didn't even bother to check if they were correct.

Emotionally disturbed.
Bipolar.
Schizoaffective disorder with transient features.
Major depression.

Those were the words, the labels, the answers that followed me everywhere. They walked ahead of me into every classroom, whispering my story before I even had the chance to speak.

The teachers accepted it. The school system filed it away. And I definitely played the part. I did everything they said I did. I had given up on school, just like school had given up on me.
But now, everything had changed.

This time, something was different. I told myself it had to be. I had a daughter now. A life I was fighting for. She was the reason I showed up at all, the reason I decided to try. I wasn't sure I knew how to succeed at school. It had been so long since I had even tried. But I couldn't afford to fail. Not for her. She deserved better, and I was determined to find a way to give it to her.

Still, trying didn't make it easy.

The first day back felt like stepping into another world. One I didn't belong to. The laughter, the whispered gossip, the buzz of students planning their next game or dance all felt like noise. I kept my head down, hoping to blend into the shadows, counting the minutes until it was over.

I sat in the back of every classroom, quiet, disconnected, doing everything I could to make myself invisible. I wasn't there to make friends or memories. I was there because I had to be.

The only part of the day that didn't feel like punishment was the ride home. Not because I liked where I was going, but because I could sit in my seat alone and disappear into my head. The noise around me barely registered. I didn't hear the arguing or the laughter.

The noise would dwindle with each stop. I was always the last student, a routine that had become both a comfort and a curse. I enjoyed the peace and quiet alone on the bus. But I wasn't alone. Mr. Thompson, the driver, was with me.

He was quiet but friendly, always greeting everyone with a nod and a soft "Hello." I barely noticed him. I was too wrapped up in my own thoughts, focused on getting through each day.

He didn't say much, but I started to notice the way he looked out for us. How he waited an extra few seconds if he saw someone running for the bus. How his eyes flicked to the mirror just a little longer than necessary, like he was checking on more than traffic. Just small things
.

Sometimes I saw him watching me through the rearview mirror, his eyes steady but never invasive.

At first, we didn't speak beyond the basics. A thank you when I stepped off the bus. A nod if our eyes met.

One day, his gaze lingered, and for the first time, I didn't look away. That was the beginning. Not a grand moment. Not even a real conversation. Just a glance that said, I see you.

Soon after, the small talk started. He'd ask about the weather or how long the ride felt that day. Simple things. But slowly, those short exchanges stretched longer. He began to ask about my life, the place I called home, and the dreams I held onto.

One afternoon, as the bus rattled along the empty road after dropping off the other students, he turned back to look at me. "Man, you're so quiet. Ever feel like nobody notices you back there?" he said with a grin.

He meant it as a joke, but it made me pause.

"Sometimes," I said with a small laugh, though inside it hit me different. Too quiet. Easy to miss. Invisible.
I knew that feeling better than most. I had been in a coma once. Silent. Still. Unreachable. I couldn't speak. Couldn't move. Couldn't scream, even when I wanted to. My body was there, but it felt like my soul had vanished. Like I had already been erased.

Even after I woke up, it sometimes felt like I never fully came back.

A few days later, he looked at me through the mirror and asked, "Do you like hamburgers?"

I blinked, caught off guard. "I guess so."

"Well, if you're ever hungry, let me know. I'll treat."

I hesitated, unsure of how to respond. "Okay," I said softly, sliding out of my seat and stepping off the bus.

The next day, he brought it up again. "How about lunch tomorrow?"

I nodded. "Okay."

It started with that one lunch. A break from the monotony of school. He picked me up the next day during my lunch period, and we drove to a small diner just a few miles away. He ordered for me, joking that he knew exactly what I'd like.

"Do you ever think about what your future might look like?" He asked between bites.

"I don't know," I said honestly. "I just want to be happy."

"That's a good goal," he replied, his smile warm and approving. "You deserve that, Marla. Don't let anyone tell you otherwise."

After that, our outings became more frequent. Sometimes, we'd skip lunch entirely and head to the mall, where he'd buy me clothes, shoes, whatever caught my eye. Other times, we'd just drive around, talking about everything and nothing, the world outside fading away.

He made me feel like I mattered. The small gifts he gave me, like bracelets, a new jacket, and my favorite snacks, felt like kindness. The way he watched me. The way he listened. It all felt like safety.

But as much as I wanted to believe in the warmth of his attention, there were moments when unease crept in. His touch lingered just a little too long, his compliments edged just a little too personal. It made me second-guess myself. Was this normal? Was this what kindness was supposed to feel like?

After everything I'd been through, I craved that feeling more than anything. I didn't see the cracks forming beneath the surface of our relationship. I didn't see the way he was shaping our closeness into something I hadn't agreed to.

For weeks, our routine became second nature. Mornings passed in crowded classrooms, afternoons on the bus with quiet conversation, and every now and then, a break for lunch or shopping. It started to feel like we were creating something that belonged only to us.

I told myself it was harmless, even as the boundaries began to blur, even as my intuition whispered warnings I refused to acknowledge.

But one day, the line between what we were and what we had no business being disappeared altogether.

CHAPTER 18

The Unspoken No

"What's the point of having a voice if you're gonna be silent in those moments you shouldn't be?"

— Angie Thomas

It started like any other outing. We had planned to meet during lunch, just another excuse to get out of school and spend time together. He was waiting near the school parking lot, his familiar smile meeting me as I slid into the passenger seat.

"How's my favorite girl?" he asked, his voice smooth, his gaze lingering.

I smiled faintly, brushing off the way his words settled uncomfortably in my chest. "I'm fine. Just hungry."

"Well, let's fix that." He shifted into drive, and we were off.

When he took a different route, I didn't question it at first. I trusted him, even when he parked in that secluded clearing and turned off the car. My pulse quickened, though I couldn't explain why. It wasn't fear. Not yet. It was confusion.

"What are we doing here?" I asked hesitantly, my voice barely above a whisper.

He smiled, but it didn't reach his eyes. "I thought we could talk. No interruptions."

I nodded slowly, still trying to make sense of the situation. He'd always been kind, always generous. Why would today be any different?

He started with small talk, the way he always did, asking about school, my foster home, and my plans for the weekend. But then his tone shifted.

"I've done so much for you, Marla," he said, his voice low but pressing. "Don't you think I deserve something in return?"

His words stung, but I didn't fully grasp what he meant until he moved closer. The air in the car felt heavier, his demeanor more insistent than before.

I didn't know how to respond. I had trusted him, leaned on him, seen him as someone who cared about me when so many others didn't. But something about this moment felt different. It felt wrong. Still, I didn't want to lose him. I didn't want to ruin the one relationship that made me feel less alone.

When he motioned to the backseat, I hesitated, the weight of his words sinking in. But I was scared of what would happen if I said no. "Come on, Marla," he coaxed. "You can trust me."

The world outside the car felt impossibly far away as I climbed into the back. My hands trembled, my breath shallow. Every instinct screamed at me to stop, but I couldn't. He had done so much for me, hadn't he?

That's what he said. And now he wanted something in return.

I told myself it was okay. I told myself this was normal, that this was what people who cared about each other did. But deep down, I knew better. I knew this wasn't right.

In the backseat, it became clear there was no going back. He was persistent but never raised his voice. The backseat was too small, too tight, the air thick and stifling. His car, a two-door coupe, offered no room to move, no space to think.

"Go ahead and take off your pants," he said, his voice low but firm. The words hung in the air, heavy and unrelenting, leaving no room for negotiation.

I froze, hoping he'd see my hesitation, that he'd change his mind. But his gaze was steady, expectant, his anticipation almost palpable. My hands moved reluctantly to the waistband of my pants, trembling as I unbuttoned them. I took my time, each motion slow and deliberate, silently begging him to stop me, to realize this wasn't what I wanted.

But he didn't. He waited, watching as I slid the fabric down my legs and set them aside. The air felt colder against my skin, amplifying the vulnerability that consumed me. I paused at my underwear, my hands lingering as I looked at him one last time, searching for even the slightest sign of regret in his face. There was none.

"Don't be shy," he urged, his tone casual, like this was something normal, something I should have been okay with.

I swallowed hard and did as he said, slipping off the last barrier between us. I felt exposed, stripped of more than just my clothing, as I sat with my legs tightly crossed, trying to shrink into the cramped space beside him. I wanted to disappear, to fold into myself and vanish. The sharp scent of the vinyl seats mixed with the faint trace of his cologne, creating a nauseating blend that clung to the air and made it hard to breathe.

He pulled one of my legs toward him, forcing his way into the narrow space between them. His movements were frantic and unsure, hands shaking as he fumbled with his clothes. I didn't move. I couldn't. My body lay still beneath him, not because I wanted to stay but because something inside me had already left. I opened my mouth, thinking I might tell him to stop, but no sound came. The words stayed lodged in my throat, thick and immovable. His weight was heavy, but it wasn't what held me there. It was the disbelief. The kind that seeps into your bones and tells you this can't be real, even while it's happening.

When his fingers reached for his waistband, I thought, maybe. Maybe he would stop. Maybe he would catch a glimpse of himself and pull away before it was too late. For one fragile second, I let myself believe that. I needed to believe it. But then he reached for me instead. His hands were cold, his touch unfeeling, and that small thread of hope unraveled all at once. My muscles tightened as he pressed against me, and then he was inside. No pause. No protection. Just the terrible, quiet knowing that it was happening and I couldn't stop any of it. Not the pain. Not the fear. Not the way my own voice had betrayed me by vanishing when I needed it most.

"Wait," I finally managed to whisper, my voice shaky and uncertain.

"It's okay," he said, cutting me off, his tone dismissive, almost impatient.

But there was no comfort in his words, only a deepening sense of dread. His assurances meant nothing as he pressed forward, the weight of him suffocating in every sense of the word. My knees bent awkwardly beneath him, the cramped backseat shaping my body into a position that accommodated submission.

I turned my face away and stared at the ceiling of the car, looking for something to hold on to. Anything. Just to get through it. But there was nowhere to go. Every sound felt too loud. The rustling of his clothes. The creaking of the seat. His labored breathing. The woods were so quiet it made everything worse. Time moved slow, like it was trying to make me feel every second of it, each thrust a reminder of how trapped I was.

The moment he finished, a wave of nausea rolled over me. I was left lying there, wet and sticky, with nothing to even clean myself. The dampness clung to me as I pulled my underwear back on, a humiliating reminder of what had just occurred. The small car offered no reprieve, no privacy, no way to reclaim even a sliver of dignity.

He spoke softly, his tone almost tender, as if that could erase what had just happened. "You're so special to me," he said.

I didn't respond. I couldn't. My voice was gone, buried under the weight of everything that had just happened. All I could do was look out the window at the tall trees.

Trees that stood as silent witnesses that would never speak. Their branches swaying gently in the breeze as if mocking the stillness that had overtaken me. My legs trembled as I climbed back into the front seat, my clothes sticking uncomfortably to my damp skin. The scent of sweat and regret clung to me, a suffocating reminder of the backseat I couldn't escape fast enough.

His eyes met mine for a brief second. Calm. Too calm. Like nothing had happened at all. I stared straight ahead, gripping the door handle. I wanted to say something, to scream, to demand answers for why my world felt like it had just shattered. But the words were stuck, lodged in my throat, silenced by fear and disbelief.

Then, casually, as if we hadn't just left a part of me broken in the backseat, he said, "Let's grab lunch."

Lunch.

The word hung in the air, absurd and insulting. My stomach churned at the thought, but I nodded anyway. Not because I was hungry. I couldn't even imagine swallowing anything. I nodded because I didn't know how to say no.

The ride to the diner was quiet, except for the hum of the engine. I stared out the window, watching the trees blur past, wishing I could fade into the scenery. Every bump in the road jolted me, each one a cruel reminder of the small, cramped backseat I'd just left. My thighs ached from the awkward position, and the sticky dampness between my legs made me feel filthy.

I hated myself. I hated that I hadn't fought, that I hadn't screamed loud enough for the world to hear. I hated that I still sat in that car, letting him drive me somewhere, pretending we were okay.

He parked outside the diner, the cheerful neon sign flickering against the twilight sky. "Come on," he said with a smile, as if we were still just two people grabbing a bite to eat. I hesitated, my fingers fumbling with the seatbelt, the weight of my shame making it impossible to move.

Inside the diner, the world seemed untouched by my discomfort. The smell of sizzling bacon and fresh coffee filled the air, mingling with the chatter of families and the clink of silverware on plates. He ordered for both of us, his voice warm and casual, like nothing had changed. Like everything was fine.

But I wasn't fine. I was shattered, sitting across from the man who had left pieces of himself inside me that felt like shards of glass. And now he was talking about the fries like nothing was wrong. My reflection in the window didn't even look like me. It looked like someone else. A stranger I didn't even recognize.

CHAPTER 19

No Turning Back

"And with every step I took it became more impossible for me to turn back."

— James Baldwin, Giovanni's Room

After that day in the backseat, nothing felt the same. I thought about ending it, about pulling away completely, but something always stopped me. Maybe it was fear. Fear of him. Fear of being alone. Fear of facing what had happened. Or maybe it was the part of me that still wanted to believe he cared, that he saw something in me no one else did.

Whatever it was, it kept me on the bus. It kept me answering his questions and laughing at his jokes, even when I didn't feel like laughing.

He wasn't just the bus driver anymore. He wasn't just Mr. Thompson. He had become something else, something I didn't have the words for. He had crossed a line, and I had followed him. Now we were stuck in this strange, tangled connection that felt too complicated to name. I didn't know if I hated him or needed him. Maybe it was both.

But as the days turned into weeks, I started to feel different too. I was more tired than usual, my body ached in ways it hadn't before, and there was a queasiness I couldn't shake. I ignored it at first, chalking it up to stress or exhaustion. But when my period didn't come, I couldn't ignore it anymore. The truth sank in slowly, then all at once, and it changed everything. Every moment we'd shared suddenly felt heavier. More complicated.

Even our lunches had become more complicated. He picked me up in his car, cheerful as always, and we drove to one of his favorite restaurants. I smiled when I was supposed to, answered his questions, laughed at his jokes, even when none of it felt real.

We slid into a booth, and while he ordered for both of us, I turned to the window, pretending to watch the world outside. In truth, I was barely holding it together. I was scared, and unsure of everything, and now I had to wonder if there was a life growing inside me. Not one I planned for. Not one I wanted. Just something left behind by a man who took what he wanted.

How could I be pregnant again? I was barely sixteen, already a mother to a daughter I didn't even have custody of. The one I chose to have. My daughter, my baby, was growing up in moments I only got to glimpse during bi-weekly visits, probably thinking I'd abandoned her the same way I had always felt my mother abandoned me.

I felt a pang of guilt and fear. What if she thought I was replacing her?

The idea twisted my stomach into knots. I had always felt replaced by the children my mother chose to foster, the kids who received the love she never had for me. How could the state even allow it? How could they let a woman raise someone else's children while turning her back on her own?

I would never want my daughter to feel that way. But with this baby growing inside me, I felt lost. This wasn't planned. It wasn't a choice. It was something forced onto me. And as much as I tried to push the thought away, I couldn't shake the fear that having another child while still fighting to get my daughter back would make her feel like she didn't matter. How could I explain this to her? How could I make her understand something I barely understood myself?

"Marla, you okay?" His voice broke through my spiraling thoughts, pulling me back to the diner, to the plate of food I hadn't touched and the man sitting across from me, watching me too closely.

I forced a nod, but it wasn't convincing. "Yeah, just tired."
He tilted his head, his eyes narrowing like he didn't believe me.
"You haven't been acting like yourself, lately."

I wanted to scream that I didn't even know who "myself" was anymore. But instead, I just shrugged, trying to swallow the lump in my throat.

"You're not eating. You're not smiling. Something's going on." He leaned forward, lowering his voice, making the space between us feel suffocating. "Marla... are you pregnant?"

The words hung in the air like a punch I didn't see coming. I froze, my mind scrambling to come up with something to say, but all I could feel was the crushing weight of reality pressing down on me. My body betrayed me, a tear slipped down my cheek before I could stop it.

"I... I think so," I whispered, my voice barely audible, as if saying it louder would make it more real.

His reaction wasn't what I expected. His face lit up with excitement, his eyes shining like this was the best news he'd ever heard. "Really?" he asked, leaning forward. "That's amazing, Marla! Do you know how special this is?"

Amazing? Special? The words rang hollow. Nothing about this felt special to me. All I could feel was dread, fear, and confusion. I was already a mother who couldn't even raise her first child. And now, I was about to be a mother again. To his child.

He reached across the table, covering my trembling hand with his. "We'll figure it out," he said, his voice full of reassurance. "You're not alone in this."

I stared at him, the emotions swirling inside me too tangled to untangle. His joy felt surreal, almost detached from the reality I was living. To him, this might have been a dream come true, but for me, it was a nightmare I couldn't wake up from.

"Yeah," I said quietly. "We'll figure it out."

The days following that lunch blurred together. I told myself I could handle it, that the pregnancy wouldn't change anything. Not yet, anyway. But everything was different. I could feel it in the way my body began to shift, in the quiet nausea that crept in each morning, in the tenderness in places that had never felt tender before. And I could feel it in the way Mr. Thompson looked at me, how his presence felt heavier, more suffocating than it ever had.

At first, he seemed excited, even happy. He'd talk about the baby like it was a gift, something that tied us together in a way I hadn't asked for and didn't want. "You'll make a great mom," he'd say, his words dripping with a sweetness that tasted bitter in my mouth. "We're going to have a beautiful baby."

But as the weeks passed, his excitement shifted. The kindness that once felt like security now carried an unspoken expectation. He'd casually remind me of everything he'd done. "I've done a lot for you," he'd say, his voice light but certain. "You see that, right?"

It didn't matter if I was tired, nauseous, or just didn't want to be around him. Every time I hesitated to meet him or questioned the arrangement we had fallen into, he reminded me of the baby. His baby. As if that justified everything. "You're not going to turn your back on me now, are you?" he'd ask, his voice soft but his eyes hard. "Not when we're in this together."

But we weren't in it together. Not really. He liked to say we were, but that was never true. I was the one carrying the child. I was the one whose body was changing, whose life was changing, whose entire world was turning upside down while his stayed the same.

Everything he expected from me, all of the guilt and confusion I had been holding in finally became too much. I couldn't keep it bottled up any longer. One day during school, I walked into the counselor's office, unsure of what I was even going to say. Ms.

Donahue was unlike anyone else at the school. She had this gentle presence, the kind that made you feel seen even when you didn't want to be. She was always asking how I was doing, pulling me aside in the hallways, or sitting me down in her office under the pretense of checking on my progress. It was surface level at first.

"How's class going?" or "Do you feel okay today?" But it was clear she cared. Maybe she didn't know everything, but with my IEP, she had some idea of the complications surrounding my life. And she never made me feel like I was a burden.

That day though, it was different.

I walked into her office feeling like I was dragging everything behind me. She looked up, her warm eyes immediately softening, and gestured for me to sit down. I didn't even know how to start, didn't even know if I wanted to tell her. But her patience, her kindness, it was like I couldn't hold it in anymore. The words just poured out.

"I need to tell you something," I said, my voice barely audible. Her expression softened, and she leaned forward slightly, giving me her full attention. "Take your time," she said.

I told her everything. About Mr. Thompson. About the time in his car and how I felt like I couldn't say no. About the gifts, the outings, and how it had all changed after that day. And then, I told her about the pregnancy. I told her no one else knew. That I was scared of what would happen next. Scared of what this meant for me. Scared of what it meant for the daughter I already had. She didn't flinch. She didn't interrupt. She just listened.

My voice cracked as I explained it, my hands gripping the arms of the chair as if they were the only thing holding me together. I told her just about everything, even admitting my own guilt and complicity.

Ms. Donahue didn't judge me. She listened, her face full of compassion, and told me I had done the right thing by coming to her.

But it didn't feel right. I felt exposed, like I had just handed her all the pieces of my broken life and wasn't sure if she'd know what to do with them. She promised to help. And she did.

Or at least, she tried to.

CHAPTER 20

Under Oath

"All truths are not to be told."

— George Herbert

Unbeknownst to me, the moment I left Ms. Donahue's office, all hell broke loose. The school contacted authorities immediately after I confided in her. Everything I shared triggered a chain reaction I didn't anticipate. Police interviews, court dates, and social workers filled my days, turning my private pain into a public storm. The charges against him, coupled with his position as a trusted school bus driver, created a scandal that swept through the small community. News outlets seized on the story, splashing his face across television screens and headlines, painting a grim picture of betrayal and abuse.

I could tell something was happening. Whispers in hallways. Closed-door meetings. Folks deciding what was best for me without asking what I wanted. I could feel it coming before anyone said a word.

I was being moved.

They said it was for my well-being. That the stress, the headlines, the pregnancy, it was all too much. Maybe they were right. But it didn't feel like help.

I didn't want to leave. Living with the Hamptons wasn't perfect, but it was better than most places I'd been. Maybe they were tired.

But leaving meant more than packing up. It meant losing what little I had started to build. School was finally manageable. Ms. Donahue was in my corner. And worst of all, it meant being separated from my daughter. Again.

No one cared.

I was placed with a new foster family, the Deangelo's', hours away in a different city. A new house. A new routine. Another move I didn't ask for.

The Deangelo's' were nice enough. Steady. Present. Their home always smelled faintly of warm vanilla from the candles Mrs. DeAngelo kept lit. The light on the walls made everything feel calm. The furniture was soft, lived-in. The kind of place where you didn't have to ask before curling up with a blanket.

But now I was hours away from my daughter. I wouldn't be able to curl up in a blanket with her. No one even told me when I'd see her again or if I'd be able to at all. I didn't know if anyone had explained why I was gone, or if she was left to make sense of it on her own. I wondered if she cried for me at night. If she thought I didn't want her. If she believed I had chosen this.

I didn't know anything.

It was a choice they made for me. Said it would be better for me, but nothing about it felt better. It felt like I was imprisoned. I wasn't in school anymore. I wasn't around anyone who knew me. I was pregnant in a stranger's house, walking around in silence like a guest who stayed too long. And the silence was the worst part, because it gave my thoughts room to fester.

And those thoughts were brutal. They told me I never should have said anything. That I was stupid for thinking people like Ms. Donahue could actually help. That I let it happen. That it was my fault. That every time they tried to fix my life, every so-called solution these people offered only made things worse.

At least Ms. DeAngelo was gentle and thoughtful. She always checked in without being pushy. She had three kids of her own but still found a way to take care of me like I mattered. She made sure

I ate. She asked if I was sleeping. She kept the house steady, and in some small way, it made things easier to breathe.

But even in a house full of warmth, I still felt alone. I helped out where I could. I said thank you. I smiled when I was supposed to. But inside, I was heavy. Pregnant. Disconnected. Missing my daughter and trying to understand what it meant to carry one child while being kept from another.

Maybe she could see it on my face. Or maybe she had just been waiting for the right moment. But one evening, while dinner simmered on the stove and the house settled into its usual quiet, Ms. DeAngelo sat me down at the kitchen table.

She didn't rush into it. She folded her hands on the table, like she was trying to make sure I knew this wasn't an ambush. Her voice was soft.

"I've been thinking about something," she said. "Not because I want to pressure you. But because I think it's important that you know what's possible."

I didn't say anything. I just stared at her hands, waiting.

"My sister has been trying to have a baby for a long time," she said. "And she's open to adoption. If that's something you ever want to talk about, I can help you explore it. Only if you want to. I just want you to know you have options."

Her words sat there between us for a minute. Not heavy, but not light either. Just there.

Adoption. I hadn't even considered it, but now the thought was impossible to ignore.

At first, I rejected the idea outright. "I don't think I could do that," I told her, my voice shaking. The thought of giving up my baby, giving up another child, was too much. But the more I thought about it, the more her words stayed with me. What kind of life could I really offer this child? I was sixteen, with no stability, no way to promise anything.

And I already had a daughter who wasn't with me. A daughter I couldn't even hold.

Still, the doubts piled up. What kind of life would my child have with them? They were white, and I was brown. Would my baby feel out of place, constantly reminded that she didn't look like her family? Would my baby grow up with questions I couldn't answer? Resent me for giving her away?

And then there was my daughter Rayna. She was still with my mother, still in a home I had no control over. Would she think I was replacing her? Would she feel like I had abandoned her completely?

I thought back to the foster kids my mother used to take in, how she cared for them more than she ever cared for me. I remembered how small and forgotten I felt, as if I didn't matter in her world. I couldn't stand the thought of my daughter feeling the same way.

I thought about it endlessly, turning every option over in my mind until it all blurred together. Adoption meant letting go. Keeping the baby meant holding on without knowing how. Either way, felt like a loss, and I was drowning in the uncertainty of it all.

But the world didn't stop to wait for me to figure it out. The system kept moving and dragged me along with it. Hearings and meetings and testimonies, each one demanding more than I had to give. The Deangelo's drove me back and forth to court without hesitation. They never complained about the long hours on the road or the time spent waiting in courthouse hallways. They didn't ask questions or push for details. They just showed up. And I needed that more than anyone probably realized.

Especially with all the media coverage.

The headlines were everywhere. Trusted school bus driver. Sixteen-year-old high school student. Pregnant. They never printed my name, but they didn't have to. I knew who they meant.

And so did she.

My mother.

She never missed a hearing. Sat right up front like she had the best seat in the house. like she was watching some blockbuster movie.

Testifying was already brutal. I had to tell them where it started. How he picked me up from school. How our conversations blurred the line between comfort and control. How I didn't even realize what was happening until it was too late. I had to explain things no sixteen-year-old should have to say out loud. And still, every word I spoke was picked apart and twisted until even I started to question if I was remembering things right.

And through all of it, she sat there. Watching.

Not listening. Not comforting. Just watching.

I begged for her to be removed. I told the court I didn't feel safe with her there. That I couldn't speak with her staring at me like that. But it didn't matter. She had rights. And she made sure everyone in that courtroom knew it.

The judge tried. Said he understood. But in the end, they couldn't make her leave.

So, she stayed.

Not to defend me. Not to stand beside me. But to sit in silence and stare.

And I felt it. Every time I opened my mouth, I could feel her peeling me apart from the inside out. Her presence louder than the lawyers, sharper than any cross-examination. I was under review by my own mother, as if she were the sitting judge deciding whether my suffering was real.

She didn't believe me. I could see it in her eyes. I could feel it in my chest.

And yet, there she was. Front row, like she had a right to my pain. The worst part? I didn't even know who I was fighting anymore.

Was it my mother, who watched and doubted and did nothing?

Was it the court that asked me to relive it all just to question every detail?

Was it the system that kept me moving from house to house, farther away from my own child?

Or was it him?

The man who violated me, leaving behind a pregnancy I had to carry, a truth I had to explain, and consequences I had to live with.

CHAPTER 21

The Room I Wasn't Ready For

"At the last moment she thought, I'm not ready. But she already knew the answer to that. Nobody was ever ready."

— L.J. Smith

I was carrying another life while figuring out my own. It wasn't new to me, but this time, both physical and emotional, it felt different. It terrified me but none of that fear could overshadow the love I already felt for the little girl growing inside me. She was my child, no matter who her father was or how she came to be. Her tiny kicks reminded me that she was real, that she was mine. I wanted her to have the world, to be loved and cherished in ways I had never been.

Sometimes, in the quiet of my room, I'd imagine a future where I could raise her, where I could prove to everyone, especially myself, that I was capable of being a good mother. Maybe if I could do right by her, they would see that I could be a good mother to Rayna too. Maybe I could finally have the family I always dreamed of, even if I had to build it from broken pieces.

Still, the questions haunted me. Could I give her the life she deserved? Would she grow up resenting me for not being enough? I didn't have the answers, but I knew I loved her fiercely, more than words could say.

At the Deangelo's' home, I found a fragile kind of solace. They didn't just give me a place to stay; they gave me space to hope. I knew they probably wouldn't have minded if I kept the baby and stayed with them longer. Still, being in a whole new city, especially a city like Camp Douglas, made the weight of my choices feel heavier.

Camp Douglas was unlike anywhere I had lived before. The town was overwhelmingly white, so white that I felt like an anomaly wherever I went. That isolation pushed me to think even harder about my daughter's future. Would she feel as out of place here as I did?

The DeAngelo's mentioned their sister once. She couldn't have children and had always dreamed of adopting. It wasn't a pushy suggestion, just something they brought up as an option. The idea lingered in my mind, though. Would giving my baby to their family mean she'd have a better life? A stable home? The kind of life I couldn't promise her? But then I thought about the whispers, the stares she'd face as a brown-skinned child in a white family.

Even with all the uncertainty, one thing never wavered: my love for her. She was mine, and I wanted to do right by her. Maybe that meant keeping her. Maybe it meant letting her go. I didn't know yet, but I knew I'd do whatever it took to give her the best chance at happiness.

I was even back to going to school every day. It had become routine, something I dreaded but followed anyway. I kept my head down, walked the same path, sat in the same seat.

There weren't many girls who looked like me, and the ones from the nearby military base stayed in their own corners. I felt different in every room I entered.

Not just different. Watched. Judged. Every glance reminded me that I didn't quite belong.

At least no one knew I was pregnant. I was already seen differently because of my skin. I wasn't ready to face scrutiny for my growing belly too. I did what I could to hide it.

I wore baggy clothes, sweatshirts and loose jeans that concealed my body, but as the weeks went on, my options dwindled.

One morning, as I stood in front of the mirror pulling at my clothes, Ms. DeAngelo suggested a dress-like shirt she thought would be perfect.

"It's cute," she said with a reassuring smile. "It'll take attention away from your belly."

I hesitated, looking at myself in the mirror. The fabric clung just enough that I could see the faint outline of my bump. "I don't know," I murmured. "I feel like I look pregnant in this."

She waved a hand dismissively. "No one will notice. You're overthinking it."

Reluctantly, I kept it on, hoping she was right. But as soon as I stepped into school, I felt a shift in the air. Maybe it was paranoia, or maybe it was real, but I swore I could feel eyes on me. The usual whispers in the hallway seemed louder, and every glance felt like it lingered too long. I kept my head down, trying to focus on getting through the day.

The breaking point came during a class when the teacher asked everyone to stand and form a circle. My heart sank as I stood. The room spun with imagined, perhaps real, judgment. As I moved into the circle, I could feel their stares burning into me. Then came the whispers. Quiet, but not quiet enough. My cheeks burned, and I dared to meet one pair of eyes, then another. All of them were wide with shock and disbelief.

"Is she pregnant?" someone whispered, loud enough for me to hear.

I wanted to disappear. My hands trembled, clutching the edges of that "cute" shirt Ms. DeAngelo had been so sure about. The teacher, noticing my distress, gently told me I could step out and go to the counselor's office. I nodded, keeping my head down as I left the room, tears threatening to spill.

In the counselor's office, the silence only amplified my shame. I felt exposed, humiliated, and angry. Angry at Ms. DeAngelo for suggesting the shirt. Angry at myself for wearing it. Angry at the entire situation.

My stomach churned with a sharp pain, and I told myself it was just anxiety. Maybe it was hunger too. I hadn't eaten anything that morning.

I had been too nervous about school and didn't have the appetite to force anything down. Now, sitting in the quiet office with a granola bar the counselor had offered still untouched in front of me, the pain grew worse. I wanted to eat, but the embarrassment of the day had taken even that small comfort away.

By the time I got home to Ms. DeAngelo's house, I was starving but still too angry to eat. My emotions churned inside me, matching the hollow ache in my stomach.

"I told you this shirt wasn't a good idea!" I snapped at her, tears streaming down my face. "You said it was fine! Now everyone knows!"

She looked stricken, but her voice was calm. "I didn't mean for that to happen. I thought you'd feel comfortable in it."

"Well, I wasn't!" I shouted before retreating to my room and slamming the door behind me.

That night, as I lay in bed, the pain in my stomach returned. I stared at the ceiling, clutching my middle. At first, I thought it was just hunger, maybe the anger I'd been holding in all day twisting itself into something physical. I tried to ignore it, curling up in bed, pulling the blanket tighter around me, and willing the ache to fade. But it didn't. Instead, it intensified, turning into something deeper, more urgent.

I got up, pacing the room, holding my belly as if I could somehow shield the life inside me from whatever was happening. My breaths came in short gasps as the pain ebbed and flowed, each wave stronger than the last. I didn't know what to do. Was this normal? Was something wrong? I didn't have the answers, and that terrified me.

Eventually, I couldn't stay quiet anymore. I knocked on Ms. DeAngelo's door, my voice trembling as I called her name. She opened it, her face immediately filled with concern when she saw me doubled over in pain.

"What's wrong?" she asked, her voice calm but urgent.

"I don't know," I managed to whisper, tears streaming down my face. "It hurts. It hurts so much."

She didn't waste a second, grabbing her keys and throwing on a jacket. "We're going to the hospital," she said firmly, guiding me out to the car.

The drive was a blur, the streetlights passing like ghosts through the car window. I tried to focus on my breathing, clutching my belly, praying that whatever was happening would stop, that my baby would be okay.

The pain was relentless now, sharp and unyielding, and deep down, I knew something was terribly wrong.

When we arrived at the hospital, the sharp scent of antiseptic filled my nose. Nurses rushed toward me, their voices loud and urgent as they asked questions I couldn't process. I didn't answer.

I just let them move me, wheeling me down the hall and into a room I wasn't ready to be in.

CHAPTER 22

The Breath of an Angel

"Some people arrive and make such a beautiful impact on your life, you can barely remember what life was like without them."

— Anna Taylor

The pain didn't stop. It didn't even ease. It grew, wave after wave, each one crashing into me harder than the last. By the time they got me into a hospital bed, it was unbearable. Nurses moved around me, checking monitors, adjusting IVs, murmuring instructions, and everything slipped out of focus.

Then, the words I'd been dreading. "We're sorry," the doctor said softly, his voice heavy with regret. "Your baby is coming."

I shook my head, refusing to believe it. "No, no, she's not ready! She's not supposed to come yet!" I cried, clutching at the blankets, at the doctor, at anything that could stop what was happening.

But ready or not, there we were. One of the nurses squeezed my hand, her expression kind but unreadable. "I know, sweetheart," she said gently, her words a poor shield against the storm raging inside me. "We're going to take care of you, okay?"

The doctor confirmed what I already feared but couldn't fully process. "You're in labor," he said, his tone low and serious. "You're going to have to deliver."

Deliver. The word hit me like a blow. My baby wasn't ready to come into the world.

The contractions were fast and unrelenting, each one stealing what little breath I had left. I wanted to scream, to cry, to run, but there was nowhere to go. I was trapped in my own body, forced to face the impossible.

They told me to push, I didn't want to push. I begged them not to make me. "Please save my baby," I cried, my voice breaking as the contractions tore through me. "Please, let her stay in. She's not ready! Don't let her come out!"

My words were frantic, desperate, a plea against what I already knew was inevitable. But the nurses and doctors exchanged looks I couldn't understand, their silence speaking louder than anything they could have said.

The pain was relentless, building and cresting like waves that threatened to drown me. My body betrayed me, forcing me to do the very thing I was begging not to. My muscles tightened on their own, and the pressure was unbearable.

I tried to refuse. Tried to hold her inside me, protect her from a world she wasn't ready for. To keep her safe, where she belonged. But my body wouldn't listen. The pain left no room for resistance, dragging me forward even as I tried to claw backward.

I screamed as I pushed, my hands gripping the sides of the bed so hard I thought they'd snap. Tears streamed down my face, hot and endless, mingling with the sweat dripping from my forehead. I didn't want this. I didn't want to lose her.

"Just one more push," someone said, their voice cutting through the chaos around me. I sobbed as another contraction hit, the force of it taking what little strength I had left.

And then, she was here.

The room went quiet, save for the faint, fragile cry that broke the silence. My baby. My daughter. They placed her on my chest, and I looked down at her tiny, impossibly small body.

Her skin was so delicate it was almost translucent, her fingers no bigger than matchsticks. She was breathing, but barely, her chest rising and falling in weak, shallow motions.

The room spun around me, voices blurring into a hum of noise I couldn't make sense of. My body ached, my mind screamed, and all I could do was pray.

"Please, God," I whispered, clutching the sheets beneath me. "Please let her live."

They took her from me, her tiny body cradled in careful hands, and placed her on the table under the bright, sterile lights. For a moment, I thought they were going to try to save her, to do something, anything, to help her fight. I clung to that hope, fragile and desperate, as I waited for them to act.

But they didn't.

The doctor's voice was steady, almost clinical. "She's too small," he said. "Too early. There's nothing we can do."

Nothing.

Those words hit me like a blow to the chest, knocking the air out of my lungs. My daughter was here, she was breathing, and they were just going to let her die? My heart shattered into pieces, the weight of their decision crushing me as I lay there, powerless to do anything but watch.

"No!" I screamed, my voice hoarse with desperation. "She's alive! Please, do something! Don't just stand there!" "Please, try." I begged "She's alive. She's fighting. Please don't give up on her."

But they didn't rush to help her or bring in machines to support her tiny lungs. The technology to save her didn't exist. They just stood there. Their faces were heavy with resignation, as if her life was already over.

My heart pounded in my chest, my cries echoing against the walls. How could they just let her die? She was breathing, her tiny chest rising and falling, and they were doing nothing.

The room spun around me, the walls closing in as the finality of it all sank in. My body ached, my mind screamed, and tears streamed down my face. "Please, God," I screamed, "Please don't let her go."

Then they brought her back to me, swaddled in a blanket that dwarfed her fragile body. She was alive, barely, but alive. Her tiny hands twitched, her chest moved with shallow breaths. I held her against my chest, her warmth faint but there, and I sobbed uncontrollably, trembling as I begged her not to leave me.

"Please, Angel," I cried, my voice cracking with a feral, desperate sob that came from a place I didn't know existed. "Stay with me, baby. Please, fight. Don't leave me. Don't go."

Her tiny chest moved slower and slower, each breath like a fragile whisper that could disappear at any moment. I could feel the fight slipping from her body, and all I could do was hold her tighter, as if my arms could keep her here, as if my love alone could be enough to save her.

The room around me disappeared; it was just her and me, and I begged her to stay. My cries turned into a guttural wail, the kind of pain that tears through your soul, leaving nothing whole behind. "I need you, Angel. Please, please don't leave me. Please…"

But her breaths grew fainter, her tiny movements stilling until there was nothing but the weight of her lifeless body against mine. We named her Angel because that's what she was. Innocent. Pure. A life too brief to make sense of, but too meaningful to ever forget.

I was shattered from Angel's loss. I couldn't eat. I couldn't sleep. I couldn't breathe without the ache of everything that had been taken from me.

I avoided mirrors, unable to face the girl staring back, the one who couldn't protect her children, who couldn't save them. Every time I closed my eyes, I saw Angel's face, her tiny hands, her struggle to breathe. I replayed the night over and over in my head, wondering if I could have done something, anything, to save her.

I had failed her, just like I had failed Rayna. What kind of mother can't hold on to either of her children? It felt like failure was the only thing I knew.

And as if feeling like a failure, tired, depressed, and worn all the way down wasn't already enough, I still had to show up. Still had to sit in that courtroom, numb and unraveling, while the case against Mr. Thompson played out like it was routine, like it didn't cost me everything.

At least the paternity test eliminated any lingering doubt. Angel was his child. That fact, now official, stamped and confirmed on record, meant they had all the evidence they needed. The case was finally closed.

But it didn't bring peace.

My oldest daughter was taken from me by a system I couldn't fight, and now Angel was gone too. There was nothing left to hold onto. Nothing left to hope for.

Even the Deangelo's' kindness couldn't reach me. They gave me space to grieve, offered quiet words of comfort and shoulders to cry on, but nothing could fill the void I was left with.

They tried to reassure me that it wasn't my fault, but how could I believe that?

The world I was living in was not a world for me. It was cruel, unrelenting, and devoid of mercy.

I couldn't do it anymore. I didn't want to exist in a world where everything I loved was taken from me.

I had to end it.

CHAPTER 23

A Broken Promise

"Losers make promises they often break. Winners make commitments they always keep."

— Denis Waitley

Just like Angel, I could drift off into a permanent sleep, softly and silently. This time, I was determined to succeed. I took so many pills I knew they wouldn't be able to save me this time.

But once again, I failed. I woke up in the emergency room, with a tube in my nose, pumping charcoal into me to counteract the pills I had swallowed.

I wanted to rip it out, to scream at them to stop, but my body wouldn't cooperate. I could feel the tears sliding down my face as the overwhelming questions consumed me: Why couldn't they just leave me alone? What gave them the right to decide I should live when I so clearly didn't want to? Why were they playing God with my life, forcing me to stay in a world I didn't want to be in? I couldn't even be allowed the dignity of leaving on my own terms.

The hospital staff called it saving my life. I definitely didn't feel saved. I felt sentenced. And when they discharged me, that sentence led straight to the psych ward.

I didn't want to hear their recycled lectures about hope and healing. I didn't want to sit in their groups where they told us to "visualize a brighter future." There was no future for me. There was no hope.

This time, things were different. I was the only patient on the child unit. There weren't any pointless group sessions since there was no one to group with.

The quiet should have been a relief, but it only amplified the noise in my head, the relentless thoughts of Angel, of my failure, of the emptiness.

The only thing I wanted, the only thing that gave me even a flicker of comfort, was to talk to Ms. DeAngelo. But for some reason, they wouldn't let me call her. Maybe it was some rule for new patients.

Maybe they thought isolation would heal me. I didn't know, and I didn't care. I just needed her voice.

Not being able to reach her made everything worse. I stopped eating. If the pills didn't work, maybe starving myself would. I wasn't hungry anyway. I didn't want their food. I wanted to talk to Ms. DeAngelo.

One afternoon, I asked the nurse if I could call her. She hesitated, then said, "If you eat all your food today, I'll let you call her." It wasn't much of a bargain, most of the food was barely edible, but I was desperate.

The tray they brought me seemed deliberately gross. Cold, soggy carrots, unseasoned mashed potatoes, and a piece of rubbery chicken. I gagged on the carrots, but I swallowed them anyway. I forced it all down, each bite a struggle. The thought of hearing Ms. DeAngelo's voice kept me eating.

When the tray was finally empty, I handed it to the nurse and looked at her expectantly. "Can I call her now?" I asked, my voice small but eager.

She smiled. A kind smile. The kind that might have seemed genuine in any other situation. "I already called her for you," she said casually. "I talked to her myself."

Her words didn't make sense at first. I blinked, trying to process. "But you said I could call her," I said, my voice trembling.
"She's doing fine," the nurse said dismissively. "Now, how about we watch a movie? I'll put something on for you."

A movie. She wanted me to watch a movie.

She probably didn't realize the magnitude of what she had just done. To her, it might have seemed like a harmless white lie. But to me, it was a betrayal of the only lifeline I had left.

"No," I said, my voice rising. "You lied to me. You said I could call her!"

The nurse's face changed, her smile faltering. "Calm down," she said, trying to pacify me while turning her back to me as she fiddled with the VHS player trying to put a movie on.

But the betrayal hit me deep, to the very core of my bones. My hands started to shake, my chest tightening with a mix of rage and hurt. She had lied to me. She had used my desperation against me, and now she was brushing me off like I was nothing.

Before I even realized what I was doing, I was on her, my hands wrapping around her neck. I didn't feel in control of my body, it was pure, unfiltered anger taking over. She had lied to me. She had broken the only promise I was clinging to.

What happened next came in flashes. Staff members rushed into the room, pulling me off her. I remember their voices shouting things I couldn't understand. Commands, accusations, and panicked questions came from every direction, none of it making sense. My ears rang as hands clamped around my arms and dragged me down the hallway, my feet barely keeping up.

Now my very sanity was under review, every step judged by the stares of the staff lined and pressed against the walls. Their eyes wide with shock and fear as I was shoved into an empty room.

One of those padded rooms, the kind you only see in movies. It was a small, empty box with no furniture, no windows. Only cold, bare walls that seemed to echo the silence after the shouting stopped. The door slammed shut, the sound reverberating in my chest. I paced the tiny space, my breath ragged, my hands shaking uncontrollably.

I stayed on my feet for a while, pacing the room in circles, trying to outrun the panic that kept crawling up my spine. My mind raced, replaying the moment over and over. Her back had been turned to me, her hands fiddling with the VHS player like it was nothing. Like I was nothing. She had lied to me, tricked me, and now her betrayal was all I could see.

Eventually, I slid to the floor, too exhausted to stand, too wired to cry. The silence stretched on. No one came. I didn't know if an hour had passed or five. I just sat there, staring at the wall in front of me, waiting for something. Anything.

At some point, the door creaked open, pulling me out of my daze. Two police officers stood there. One held cuffs, and the other looked at me with a mix of caution and disdain. I didn't know how long I had been in that room. All I knew was that the only brown girl in the whole city was about to be taken to jail. Not protected. Not comforted. Arrested.

"Turn around," the first officer ordered. His voice was sharp, and I knew there was no room for negotiation.

I turned slowly, my movements mechanical. Cold metal clamped around my wrists.

"You're under arrest for battery," the officer said. "The nurse is pressing charges."

She feared for her life. I didn't even want mine. At least she got what she wanted.

At seventeen, they decided I was an adult. Locked up in a hospital one moment, locked up in jail the next.

What happened to temporary insanity? Wasn't that the point of a mental hospital?

As we drove off in the back of the squad car, I stared out the window, watching the facility disappear behind me.

In the silence, one question lingered.

This is what they saved me for?

CHAPTER 24

Mother, May I?

"Our mothers always remain the strangest, craziest people we've ever met."

— Marguerite Duras

If they had just let me call her like promised, none of this would have happened. I wouldn't be sitting in a cold jail cell, not knowing what was going to happen or how long I was going to be there. Time passed slower than molasses.

When they finally came to get me, I didn't know whether to feel relieved or afraid. I had no idea what was waiting for me on the other side of those loud, banging doors.

But as they led me into the lobby, there she was.

Ms. DeAngelo.

Her face was a mix of disappointment. Worry. A quiet kind of frustration that stung more than yelling ever could. She didn't say a word, just gestured for me to follow her.

The silence between us as we walked to her car felt more suffocating than the cell I'd just left.

I kept my eyes on the ground, wondering if she was angry or if she just didn't know what to say.

Once we were inside, she finally spoke, her voice low but firm. "What happened, Marla?"

I couldn't look at her. My gaze stayed fixed on my lap as I tried to find the words. "She lied to me," I muttered.
"Who lied to you?"

"The nurse," I said, my voice barely above a whisper. "She told me I could call you if I ate, and then she didn't let me. She said she already called you."

Ms. DeAngelo sighed, her breath thick with disappointment, filling the small space of the car. "Marla, you can't just attack people."

I slowly shook my head, my hands tightening in my lap.
"She lied to me," I said again, louder now, the words clawing their way out. "She lied."

I could feel it rising in me, every wound, every broken promise, every time someone turned their back. I couldn't hold it anymore.

"Everybody lies," I snapped. "They lie, and they break promises, and they make everything worse. No one ever means what they say. No one ever keeps their word to me. And I am so sick of it?"

I looked at her, my voice trembling, then cracking open wide.

"I was born into a family that doesn't even want me. My father is addicted to drugs and alcohol. My mother hates my guts for some unbeknownst reason. She threw me out with no shoes on my feet when I was ten years old. TEN! I was almost raped! And she couldn't have cared less! She left me in a treatment center without so much as a goodbye. She didn't even have the common decency to tell me I would be staying there!

She's literally raising other people's kids while her own daughter is in foster care. The state took me and left my baby behind. They separated me from my daughter! My own sister let them arrest me like I was some kind of criminal for no other reason than wanting to see my child."

I couldn't stop. My voice was shaking, rising, spilling out everything I had buried.

"I was in a coma for days. The media plastered a story about a 16-year-old student sleeping with her bus driver!! And Angel? My baby. She died in my arms because the hospital refused to save her.

I could barely catch my breath. My chest felt tight. My voice cracked again.

I'm not even allowed to die in peace. I can't even have that."
Tears stung my eyes, but I didn't wipe them away. My whole body felt like it was on fire.

"All I wanted was to call you. That's it. That's all I asked for. She said if I ate the damn food, I could call. So I did. I ate every bit of that nasty ass food, because I needed you. I ate the damn food. And she lied! She stood there, smiled in my face and lied!"

I wasn't yelling anymore, but it still felt like a scream. Every word slammed against the inside of the car.

"She lied. Just like everybody else."

Her hand tightened on the steering wheel, but she didn't speak. Her jaw clenched. I could see it from the side, the way her lips pressed together like she was holding something back, whether words or tears, she didn't want me to see. Her eyes stayed on the road, unmoving, like if she looked at me too long, she might fall apart too.

The silence stretched. For a second, I thought maybe she wasn't going to say anything at all. Maybe she'd just drive me somewhere and drop me off like everyone else had.

But then, she spoke.

"You didn't deserve any of that," she said quietly. "Not a single part." You can't control what other people do. But you can control what you do. Do you understand how serious this is? Do you know what could've happened to you?"

"I don't care," I muttered, my voice low. "I don't care about any of it. Let them do what they want like they always do."

Her knuckles turned white, and I could tell she was struggling to find the right words. It felt like the car itself was holding its breath, waiting for one of us to break the silence.

"Marla," she said, quieter now but still steady, "I know you're hurting. I know you've been through more than anyone should ever have to. But you can't..." she paused, exhaling deeply, "you can't lash out like this. What you did, it has consequences. Real ones. They are ready to send you to jail."

"I don't care about their consequences," I snapped. "I didn't ask to be here. I didn't ask for any of this. No one ever cares about me, so why should I?"

The car jerked to a stop on the side of the road. I flinched, caught off guard. For a second, I didn't know if something was wrong with the car or with her. She turned to face me slowly, her eyes searching mine. Her expression was hard to read. Not anger. Not sadness. Just a stillness that made my chest tighten, like she was holding something in and didn't know where to put it.

"Marla," she said, her voice trembling slightly, "I care. I care about you more than you'll ever know. But you're making it so damn hard for anyone to help you when you keep pushing everyone away."

I didn't say anything. I couldn't. My throat was tight, and the tears I thought were gone started building again. I turned to the window and stared outside, trying to keep it together.

The rest of the drive passed in silence. No talking. No music. Just the sound of the road and everything we didn't say.

When we pulled into the driveway, she parked the car and just sat there. Neither of us moved.

"They're saying you need to be closer to your mother," she said quietly, her voice thin like she already knew how I'd take it. "That being far away makes it harder for her to stay involved."

I stared at her, my pulse thudding in my ears. For a second, I thought I misheard. Closer to my mother? The woman who hadn't wanted me around? Who had me deemed crazy, locked up and treated me like a burden until the day I left?

"What?"

I could barely get the word out. My stomach twisted, not from shock but from the sharp sting of knowing I had just told her no one cared what I wanted, and here she was, proving me right.

"She's never been involved," I said, the words sharp now. "She doesn't even want me."

She doesn't even want them sending me to her. Just near her. Like that was supposed to mean something. Like being a few miles closer would change the fact that she didn't give a damn about me.

They put my life under review, made decisions about what was best for me, with no regard for what I wanted, no regard for what I had already survived. And their verdict would have nothing to do with what I wanted.

Ms. DeAngelo looked like she wanted to say something that might undo what she had just told me. But nothing came. Just silence.

"Are they taking me?" I asked. My voice didn't even sound like mine anymore. It was hollow. Resigned.

"I'm fighting it," she said softly, trying to sound sure. "This is your home. I want you here. I'm not going to allow them to take you away."

Her intentions may have been good. Maybe she really believed she could stop it. But her good intentions weren't enough to conquer the wrath of my mother's demands.

CHAPTER 25

Uprooted

"Uprooting is by far the most dangerous of the ills of human society, for it perpetuates itself."

— Simone Weil

After the car ride, after watching me fall apart right in front of her, she was desperate. Desperate to keep me with her. Desperate not to let them take me. This morning, she wasn't calm. She was scrambling. On the phone nonstop, reaching for anyone who might listen.

I stayed out of sight in the hallway, close enough to hear but far enough not to be seen. Her voice moved between steady and strained, like she was trying to hold herself together while everything else was slipping.

"This is her home," she said. "I've been the one here, supporting her through everything. She's been through more than any child should ever have to endure, and now you want to rip her away again? For what?"

The caseworker's voice came through flat and muffled, too calm for what was being asked. Like none of it was personal.

"She's just lost her baby," Ms. DeAngelo said, her voice breaking for real this time. "What kind of stability do you think you're giving her by uprooting her again?"

The silence that followed felt worse than the arguing. She kept talking, kept pushing, but the tone had shifted. The answer was already no. She knew it. I knew it.

They said it was about my mother. About giving her another chance to be involved.

But I knew what it really was.

Another reminder that I didn't get a say.

Ms. DeAngelo sat down at the kitchen table, her head in her hands. I approached cautiously, unsure if I should say anything. When she looked up, her eyes were red, and her face carried all of it. Exhaustion. Heartbreak. Guilt. Shame. Failure.

"They've given us a few days," she said, her voice strained but steady. "I'm not giving up, Marla. I promise you that."

I wanted to believe her, to hold on to that promise. But promises didn't stop the car from coming to take me away.

The car ride to Racine was long and silent, the caseworker occasionally glancing at me in the rearview mirror but saying nothing. I had nothing to say either. My head throbbed with a mix of anger, sadness, and fear as the miles ticked by, carrying me further from the DeAngelo family.

When we pulled up to the Mendez home, the sight was enough to make my stomach turn. The house sat crooked on its foundation, paint peeling from the walls like a snake shedding its skin. Trash littered the yard. Cans, broken toys, and what looked like an old mattress sagged against the side of the house. Inside, it was worse.

The air was stale, thick with grease and mildew that hit me the second the door opened. The furniture was stained, sagging under years of neglect. I clutched my bag tightly, hesitant to even step inside.

Mrs. Mendez, a stout woman with an air of indifference, greeted us with a half-hearted smile. She waved toward a corner of the living room. "You can put your things over there for now," she said, her voice flat.

I didn't move. The corner she pointed to was piled high with clothes, toys, and random junk.

"Is there... a room I can put them in?" I asked, keeping my voice even.

She shrugged. "We'll figure that out later."

The caseworker, sensing my hesitation, placed a hand on my shoulder. "It's just temporary," she murmured, though her words carried no conviction. "I'll check in with you soon."

As the door closed behind her, I stood there, frozen. I didn't want to put my bags down. I didn't even want to touch anything.

The other foster kids wandered around, some staring at me, others ignoring me completely. A few of them laughed, their voices sharp and mocking, though I couldn't make out what they said.

That night, I couldn't sleep. The smell, the mess, the unfamiliar noise and movement in the filthy house were too much. So I did the only thing I could think of. I cleaned. I stayed up all night, scrubbing the floors, wiping down counters, trying to make sense of the disaster I had been dropped into. By the time the sun rose, my body ached, but at least I could breathe a little easier in the space I had carved out.

It didn't last. Within two days, the mess returned. Dishes piled up, food was left out, wrappers and clothes scattered the floor like no one even noticed what I had done. Maybe they thought I was going to keep cleaning. Maybe they expected it.

A few days passed before the caseworker came back. When she finally did, I didn't hold back. "I can't stay here," I said, my voice firm. "This house is disgusting. I stayed up all night cleaning because I can't live like this."

She glanced around but said nothing about the condition of the place. "I'll talk to Mrs. Mendez," she said.

I stopped bothering after that. I kept to myself, stayed quiet, and waited for something to change. A few days later, I spent the day with some older friends in the neighborhood, not ready to return to the filth and silence that waited behind that door. By the time I finally returned, the house was dark. I knocked on the door, expecting someone to let me in, but no one answered. I knocked again, louder this time. Still nothing.

I could hear faint whispers and movement inside. They were awake. They just didn't want to open the door.

Frustrated and pissed off, I went to a neighbor's house. They let me crash on their couch for the night, offering a small moment of relief in the middle of everything.

When the caseworker came back again a few days later to check in, I told her exactly what happened.

"She locked me out," I said bluntly, my voice trembling with anger. "She wouldn't let me back in."

Mrs. Mendez had already gotten to the caseworker, twisting the story before I even had a chance to speak. She claimed I didn't get along with the other kids, that I was disruptive and threatening. But I hadn't even spoken to those kids. I barely looked at them. I didn't care what lie she told. I didn't want to be there anyway.

I told the caseworker I wasn't staying there another minute. I didn't care what the consequences were. She asked Ms. Mendez to retrieve my belongings, and what she brought out wasn't even half of my stuff. I hadn't even unpacked, but somehow most of it was already gone.

And then it hit me.

The angel.

I tore through what was left, hands shaking, praying I was wrong. But it wasn't there.

It wasn't just an ornament. It was the ornament Ms. DeAngelo had given me, the one that had been in her family for years. She gave it to me the day I left, not just as something to hold onto, but to show me she was keeping her word. That she was going to fight for me. That she was bringing me back. She had placed it in my hand like it meant something, like I meant something. She told me to keep it safe, to bring it back when I came home. It was a piece of her family that she had given to me like I belonged in it.

I was ready to kill her. "Give me the angel," I screamed. "She stole my angel."

The caseworker's face twisted into a mix of fear and confusion as she tried to defuse the situation. Ms. Mendez acted like she had no idea what I was talking about. The caseworker asked her to get the angel. She pleaded with her. Ms. Mendez pretended to look for it, then claimed they didn't have it and promised they'd call if they found it.

Lies.

The angel was white as snow, clearly cherished and well-loved, its beauty unmistakable. It wasn't something that could have been overlooked or accidentally misplaced. They had taken it deliberately, out of spite for my complaints about their filthy home.

I wanted to burn the whole place down. My fists clenched so tight my nails cut into my palms.

While I was ready to kill each one of them, I wasn't about to give them the satisfaction.

I would buy Ms. DeAngelo a new one. Something just as beautiful.

Maybe even better.

And when I brought it back, she would know I kept my word too.

CHAPTER 26

Not Like Us

"Your assumptions are your windows on the world. Scrub them off every once in a while, or the light won't come in."

— Alan Alda

I didn't say anything when we pulled off. There was nothing left to say. I sat there, arms folded, jaw clenched, doing everything I could not to explode.

The caseworker said I'd be placed somewhere new. She made a few calls, flipping through options, doing her best to make it right. Eventually, she landed on the only placement still available. The James family. The same house I had refused once before.

Back then, I couldn't imagine living with a brown family. Every time I had been around my own, it ended in yelling, silence, or bruises. To me, brown families meant coldness, cruelty, toxic, careless, harsh, unstable, fake, unsupportive, and dysfunctional.

This time, I didn't have a choice.

As we pulled up to the James residence, the car came to a smooth stop in front of the beautiful ranch-style home. It looked even more pristine than I remembered, especially after the hellhole I had just left.

The caseworker glanced at me with a smile, clearly hoping the outward charm of the home would soften my resistance. "It's a nice place," she said, her tone light and optimistic.

I nodded slightly but kept my thoughts to myself. The house might have been picture-perfect on the outside, but that didn't mean anything to me. A pretty house didn't guarantee a happy home. I had already learned that lesson.

We walked up the driveway as Mrs. James greeted us at the door, her expression warm and welcoming. She wore a bright floral house dress and carried the air of someone who took pride in maintaining a pristine home.

Mrs. James was the epitome of warmth. She was a short, round woman with a rich dark complexion, and her kindness seemed to radiate from her every move.

"Welcome," she said, stepping aside to let us in. "We're so glad to have you." Her soft smile and tidy home felt like another world entirely, one I wasn't sure I belonged in.

I followed the caseworker inside, where the house's interior mirrored its exterior charm. Clean, quiet, almost too perfect. The floors gleamed, the furniture was polished, and there wasn't a speck of dust to be seen. The scent of something freshly baked hung in the air, mingling with the faint notes of lemon-scented cleaner. Everything about the place was beautiful. Comfortable. Even cozy.

Mrs. James led me down the hallway to a small pale-yellow bedroom. "This will be your space," she said, gesturing toward the twin bed, a perfectly arranged dresser, and a small desk tucked in the corner.

It was a sharp contrast from the Mendez house, where four people shared one bedroom. For a second, I wondered if it was really mine or just something they were showing me while the caseworker was still here. I nodded, setting my bags down carefully. It was nice. Too nice.

Was this a show? Would I be moved somewhere else once the caseworker left? My eyes scanned the room again, taking in every detail like it might disappear at any moment. It wasn't home. It wasn't what I wanted. But it appeared clean, safe, and quiet.

Mrs. James gave me a gentle pat on the arm before stepping out to walk the caseworker to the door. I sat on the edge of the bed, hands resting in my lap, listening to the soft murmur of their voices in the distance.

My mind wandered to the angel ornament and how they had deliberately stolen it. I wondered what Ms. DeAngelo would say if she knew it was gone. I thought about all the places I had been. I thought about my mother and why she would even want me back here. And I thought about Rayna. We were closer now. Maybe that meant I could see her. Maybe the visits could start again.

The front door closed softly, pulling me out of my thoughts. Footsteps made their way down the hall, steady and unhurried. Mrs. James peeked into the room, her smile still warm.

"You want a sammich?" she asked, her words rolling together like they had always been said that way.

I paused, unsure what she meant. "A what?"

"A sammich," she repeated, gesturing toward the kitchen.

And then it clicked. A sammich was a sandwich.

The memory of our first encounter flooded back to me, when she had offered me a sammich while I sat stubbornly in the car. I had refused then, partly because I didn't know what she was talking about and partly because I was too angry to care. But now, something about the way she asked felt different. Warmer. Gentler. Like maybe this place wouldn't be so bad after all.

Mrs. James believed a sammich was the answer to everything. Feeling sad? You needed a sammich. Feeling tired? A sammich would fix you right up. It was her way of showing love, of trying to make the world a little less heavy for those around her.

I couldn't deny that Mrs. James had a way of softening the edges of my anger. She didn't push me to open up. She just hovered in the background, offering little things like a plate of food, a gentle reminder to take care of myself, or a simple, "You doing okay, baby?" Even with her warmth, I kept my guard up. Trusting had never gotten me very far in life, and I wasn't about to let my defenses down now.

Mr. James, on the other hand, stayed in the background, gruff and distant. He was an older man with a perpetually grumpy demeanor. I don't think he ever smiled. At least, not that I saw. He wasn't mean exactly, but he wasn't welcoming either.

He seemed annoyed by the steady flow of foster kids in their home, like he was only putting up with it for Mrs. James' sake. He was the kind of man who barked out a command like "Take your shoes off at the door," and then sank back into his chair, leaving everything else to his wife.

Still, the house itself was a far cry from the disaster I'd imagined when I first resisted being placed with a brown family. The James' were not like us. Their home was neat and tidy, the walls lined with family photos and religious quotes in ornate frames. There was a sense of order here, a rhythm to the way things were done.

Dinner was served at the same time every night. Chores were divided and expected to be done without complaint. Mrs. James ruled the house with love, while Mr. James enforced the rules with his stern presence.

The James' grandchildren filled the house with noise and laughter. We got along, joked, even laughed together sometimes. But no matter how easy it was, I was just passing through. A visitor in someone else's life.

CHAPTER 27

Never Lost Sight

"The best way to predict your future is to create it."

— Abraham Lincoln

The first morning back, I stood outside the school longer than I meant to. Buses rumbled behind me, their engines loud and impatient, but I didn't move. I stared at the building like it was something I didn't recognize, even though I knew every inch of it. The entrance was still flanked by those same grimy windows, chipped around the edges like nobody had touched them in years. The smell in the air hadn't changed either. Metal, sweat, old cafeteria grease, and something I could never quite name.

Eventually, I walked in.

The floors still had the same stains in the same places. The lockers still slammed too loud. The overhead lights buzzed with that same hollow sound.

This was the same school where I used to ride in on Mr. Thompson's bus. The same school where I sat in class with my hands in my lap, pretending everything was fine while my world quietly fell apart.

I was back. And this time felt different.

I was living with the James family now. That came with rules. School was one of them. My attendance had always been mandatory, but for years it was more of a rumor than a routine.

Now I was here. Showing up. Trying again.

Some things were still the same. But not everything.

Ms. Donahue was gone. They said she moved to Colorado.

She had been one of the few adults I ever really trusted like that. I had sat in her office, voice shaking, hands curled in my lap, and told her things I hadn't said to anybody else. About the bus. About him. About the parts of me I didn't know how to handle on my own. She told me she believed me. She told me she would always be there.

But she wasn't.

At least no one else knew. That part was a blessing. The scandal had faded. There were no stares. No whispers. Just faces. Some I recognized. Some I didn't. All of them rushing past like I had never gone missing at all.

That was fine.

I wasn't there to be noticed.

Until I was.

By him. Noah.

Noah had a homely look to him, like someone who was used to making do with what little he had. His clothes always looked like they had been handed down more than once. The hems of his pants stopped short above his ankles, his shirts stretched tightly across his shoulders, and the sleeves never quite reached his wrists. Nothing fit the way it was supposed to.

But he didn't seem to care. He didn't spend time adjusting his clothes or trying to blend in. He moved through the halls like someone who was comfortable in his own skin, even if that skin came wrapped in secondhand fabric.

He was quiet. Almost shy. The kind of quiet that didn't feel awkward or unsure, just natural. He didn't speak unless there was

142

something to say, and even then, his voice was soft, like he never wanted to take up too much space.

His skin was warm and caramel-colored, his haircut low and brushed into perfect waves. His features were sharp in a way that pulled your eyes to him, even when he wasn't trying. Maybe especially when he wasn't trying.

The girls at school definitely noticed him, even if his ill-fitting clothes suggested he came from modest means. But Noah didn't flirt. He didn't show off. He didn't move like someone who knew people were watching.

One day during lunch, Noah passed me a folded note.

I opened it cautiously, unsure of what he could possibly have to say to me. Inside, written in uneven handwriting, were just a few simple words.

Would you go out with me?

I stared at the note, not sure how to react. No one had ever asked me out before. My experiences with boys had never involved notes or questions or anything that resembled care. They were fast, shallow, and always left me feeling smaller than before. But this felt different. It felt sincere.

I looked over at him. He was sitting a few seats away, his eyes fixed on the table, clearly waiting for some kind of response. He didn't glance up, didn't try to pressure me with a smile or a joke. He just waited.

I didn't know what to say, so I nodded.

His face lit up, slow and unsure at first, like he didn't quite believe what he saw. Then a shy smile spread across his lips, soft and full of something almost sweet. It was the first time I'd seen him look that vulnerable. And something about it made me smile too.

After that, we started spending more time together.

We sat side by side on the bus ride home, our knees sometimes brushing, our conversations stretching out between us. Sometimes we talked about everything. Sometimes we talked about nothing at all. But it never felt forced.

Noah was different from anyone I had ever known. He was gentle. Kind. Curious in a way that didn't feel nosy or invasive.

He didn't ask questions to pull stories out of me. He just wanted to know me. And for the first time in a long time, that felt okay.

One afternoon, as Noah and I sat together on the bus ride home, his sister Carey turned around in her seat to look at me. She was younger than him, with the same caramel skin and sharp features, but her demeanor was sharper. There was something in her tone that always felt a little sarcastic, like she knew more than everyone else and wasn't afraid to say it out loud.

"You know he's nineteen, right?" she asked, her voice just loud enough for the other students nearby to hear. She smirked, clearly trying to embarrass him.

I blinked, caught off guard. Nineteen? It hadn't even crossed my mind to wonder.

"No, I didn't know," I said, glancing over at Noah. He was clearly uncomfortable, his shoulders stiff, eyes locked on the seat in front of him.

Carey leaned back and raised an eyebrow. "You don't think it's weird? Him being nineteen and still in high school?" Her voice was full of mockery, like she had just dropped some kind of bomb.

Noah stayed quiet. He didn't argue or explain. Just sat there, tense and silent.

For a moment, I didn't know what to say. I looked at him, really looked at him. The same boy who had passed me that note at lunch. The one who walked me home every day. The one who never pushed, never played games, never tried to be anything other than kind.

I shrugged. "It doesn't matter."

Carey rolled her eyes, clearly annoyed that her attempt to clown him hadn't worked. She turned back around without another word. Noah let out a slow breath and looked over at me. His smile small, and quiet.

Later, as he walked me home, I turned to him.
"Why are you still in high school?" I asked gently, trying to understand.

He hesitated, kicking a pebble down the sidewalk. "I've got trouble with English," he admitted. "Reading, writing, all of it. I keep failing, so I have to keep retaking the class."

His honesty surprised me. And the fact that he trusted me with it meant more than I expected. Instead of judging him, I felt this strange urge to help.

"Well," I said, nudging him playfully, "you're lucky I like English. Maybe I can help you."

The more time we spent together, the more I noticed the way he made space for me without even trying. Noah didn't ask for much. He didn't push, didn't pry. He just listened. Walked with me. Showed up every day like it was the most natural thing in the world.

I wasn't used to that.

Most days, we talked about everything and nothing as we walked home from the bus stop. It wasn't about what we said. It was about how easy it felt to be around him. Quiet, but safe. Simple, but different. And slowly, I started to look forward to those walks.

To him.

One afternoon, as we turned down the block near my street, Noah turned to me with a thoughtful look on his face. "Has anyone ever told you that you look like Scotty Pippen?"

I stopped in my tracks, staring at him in disbelief. "Scotty Pippen? The basketball player?" My voice was a mix of confusion and amusement.

"Yeah," he said, completely serious. "You've got that nose."
I stared at him, then burst out laughing. A deep, genuine laugh I hadn't felt in a long time.

"So, out of all the people in the world, you think I look like Scotty Pippen?"

He shrugged, his expression as sincere as ever. "I mean, nobody else sees it?"

"No!" I said, still laughing. "Nobody has ever said that."

"Well," he said with a grin, "I'm just saying, Scotty Pippen's a legend."

I'm not sure if that was his idea of a pickup line, but it definitely needed some work.

I rolled my eyes, shaking my head at the absurdity of it all, but secretly, I couldn't stop smiling. His honesty, however ridiculous, was oddly charming.

Just Noah being Noah.

CHAPTER 28

When Life Throws a Curveball

"Life throws many curve balls, and if you don't swing... you're never going to hit any!"

— Taylor Hicks

Life swung hard again, but this time, it didn't come for me. It came for Noah.

His family was being evicted. His mother, doing what she could with what little she had, had crammed all five of her children and her granddaughter into a small two-bedroom apartment. It was all she could afford, and for a while she managed to keep it hidden. But once the landlord found out how many people were really living there, he told them they had to leave.

They ended up at the shelter. It had space for her and the younger kids, including Frankie and Allie. I had grown close to them in those days. Frankie, the youngest, was bold and full of energy. Allie was quieter, still sucking her fingers like a toddler, trailing after me just to talk even when she had nothing to say. They were sweet girls, and knowing they were safe gave me some peace.

But not everyone could stay. At nineteen, Noah was considered an adult. And men weren't allowed.

The possibility of him sleeping outside cold, scared, all by himself was something I couldn't accept. Not to someone who had been there for me, even in the short time we'd known each other. So I snuck him into the James' house.

It wasn't much, but it was better than leaving him out in the cold. We cleared a space in my closet, spread out a few blankets, and added a pillow. Quiet. Hidden. Warm. Every night, Noah slipped in after everyone went to bed, and every morning he slipped back out before the house woke up. We fell into a rhythm, careful and quiet. And for a little while, it worked.

Until the day it didn't.

The James family was getting ready for a funeral, and Mrs. James needed something from my closet. She swung the door open without warning.

There he was. Curled up, half-asleep on the floor, eyes wide as the light poured in.

Her gasp cut through the room. "What is he doing in here?" she said, her voice sharp, hovering somewhere between shock and anger.

I stumbled over my words, trying to explain, but Mrs. James was already halfway out the door. Her frustration was clear.
"He has to go," she said, her voice low and firm. "And this better not ever happen again."

After he got caught, there was no hiding him anymore. Noah spent the whole day trying to find somewhere else to go. He called shelters. He called friends, old neighbors, anyone he thought might have a couch or a spare bed, but every answer was the same. No room. No help. No luck.

By late afternoon, his mom finally stepped in. She managed to track down a distant relative he hadn't spoken to in years. They agreed to let him stay, but they lived in Green Bay, hours away.

Going there meant more than just leaving the house. It meant leaving school too. Still, it was the only option left.

That night, he was gone.
His absence created an emptiness I couldn't quite explain. I missed him.

But I didn't have much time to dwell on it.

I was still in school, determined to finish no matter what. Every morning, I showed up to class. And every afternoon, once the final bell rang, I headed straight to my job at Family Dollar. I stayed until closing, stocking shelves and running the register, saying yes to every shift they offered. The work was exhausting, but it gave me purpose. Every paycheck brought me closer to the home I imagined for my daughter and me.

Even Noah, miles away, put his paycheck toward our dream. He had found a job doing housekeeping at a hotel in Green Bay, and at least once a month, without fail, I'd find a letter waiting for me. Inside was always the same: a few handwritten lines from Noah and a crisp hundred-dollar bill.

"I just want to help," he wrote in one of them. "This is for her. For us. For the future."

It wasn't just money. It was his way of staying connected, of reminding me that even from a distance, he believed in me. And that quiet, unwavering belief carried me through some of the hardest days.

But belief alone couldn't fix the tension building in the James' house. Mrs. James stayed kind, offering me her famous "sammiches" and treating me like one of her own, but Mr. James had grown colder. He was never especially warm, but after he found out that Noah had been sleeping in my closet, the tension in the house turned sharp. I could feel his eyes on me differently, like I had betrayed some unspoken rule.

I had explained everything to Mrs. James, told her how I couldn't stand the thought of him outside with nowhere to go. My voice was shaky, but I didn't hold back. I admitted I should have come to her first. I knew I had crossed a line, but I needed her to understand why.

I told her about the shelter, how they had room for everyone except Noah. He was nineteen, and that made him an adult in their eyes. But to me, he was still just a boy trying to stay off the streets. I couldn't watch him sleep outside. Not after everything he had done to support me. Not when he could be warm, even if it was just on a closet floor.

"We weren't doing anything," I said. "He came in late, kept quiet, and left before anyone woke up. I just didn't want him to be out there alone."

Then I looked her in the eye and told her the truth that had been sitting in my chest all day. "You took me in when I had no one. You gave me a chance. I was only trying to do the same for him."

She didn't say much in response, but I could see something shift. Her face softened, and I knew she understood. I was just trying to do for Noah what they had once done for me. She had always been fair. She saw my heart.

Mr. James didn't. He didn't care about my reasons. He had never wanted foster kids in his home to begin with, and now, he had a reason to push me out and he was determined to use it.

It started in small ways. He stopped speaking to me altogether. When I walked into a room, he'd walk out. If I asked a question, he'd pretend not to hear it.

I tried to stay out of the way, moving quietly through the house, careful not to give him any more reasons to be angry. But it was like living in a room slowly filling with smoke. I could feel it creeping in, thickening the air around me, making it impossible to ignore.
And eventually, it all caught fire.

He snapped over something small. I don't even remember what it was. Maybe a dish left in the sink, or a light left on. But it was never really about that. It had been simmering beneath the surface for days, maybe weeks, and that moment gave him permission to let it all out.

His voice erupted through the house, deep and furious, shaking the walls and rattling something in me I thought I had buried. I tried to stay calm at first, to explain myself, to make him understand, but he didn't want to hear it. He wanted to be angry. And I had carried too much for too long to take it quietly.

I fired back.

My voice didn't even sound like my own. It was louder, sharper, filled with everything I had tried to swallow just to keep the peace. The room spun with the kind of heat that makes you feel like anything could happen. And for a second, I wasn't sure what would. He stepped forward. I didn't flinch.

I had the broom in my hand, and I wasn't scared to use it.

Mrs. James rushed in and planted herself between us. "Enough," she said. Her voice was trembling, but her presence was solid. She looked at both of us like we were children.

Neither of us said another word.

But the damage had already been done.

I made up my mind. I couldn't stay in that house any longer.

When I wasn't at work or in class, I was searching for somewhere new. A place where my daughter could walk through the door and feel safe. A place where no one could make me feel like I didn't belong.

After weeks, I finally found it.

The apartment was everything I hadn't dared to ask for. A beautiful two-bedroom apartment. Not just decent but spacious, clean, a perfect neighborhood, a huge shopping center within walking distance and somehow still affordable.

I could picture Rayna there instantly, her tiny feet running across the floor, her laughter bouncing off the walls. It felt like the first real answer to every prayer I had.

Noah was so excited for us, he caught the Greyhound down just to be there to sign the lease. Since I was only seventeen, the lease had to go in his name as well. He didn't flinch. No hesitation. No second thoughts. He just showed up and stood beside me.

The furniture I had spent months paying off was scheduled for delivery the next morning.

I watched as each piece was carried inside, filling the empty space with more than just furniture. It was hope, purpose, and proof. The cream-colored living room set. The white bedroom set I had picked out for Rayna.

It had all been sitting on layaway for months. Every check, every extra shift, had gone toward those payments. And now, here it was. Real. Solid. Mine.

I stood in the middle of the living room, looking at it all, and let out a slow breath. I had a home. Not someday. Not eventually. Right now. For the first time in what felt like forever, I let myself believe. Maybe, just maybe, things were finally falling into place.

Life had thrown every curveball imaginable. But this time? This time, I was hitting it out of the park.

CHAPTER 29

A New Beginning

"The beginning is the most important part of the work."

— Plato

The apartment was a start, but it didn't feel like home, not yet. Every time I walked past the second bedroom, the one I had carefully furnished for Rayna, I felt the emptiness of what was missing. The bed was made, the dresser perfectly positioned, but the space felt hollow. I had done everything I could to build a home, but until she was here it would never feel complete.

Still, even with that emptiness, Noah and I found an easy rhythm. I was in school, we both worked, and somehow, we made it work. We didn't have fancy dinners or expensive dates, but we had our own dates. Nights at the park. We sat side by side on the swings, talking and laughing as we tried to see who could go higher. Some nights we ended up on the merry-go-round, stretched out in the quiet, looking up at the stars.

Another favorite date night was at the dog track. We couldn't place bets, but that didn't stop us from picking our favorites and cheering them on from the stands. Noah always chose the sleekest, fastest-looking dogs, while I liked to root for the underdogs. "Number seven's got heart," I would tell him, grinning as he shook his head, laughing at my stubborn optimism.

We didn't need money to make memories. In those moments, it felt like we had everything we needed. Maybe happiness wasn't so far out of reach. Especially with Noah. He had a way of surprising me with his quiet acts of kindness. He wasn't the type for grand gestures, but his thoughtfulness spoke volumes. Some days he would bring me a single rose or leave a note scribbled on the back of a receipt just to let me know he cared.

I'll never forget the night of the blizzard. The streets were buried in snow and the buses weren't running. I offhandedly mentioned needing something from the store, not really expecting him to do anything about it. But before I knew it, he was bundling up and heading out into the storm. I thought he was insane, risking frostbite just to grab a few groceries. But when he came back, cheeks red from the cold and bags in hand, I couldn't help but laugh.

"You're crazy," I told him. But deep down, I was touched. Moments like that showed me how much Noah loved me.

And yet, even in that safety, something unsettled me. His mother was always there. Not in our apartment, but in every conversation and every decision. At first, I chalked it up to them being close, something I couldn't relate to given my own rocky history with my mother. But as time went on, it started to feel like she had more influence over our lives than I did. While I often felt like Wilma was a third wheel, somewhere beneath that frustration, I found a strange comfort in it. Maybe it was hope. Hope that one day, when Rayna was finally home, I could build that kind of closeness with her too.

And just as I was holding onto that hope, something new unfolded.

I was late.

At first, I brushed it off as stress, but the signs became impossible to ignore. Nausea, fatigue, the subtle tenderness. I had been here before, and deep down, I already knew. I was pregnant.

The realization should have been overwhelming, but instead it settled over me quietly, like something I had already accepted before my mind had fully caught up. A new life was growing inside me, bringing emotions I wasn't sure how to untangle, excitement, fear, and guilt all at once. I worried about how this would impact Rayna, especially when I was still trying to bring her home.
Noah, on the other hand, couldn't have been more thrilled. "We're going to be parents," he said, his eyes lighting up like a kid on

Christmas morning. His excitement was infectious. For once, it felt like everything might actually work out.

"We're going to give her everything," he said one night, his voice steady with conviction. "Everything we didn't have growing up."

I nodded, tears welling in my eyes. Noah squeezed my hand and smiled quietly. His optimism steadied me when my fears threatened to take over. Would we be good parents? Could I protect Rayna's place in this new chapter? These questions swirled inside me as the due date drew near.

Pregnancy made our nights in the park rare, but Noah still found ways to make me feel special. On evenings when I was too exhausted to go anywhere, he brought me flowers, roses in shades of red, pink, or yellow, and set them on the kitchen table like a centerpiece of love. He sat beside me on the couch, his hand resting protectively on my belly, and we dreamed about the future.

One crisp fall evening, Noah and I sat together on the couch.

The room was dimly lit by the soft glow of the TV. He held my hand, his thumb tracing small circles against my skin.

"Do you think we're ready for this?" I asked, my voice barely above a whisper.

He looked at me, his eyes calm and certain. "We don't have to be ready," he said. "We'll figure it out."

Maybe he was right. Maybe I didn't need to have all the answers.

I leaned into him, letting the steady rhythm of his heartbeat quiet the storm inside me.

CHAPTER 30

Ours

"Alone we can do so little; together we can do so much."

— Helen Keller

The morning our daughter was born felt like a race against time. I'd been having contractions through the night, but when I woke up and went to the bathroom and saw that bright red blood on the toilet paper, I knew this baby wasn't going to wait.

I called my mom, hoping she could take us to the hospital. She was the only person we knew with a car, and at the time, it felt like the simplest solution.

"I'll be there soon," she said.

But the minutes dragged, and the contractions got stronger, sharper. By the time an hour had passed, I realized "soon" wasn't going to be soon enough. The baby was coming, with or without her.

"Noah, we've got to go," I said, gripping his arm as another wave of pain hit me.

"But how?" he asked, wide-eyed and terrified. "We don't have a car."

I gave him a look. "Noah... have we ever had a car?"

He blinked like I'd just asked him to write an essay or something.

"We'll take the bus," I said, more determined than scared. We'd taken it a hundred times. The stop was right in front of our apartment complex, and the drivers knew us pretty well since we rode it so often.

Getting to that stop while in labor was a different story. I moved slow, stopping once or twice to catch my breath, but we made it.

A bus pulled up within minutes. The driver took one look at me, doubled over with a contraction, and her eyes widened.

"You're in labor?" she asked, almost incredulously.

"Yes, ma'am," I managed to gasp, clutching Noah's hand.

"Hurry." She waved us on without a second thought and, drove us as close to the hospital entrance as she could.

"Good luck!" she called as we made our way off the bus, her voice full of encouragement.

We made it through the hospital doors, but every step was agony, each contraction exploding through me like a firework display with nowhere to go. I barely made it to the check-in desk before doubling over, gripping the counter as another wave of pain tore through me. "She's coming!" I cried, feeling the unmistakable pressure of her arrival.

Within seconds, nurses sprang into action, whisking me toward the maternity floor. But Alyra was done waiting. She was born right there in the hallway.

It was the first time I had ever delivered without pain medicine, and I swore it would be the last. The pain was loud and raw, and so was I. I'm sure half the hospital heard me screaming. But in that moment, it didn't matter. She was here. My Alyra was here.

Noah was there somewhere. I think. It all happened so fast I couldn't tell you exactly where he was. One minute I was being rushed down a hallway, and the next she was crying.

Everything after that is a blur. I don't remember pushing. I don't remember what they did with the baby when we finally got to the room. The only thing I remember is waiting. I kept looking toward the door, eager for them to bring her back so Noah and I could share that moment together.

But when they finally handed her to me, Noah wasn't there. "Where did he go?" I asked the nurse, my voice laced with confusion and exhaustion.

"He said he'd be back," she replied, her tone neutral.

It didn't take long for me to figure out where he had gone. Noah had left to get his mom, Wilma.

While I was in the room, holding our daughter for the very first time, he was making his way across town to bring her to the hospital. I sat there in silence, Alyra tucked in my arms, still reeling from everything that had just happened. The pain, the delivery, the hallway, the way it all happened so fast, and now this.

The room felt both full and empty. Full of the love I already had for my daughter and empty because Noah wasn't beside me. I had pictured this moment so many times, us holding her together, smiling at each other like we had finally arrived. But instead, it felt off. Fragmented. Like something sacred had been broken without anyone meaning to break it.

I stared at Alyra's tiny face, overwhelmed by love and exhaustion and disappointment. This was supposed to be our moment. And yet I was alone, cradling the daughter we had created together while he went to bring his mother into it.

I knew Noah loved her. I knew their bond ran deep. But in that moment, it felt like she came before me. Before us. And even though I didn't want it to, it hurt.

Still, I pushed the feeling aside. Alyra was here. And no matter what was missing, that was everything.

It was long before the door opened, and Noah walked in with his mother, Wilma, beside him. I looked up, still holding our daughter, and did my best to suppress the frustration building inside me.

Wilma went straight to Alyra, cooing over her soft cheeks and tiny fingers like she had been the one waiting for this moment. I sat there quietly, trying to convince myself that this was just his way of showing love. That he was proud and wanted to share our daughter with the woman who raised him.

But deep down, it stung.

It felt like my presence had been pushed to the side, like his need for her to be part of this moment had overshadowed what it was supposed to be. Ours.

The days following Alyra's birth were a blur of exhaustion. I was sore, sleep-deprived, and overwhelmed by the constant demands of caring for a newborn. With Noah back at work, most of the responsibility of keeping our little home running fell on me. On top of everything else, his mother became a regular visitor, often showing up unannounced to help. Sometimes it was comforting to have another set of hands, but other times it felt intrusive.

Despite everything, I poured myself into being the best mother I could. Late at night, when it was just Alyra and me, I would watch her tiny chest rise and fall as she slept. I would stroke her course hair and whisper promises about the life I wanted to give her. A life full of love, stability, and all the things I had missed growing up. All the things it was time to give Rayna.

It was time to get her back.

CHAPTER 31

I Do

"To the world, you may be one person, but to one person you are the world."

— Dr. Seuss

Noah and I sat side by side in the small office at the agency, our knees almost touching, our hands knotted together beneath the table. The counselor looked at us with a kind smile, her notepad resting on the table in front of her.

"When judges are deciding custody," she explained, "they look for stability. Things like secure housing, consistent income, marriage, and siblings. It all paints a picture of a stable environment."

She glanced down at her notes, then looked back at us. "They also consider mental and emotional health. If either parent has any untreated conditions, especially if there's a history of instability, it raises concerns. The physical environment matters too. The home needs to be clean, safe, and appropriate for a young child."

Her voice was calm, but the weight of her words pressed against my chest.

"And of course," she added, "any criminal history or involvement with CPS will come up. The court looks at the full picture."

I nodded, but inside I was already building that picture for her.

Rayna had a sibling. A baby sister we were raising. We had a two-bedroom apartment in a quiet, safe area right on the bus line. Rayna's room was already ready for her. She had a beautiful white bedroom set with a matching mirror, and a closet full of clothes I had picked out one by one from Family Dollar using my employee discount. The bedding was soft. The dresser was clean. It felt like

161

a room fit for a princess. For two princesses, once Alyra was old enough to share it with her.

I had finished school. We had income. It wasn't perfect, but it was enough. Noah and I had worked out a plan. I would work during the day. He would take shifts in the evening. One of us would always be home with the girls.

And when our schedules overlapped, Wilma could help. As much as she got on my nerves, I knew she would love every second she spent with her granddaughters.

As for my record, there was nothing open. That battery charge had been amended down to a disorderly conduct and case closed.

There was nothing wrong with my mental health, no matter what my mother's paperwork claimed. I knew what she was capable of. I knew how far she would go to twist the truth, to make me seem unstable. But I wasn't. And I was ready to prove that to anyone who needed to know it.

I sat there in that chair, listening to everything the counselor said the court would want. And I knew we had it. Maybe not in the way it showed up on paper. Maybe not in the language they used in reports and checklists. But we had it.

I just needed the court to see it.

Later that night, as we were getting ready for bed, Noah was hopeful. He was just as excited about the possibility of bringing Rayna home as I was. He mentioned that we had almost everything the court would be looking for.

Noah understood what this moment meant. He didn't need to be convinced of what I was willing to do to bring her home. He had been with me through everything: every setback, every breakthrough, every painful step toward this moment. When I told him I was ready to fight for Rayna, he didn't blink.

"If marriage is what they need to see," he continued, "then let's give them that."

It wasn't a proposal in the traditional sense. There were no flowers, no rings, no grand gestures. It wasn't romantic. It was real. It was the kind I needed. The kind that could offer the structure and security the courts were looking for. The kind that could move me one step closer to getting my daughter back.

Once the decision was made, everything moved quickly. It wasn't about planning the perfect wedding or dream venues. It was about showing the court that we were serious, that our home and our commitment could stand the weight of someone else's judgment. It was also our promise to build a life together. Not just for the court. For us.

But even before the day arrived, we had to get through moments of panic and unexpected drama.

Noah's father, Trenton, refused to come. He believed Noah was too young to get married and straight out refused to attend. While Noah tried to play it off, I could see the hurt in his face. He wanted his father to stand beside him, not just because it was tradition, but because it mattered.

It was mind-boggling to me that Trenton suddenly found righteous conviction when it came to Noah marrying me. This was the same man who had crossed the line with me more than once, calling when Noah wasn't around and saying things no father should ever say to his son's girlfriend. Apparently, I was good enough for him but not good enough for his son. The hypocrisy was disgusting. Whether Noah was ready or not, Trenton was going to be by his side on his wedding day if I had anything to do with it. He wasn't just crossing a line with me. He was about to cross one with his son. And I wasn't going to let that happen.

I picked up the phone and called Trenton myself. I told him if he didn't show up to his son's wedding, I had a recording of one of our conversations and I wouldn't hesitate to let his wife, and his son hear it. It wasn't true. I didn't have a recording. But I said it with enough certainty that he didn't know that.

Unfortunately, that wasn't the only hiccup.

For some reason the day of the wedding, Noah decided to drive with his cousin all the way to Chicago to pick up the wedding cake. He figured they had more than enough time to get there and back before the ceremony started.

Our wedding was scheduled for two o'clock. Now it was past 4, and they still weren't back.

I sat in the little dressing room off to the side of the church. My dress hung nearby, still untouched. I couldn't bring myself to put it on. Not yet. Not until I knew he was back.

Guests were starting to leave. The food was getting cold. Every so often, someone would peek in to check on me, but no one had any answers. And no one could hide the pity in their eyes.

The whispers were growing louder in the sanctuary. I could feel them from where I sat. The longer I waited, the heavier it all became. What if he had changed his mind? What if I was sitting here, half-dressed and fully humiliated, waiting for a wedding that wasn't going to happen?

I hadn't cried yet. But my chest was tight, my hands were cold, and the knot in my throat was getting harder to swallow.

Just when I was about to call it quits, the dressing room door flew open. Noah's cousin and his sisters, Allie and Frankie, came rushing in, breathless and wide-eyed. His cousin was nearly in tears, her hands fluttering as she tried to explain, apologizing over and over. They had taken a wrong turn, gotten completely lost, and no one had a working phone. But she looked me in the eyes and said the words I needed most. He hadn't left me. He hadn't changed his mind. Noah was here. He was ready.

I stood there in silence, overwhelmed. My heart was racing. For a moment, I didn't know if I could go through with it. The fear was thick, pressing against my chest. I had been so sure, but the waiting, the silence, the uncertainty, it had shaken something in me. I almost walked out that door. I almost let the what-ifs win.

Then she stood beside me, her hands steady as she helped lift the dress from its hanger. As she pulled it over my head, her voice softened. She told me Noah had spent the entire drive talking about me. About how excited he was. About how much he loved me. About how all he wanted was to get back to his bride.

She knelt in front of me, smoothing the fabric along my waist, her fingers steady even as her voice trembled. Then she looked up and asked gently, "Do you love him?"

I didn't hesitate. "I do."

She smiled, the kind of smile that reaches past nerves and doubt, and squeezed my hands. "Then this is for you. For both of you. Don't let fear take this from you." It was so beautiful that I had to turn my face away. My eyes burned, and I could feel the tears spilling before I could stop them.

Her words held me. Her calm became mine. And somewhere beneath the nerves, I still wanted it. Not the ceremony or the pictures, but the life we had been building. The man who had chosen me, again and again.

She helped clean the streaks beneath my eyes, fixed my veil, and just like that, it was time. Thankfully, the church had given it to us.

The ceremony began with the bridesmaids gliding down the aisle in white dresses that trailed behind them like soft streams of light. My mother had chosen the gowns, and despite everything between us, she had picked well. The dresses caught the light just right, adding an unexpected grace to the moment.

Then came Rayna.

She stepped into the aisle with a basket held tightly in her small hands, her little face focused and serious. Each time she dropped a handful of petals, it felt like a blessing. She was so small, yet she carried the weight of the moment with quiet purpose, scattering color with every step. Watching her was like watching a dream come to life. My daughter, my hope, leading the way.

Junior had planned to walk me down the aisle, but the long delay had taken a toll on him. He needed to rest. My cousin James stepped in without hesitation. He offered his arm with quiet strength, and I took it, feeling the moment settle around me. My heart was racing, but as the doors opened, the room stilled. Every whisper faded. Every doubt quieted.

Then Aunt Viv began to sing.

Her voice floated through the air, gentle and clear, wrapping around me like a prayer. "You are so beautiful," she sang, and every note carried the weight of what this day meant. I hadn't expected more tears, but as her voice filled the church, tears found their way down my cheeks. It was more than a song. It was a blessing, a reminder that despite everything, I was worthy of love, of joy, of this moment.

The church was still full. Most of our guests had waited, their patience a quiet act of love. The soft hum of music wove around Aunt Viv's voice, and together, James and I began that walk. Step by step, the day unfolded in front of me.

At the altar, Noah stood beside his father, both of them in matching cream-colored suits. But it was Noah's face that held me. His smile, wide and unwavering. His eyes, warm and steady.

He looked like he belonged there, like there was no place in the world he would rather be. In that moment, it no longer mattered how chaotic the day had been or how long we had waited.

166

As I walked toward Noah, I thought of Rayna and Alyra. I wasn't just walking toward him. I was walking toward our family, toward the life we were building together.

CHAPTER 32

Only Temporary

"Being temporary doesn't make something matter any less, because the point isn't for how long, the point is that it happened."

— Robyn Schneider, Extraordinary Means

Filing the petition to bring Rayna home sent my anxiety into overdrive. The forms were thick, and half the words didn't even make sense to me. I kept rereading the same sentences, terrified that one wrong checkmark would ruin everything.

Thankfully, the agency helped me through it, translating the legal maze into plain English, guiding my pen until every I was dotted and every T crossed. It wasn't easy, but it was the first real step toward bringing my daughter home.

At that point in my life, things with my mother were actually calm, for once. We weren't close, but we weren't at war either. We could talk without yelling, hang up the phone without slamming it, and make it through a conversation without digging up the past. It wasn't perfect, but it was something.

But she still had custody of my daughter. And once the court papers landed in her mailbox, that calmness went up in flames.

She was pissed. She called, furious, her voice spitting through the line. No one loved Rayna more than she did, she said. No judge would ever hand that baby back to me.

But when the court appointed a guardian ad litem to represent Rayna's best interest, her anger shifted into all-out war. To her, it wasn't just a slap in the face. It was an attack on her authority. In her mind, she was the only one who could speak for Rayna. The only one who mattered. The idea that someone else, especially someone from the court, could step into that role lit a fire in her I hadn't seen in a long time.

She was on a mission after that, calling anyone she thought would listen, trying to rally support.

If it was up to her, I would never have seen my daughter again after filing those papers. But it wasn't up to her anymore. And I wasn't that quiet little girl who always backed down.

I will admit, the scrutiny that followed was intense. Just like the counselor had warned, our entire life was under review. The guardian ad litem and social worker came to our home multiple times. They asked questions, took notes, checked where the baby slept, what she ate, who changed her, who bathed her, and how we handled everyday life. They watched me and Noah together, how we shared responsibilities, how we treated each other, and whether the environment felt safe and stable.

I didn't have to fake anything. I was doing it all anyway. It wasn't perfect, but it was real, and it was ours.

After weeks of interviews and home visits, it was finally time for court.

One by one, the professionals gave their reports. The guardian ad litem spoke first, recommending that Rayna be placed with me. The social worker followed, echoing her words. It was the first time I felt like someone in a courtroom saw me for who I was, not the version of me she had created in the past.

My mother sat on the other side of the courtroom shaking her head, waiting for her turn. And when it came, she unleashed everything she had. She brought up things I'd done as a teenager. She called me irresponsible, selfish, reckless.

Each word stung, but I stood silent, hands clasped, trusting that the life I had built would speak louder than her.

The judge leaned back, quiet for a moment that felt like forever. My chest was tight, my pulse thundering. And then finally, he spoke.

"I award temporary custody to Mother. Oversight to continue."
Relief roared through me. Temporary or not, it was a beginning. One step closer to bringing my daughter home for good.

Across the room, my mother was livid. She didn't care that the decision had already been made. She tried to fight it. She tried to get the judge to reconsider, throwing out the same arguments as before, refusing to accept that it was done. She wasn't used to losing.

No matter how hard she fought, she lost that day.

Rayna was coming home.

CHAPTER 33

The Knock at the Door

"Anyone can be a father, but it takes someone special to be a dad."

— Wade Boggs

Having Rayna home, even temporarily, felt surreal. Every morning, I woke up and had to remind myself it was real. She was really there, curled up in her little bed, breathing soft and steady under the same roof as me. It felt like waking up inside a movie, one of those scenes where everything is perfect and no one's pretending. For the first time in years, everything felt like it was falling into place.

What amazed me most was how naturally she slipped back into my life, like she had never left. She knew I was her mommy. There was no hesitation, no confusion. She didn't treat me like a stranger. She held my hand, climbed into my lap, leaned into me when she was tired. It was beautiful. Like all the love I had stored up in my heart finally had somewhere to go again.

Breakfast was Rayna's favorite part of the day. She loved fried hot dogs and asked for them almost every morning. Noah would slice them just the way she liked, always making sure her plate was ready first. It became a little ritual, her sitting at the kitchen table kicking her feet and humming while she ate, Alyra babbling nearby, and me standing at the stove watching it all, trying to soak in every second.

Adjusting to a routine came easier than I expected. Our days were simple but steady. Rayna, four years old now, had just started preschool and loved it. She'd come home with little crafts and glittery stars, so proud of her work, grinning from ear to ear. Alyra was still a baby, her coos and giggles filling up every quiet space in the house. She was the heart of our home, the soft background to all the joy that started pouring in.

Noah and I worked opposite shifts whenever we could so that one of us was always home with the girls. It wasn't easy, but it worked. We were a team, and we made sure they never went without attention, love, or care. On the rare days when our schedules overlapped, Wilma, Noah's mother, would help out and watch the girls for a few hours. She didn't do it often, but when she did, it gave us peace of mind knowing they were in loving hands.

For a while, it felt like we had finally found our rhythm. We were building a home that was steady and full of love. The bond between the four of us was growing stronger every day. Rayna was thriving, and everything about it felt right.

But my mother couldn't take it.

Her anger only deepened when she realized those loving hands weren't hers. She couldn't stand that someone else was doing the job she believed belonged to her. And it didn't matter how well we were doing or how happy Rayna was. She had lost control, and she was determined to get it back, no matter what it cost or who got hurt.

But we refused to let her stop us from living our lives.

We kept moving forward, finding joy in the small things. That morning, we were getting the girls ready for a trip to the dog track. Rayna loved it. She'd stand at the fence pointing at the greyhounds, cheering like she had money on the race.

Noah was packing snacks, I was getting bottles ready, Rayna was already at the door with her shoes on the wrong feet. Everything felt light.

And then came the knock.
I wasn't expecting anyone. And when I opened the door, my heart nearly stopped.

LaMont.

Rayna's sperm donor.

Standing there like no time had passed.

I hadn't seen him in years. Not since long before Rayna was born. I didn't even know he knew where I lived. I didn't know what he wanted and didn't care either.

The second I saw his face, I knew I never wanted to see it again. "LaMont," I said, my voice tinged with shock. "What are you doing here?"

He barely hesitated before replying, his tone casual, almost as if this wasn't completely out of the blue. "I came to see my daughter. Can I take her for a little while?"

The words hit me like a slap. *Your daughter?* The same daughter you had denied even existed? The same daughter you ignored for years while I did everything I could to bring her home? I wanted to scream at him, but I bit my tongue. Instead, I just stood there, frozen, staring at him as I tried to process the audacity of his request.

LaMont and I didn't have a relationship in any real sense of the word. We had hooked up a few times for no reason other than the fact that my mom hated him. She used to work at a group home where LaMont was one of the residents, and she would come home and rant about how much she couldn't stand him. I didn't know much about him then, but her anger only made him more appealing to my teenage rebellion. I used to sneak him into her house while she was at work, thinking I was so clever for getting one over on her.

It wasn't love, or even lust. It was just a way to push back against my mother's control. One of those quick hookups, led to the pregnancy I had been hoping for and when I told LaMont, he acted like I was a stranger. He swore we had never even been together and that I must have mistaken him for someone else. The humiliation stuck with me, but I moved on, I actually didn't care one way or the other, I just wanted my baby. Now, here he was, years later, standing in front of my door, acting like he'd always been a part of her life.

I hesitated, unsure of what to do. Part of me wanted to slam the door in his face. But another part of me, the part that wanted to be better than my mother, felt conflicted. I didn't want to keep Rayna away from her biological father, even if he didn't deserve the chance to know her.

I glanced at Noah, hoping he would back me up, but he surprised me.

"I think you should let her go," he said gently, as if he could sense my hesitation.

I pulled him aside, my voice low but firm. "I don't think this is a good idea. I haven't seen him in years, Noah. I don't trust him."
Noah sighed, running a hand through his hair. "I get it. I really do.

But think about it. What if someone tried to keep me from seeing Alyra? I'd be crushed. You've got placement of Rayna now. He's her dad. Maybe letting him take her, even just for a little while, is the right thing."

His words pressed against everything in me that was screaming no. My whole body buzzed with resistance. I wanted to slam the door in LaMont's face, lock it, and never open it again. But I could see Noah's point, and the quiet plea in his eyes made me feel like saying no would make me the same as my mother.

My gut told me something wasn't right, but I pushed the feeling down, trying to convince myself it was just my overprotective nature.
"Okay," I said finally, turning back to LaMont. "You can take her, but just for a few hours."

He nodded, as if the arrangement was completely reasonable. Rayna was excited to go, her little face lighting up at the idea of a new adventure.

I kissed her forehead, and stood in the doorway as she skipped off beside him. My stomach twisted. The dread in my chest spread like wildfire until it drowned out everything else.

I couldn't shake it. I knew I had just made a mistake.

CHAPTER 34

Battle Lines Drawn

"The truth will set you free, but first it will make you miserable."

— James A. Garfield

I had been calling and calling, trying to figure out where Rayna was. It was getting late, and no one had brought her home. I was seconds away from calling the police when a neighbor knocked on my door with their phone.

It was my mother.

"You need to check on your daughter," she said. "The doctors at the hospital said she was brutally assaulted."

My whole body went numb. I could barely hold the phone. I started calling every hospital I could think of, panicked and shaking, until someone finally confirmed it. Rayna had been brought to the ER. LaMont and his girlfriend had reported Rayna was complaining of pain in her private area and claimed Noah had been touching her there.

They couldn't tell me much more, but they didn't need to. For now, Rayna was with my mother. And I knew exactly what had happened.

They were never planning to take her out for a visit. That was just the lie they told me. From the moment LaMont showed up, the plan was already set. My mother had convinced him to take Rayna straight to the hospital and tell them she'd been sexually abused. And not just by anyone. By Noah.

My heart shattered.

179

Noah adored Rayna like she was his own. Since we brought her home, he had treated her with the same love and care he gave to Alyra, never once drawing a line between "yours" and "ours." From bedtime stories to school drop-offs, he was there for all of it. Every moment. Every tear. Every laugh.

To him, Rayna wasn't just my daughter. She was ours.

When I told him what was being said, he collapsed into the couch. His face dropped into his hands, his body trembling with silent sobs. I knelt beside him and wrapped my arms around his shoulders, feeling the weight of his grief pressing down on both of us.

"Why would she do this to me?" he asked, his voice breaking. "I've done nothing but respect her. Help her. I've loved Rayna like my own. How could she say these things about me?"

He wasn't yelling. He wasn't angry. He was devastated.

To Noah, these accusations were worse than death. His entire character, everything he stood for, was being ripped apart by someone he thought was family. My mother's lies didn't just question his actions. They attacked the core of who he was.

He couldn't understand how anyone could create something so cruel out of thin air, especially about a child he had never done anything but love.

"I've never hurt her," he said, shaking his head, still trying to make sense of it all. "I would never hurt her. I don't even know how to prove that I haven't done something I didn't do."

I tried to comfort him, holding him as he cried, whispering whatever I could to ease his pain. But how could I promise it would all be okay when I didn't know what my mother might do next?

Noah wasn't just afraid for himself. He was afraid for us. For Rayna. He knew how damaging these kinds of accusations could be. How quickly people believe the worst. How hard it is to wash away a stain once it sticks.

At one point, he went quiet. His eyes drifted off, like he was somewhere else entirely. When he finally spoke, his voice was soft, uncertain.

"Maybe she'll stop if I'm not around."

The words hung between us. He wasn't trying to give up. He was trying to protect us. And as much as I hated to hear it, I understood why he said it. What my mother had done didn't just hurt him. It made him question whether his love, his goodness, his presence was enough. Whether staying meant safety or more destruction.

But I couldn't let that happen. Not after everything we had been through to bring Rayna home. I wasn't about to let my mother take that away from us. Not now. Not like this. If she was determined to go to war, then I was determined to give it to her.

The next morning, Noah and I went straight to the hospital. We needed to see the report with our own eyes. We needed to know exactly what was said, what was found, what was done. And what we learned only confirmed what we already knew. There was no abuse. No reason for any of this. No reason for the visit, no reason for the panic, no reason to rip our lives apart.

Rayna told the doctors the truth. No one had touched her. Nothing bad had happened. They ran a full exam and found a mild infection, the kind little girls sometimes get when they don't wipe well. No signs of trauma. No signs of abuse. But that didn't matter to my mother. She wasn't looking for truth. She was looking for ammunition.

I wasn't taking any chances. Noah and I went straight to the police.

We sat together in that small room as I explained everything to the detective: the court order, the exam results, the false report, the long history behind it all. He listened carefully, flipping through the hospital file as I spoke.

The whole time it felt like every word I spoke was being measured against lies that never should have been told.

But when I finished, he looked up at us and said exactly what we had been thinking all along.

"There's nothing here to suggest abuse. This looks like someone trying to hold on to custody, no matter who they have to destroy to do it."

Relief washed over me, but it wasn't over yet. I told him my mother was refusing to give Rayna back, and he nodded, understanding the urgency of the situation. "Meet us at her house at 5 p.m.," he said. "We'll get your daughter for you."

The hours between that meeting and 5 p.m. felt like days. When the time finally came, we arrived at my mother's house with the police. She greeted them with her usual fire, shouting accusations and inventing new lies on the spot. She insisted she had been advised to keep Rayna because of the alleged abuse, spinning more absurd stories as if sheer volume could make them believable. But the officers didn't entertain her theatrics.

"This is a court order," one of them said firmly. "You don't have a choice."

She screamed, threatened, and argued, but it didn't matter. Watching the officers block her path as they picked up Rayna and placed her in my arms felt like justice. Rayna's little body clung to mine like she knew exactly where she belonged. I could finally breathe. The fight wasn't over, but for now, my daughter was safe, and she was coming back home.

My mother had done everything she could to hold on to her, but she had gone too far this time, and the consequences were finally catching up to her.

When the courts learned of my mother's actions, they didn't hesitate to take a stand. At the next status hearing, I sat stiffly in my seat, anxiety tightening my chest as the judge called the case to order. The air in the room felt heavy with tension, my mother seated across the aisle, her expression as defiant as ever. She held her head high, as though the lies she'd spun hadn't already started to unravel.

The guardian ad litem presented the findings first, a detailed report that left no room for doubt about the fabricated allegations. The medical reports, the interviews, the complete lack of evidence were all laid bare for the court to see. Then came the judge's voice, firm and unwavering:

"It is the decision of this court that a psychological evaluation of the maternal grandmother is necessary before proceeding further."

For years, I had been telling everyone that my mother was the one who was nuts, but no one believed me. To finally hear the court acknowledge it felt like validation after years of being dismissed and gaslit. I fought the urge to turn and look at her, to see the expression on her face as her carefully constructed facade cracked. But I didn't need to look. I could feel it. The shift in the room as everyone else started to see what I had always known.

The days leading up to the final determination hearing were some of the most grueling I'd ever endured. Even with the court ordering my mother to undergo a psychological evaluation, I couldn't shake the feeling that she had something else up her sleeve. She always did.

I barely slept, my mind racing with "what ifs." What if she convinced the court I wasn't fit? What if she spun her lies into something more believable? What if all my work still wasn't enough?

The fear gnawed at me, but I channeled it into preparation. I went over every document, every report, every note from the guardian ad litem, determined to be ready for anything.

But amid all the tension and endless preparation, nothing could have prepared me for what actually happened at the final determination hearing.

I had come armed for battle, every document, every detail meticulously organized. I was ready for another round of accusations, more lies, and the exhausting process of defending myself yet again. But as the hearing began, I noticed the empty chair across the aisle.

My mother hadn't shown up.

Confused murmurs rippled through the courtroom as her absence became clear. Then the bailiff handed the judge a letter, sealed in a crisp white envelope. "This is a letter from the maternal grandmother," the judge announced, opening it carefully. His brow furrowed as he read the contents, and when he looked up, his expression was unreadable.

"I will now read this into the record," he said. The courtroom fell silent, the kind of silence that makes you hyper-aware of every breath, every creak of the floor beneath you.

"To the court, I am writing to formally state that I am no longer contesting custody of my granddaughter, Rayna. After careful consideration, I believe her mother has shown herself to be capable of providing a stable and loving home. I trust that she will be a good mother to Rayna."

The words didn't make sense at first. I heard them, but my mind refused to believe them. My mother had fought tooth and nail to keep my daughter from me. She ranted. She manipulated every system she could. She even accused the man I loved of molestation. And now she was just surrendering?

I glanced at the attorneys, the social workers, even the judge. Their faces mirrored my own shock, eyes wide, mouths slightly agape. The unspoken question lingered: *What just happened?*

The judge cleared his throat, his voice regaining its authoritative tone. "Based on the lack of opposition, this court awards full custody of Rayna to her mother."

For a moment, I couldn't move. Those were the words I had been fighting years to hear, yet my body stayed frozen, my mind refusing to believe it. Slowly, the truth settled in. It was over. The lies. The accusations. The endless war.

After everything she had put me through, it didn't end with another battle. It ended with a letter. A piece of paper that gave me back what I had bled and clawed for all along.

I walked out of that courtroom with every sleepless night, every false accusation, every tear shed in fear and fury still clinging to me. But none of it mattered anymore. Rayna was mine.

Completely and officially mine.

CHAPTER 35

Get Out

"The greatest glory in living lies not in never falling, but in rising every time we fall."

— Nelson Mandela

Having Rayna back for good was everything I had hoped for. Each night, as I tucked her in, I felt pride knowing I hadn't just fought for this moment. I had won.

She was home.

While I wasn't happy I had missed so many of her special moments, I was grateful that Rayna still felt loved. My sister and mother had been the ones to get her dressed in the mornings, hold her when she cried, and tuck her in at night. I never wanted to take that away from her. I let them call and visit, and I made space for their bond. I knew what it felt like to be separated from people you love. I didn't want that for Rayna.

At the time, things felt good. We were all getting along, and for once, it felt like everyone was rooting for the same outcome. My sister, Makayla, who managed a local grocery store, even helped Noah get a better-paying job there. It wasn't just the money. It was the way he carried himself after that. He stood a little straighter, smiled a little more, started paying attention to how he looked and what he wore. You could see it in the way he walked.

With his first few paychecks, we decided to update his wardrobe. We went on a thrift store spree, one of my favorite kinds of shopping since that's where my mother always shopped when I was growing up. Noah picked out all kinds of name-brand clothes for a fraction of the price, and for the first time in a long time, he actually felt good about how he looked.

The confidence boost was immediate, and honestly, it caught me off guard. Noah had never really cared about how he looked before. Clothes were just something to throw on, and his shoes were usually beat up. But now he was checking the mirror before work, matching his outfits, and collecting Jordans with every paycheck. There was a new energy in him. He walked differently. He talked differently. He didn't want to look like a bum anymore, and at first, I was happy for him.

But the more his confidence grew, the more I started to feel something else. I couldn't quite put my finger on it at the time. It wasn't anything obvious. Nothing I could point to. That is, until my sister Makayla said something.

She came to me one day with that look. That sibling look that holds both concern and a little bit of satisfaction. The kind that says, I'm about to tell you something you need to hear, but I'm also kind of glad it's not me.

"Have you noticed anything different about Noah?" she asked, tilting her head like the answer was already obvious.

I shook my head, not sure what she meant.

"Well, I have. He's been real flirty at work. Always grinning, humming, whistling, walking around like he's on top of the world. And there's this girl who's always around him."

Tiffany.

Her words hit hard. I didn't want to believe it. Not about Noah. But Makayla wasn't the type to make something up just to stir things.

I told myself she was probably overthinking it, that maybe he was just being friendly. But I couldn't shake it. The more I thought about it, the more it stayed with me.

I started noticing things I hadn't paid attention to before. How Noah spent more time getting ready for work. How he'd linger in the mirror, brushing his hair, adjusting his clothes, checking himself one more time before heading out. He used to barely care what he had on. Now he was leaving the house like he was Don Juan, convinced his looks were the most important thing in the world. Then there were the late nights, the vague stories, the times he wasn't home when he said he would be.

I didn't want to believe anything was going on or accuse Noah without proof, but the pieces weren't adding up, and my patience was running thin.

I didn't go looking through his stuff or anything like that, but I brought it up to my friend Tiana one day. Told her there was someone named Tiffany at Noah's job that Makayla had seen around him a lot. Tiana knew exactly who I was talking about and gave me her last name.

That was all I needed. We still had phone books back then. After I put the girls to bed, I looked it up, and there it was. The last name. Her number. Just sitting there on the page.

I stared at it for a while before I picked up the phone. I wasn't even sure what I expected to hear. Part of me hoped she wouldn't answer. But I called.

She picked up almost right away.

I told her I was Noah's sister, Carey. Said I had been trying to get in touch with him and figured she might know where he was. I kept my voice light, like it was just a casual call, nothing serious. The second she heard who I was, her tone changed.

"Oh my God," she said. "I've only met one of his sisters, but I've always wanted to meet more. I'm so happy you called."

She was excited. Too excited. Talking so fast, she started offering details she probably thought a sister would know.

I asked how long they had been seeing each other.

She paused for a second, like she was thinking back.

"A couple of months now." Her voice changing as she said it. Softer. Almost dreamy.

"I think it's pretty serious," she added.

And then, without me even asking, she started telling me how it all began. The more she said, the more comfortable she got. I didn't ask much. I didn't need to. She filled in the gaps herself, like someone who had been waiting for this conversation. Waiting to be seen. Waiting to be accepted by his people.

Then her tone shifted, just slightly.

"I still remember the first night," she said, her voice soft, like she was letting me in on something special. "In my kitchen. He came over one night, and we were just talking, laughing, playing around. I don't even know how we got there. But it just happened. It felt right. Like magic."

I stayed quiet. Just listened. She talked like no one else was on the line, lost in a world where he only belonged to her.

Her words reminded me of that old song. The one about the stars, the moon, the mountains, and the rivers. That was how she saw it. Some kind of love story.

And as much as it hurt to hear, I couldn't be mad at her. She didn't know. She had no idea he had a wife, and two daughters at home. To her, he was just this amazing guy who showed up, laughed with her, and made her feel special.

I thanked her, told her I hoped we'd get to meet soon, and asked her to let my "brother" know I was looking for him when she saw him.

As I hung up the phone, my hands shook with a mixture of rage and heartbreak. I did not know how to hold back the storm brewing inside me.

I was livid. The betrayal cut deep. It wasn't just that he cheated. It was where he did it. At the store where my sister worked. The same sister who helped him get the job in the first place. Like she wouldn't notice. Like she wouldn't tell me.

It was humiliating. Not just the betrayal, but the way he did it. Loud. Sloppy. Public. He didn't just break my heart. He embarrassed me.

I could not believe the disrespect. Like I wasn't the one who held him down when he had nowhere to go. Like I wasn't the reason he even had clothes on his back.

I paced the house for a while, trying to collect myself, but I couldn't. Every corner I turned felt like a reminder of him. His sneakers by the door. His cologne still lingering in the hallway.

The sound of his laugh rising from some distant memory. I was unraveling, and I knew it. But I didn't want to cry. I didn't want to talk. I wanted him to feel what I felt.

I gathered every pair of Jordans he owned. His pride and joy. The ones he used to line up in perfect rows and wipe down like they were trophies. I took the collector's editions out of their boxes. The ones he admired most. I laid them all out and started tearing through them, one by one. Scissors. Knives. My bare hands. It didn't matter. Foam and leather flew through the air like confetti.

Then came the clothes. The ones we picked out together after his first real paycheck. The ones that made him feel like a new man. I ripped every thread apart. Shirts. Jeans. Jackets. Nothing was safe. Every piece a reminder of how I had poured into him while he poured himself into someone else.

By the time I was done, I was breathing hard. My heart pounded in my chest. The living room looked like a storm had swept through it, and maybe one had. I sat in silence, waiting.

When Noah came home that evening, he walked straight into the aftermath. At first, he didn't say a word. His eyes scanned the room and landed on the pile of shredded clothes and the broken remains of his precious sneakers. His usual cocky confidence faded. He opened his mouth like he might speak, but nothing came out.

And I didn't speak either. I just stood there, watching him take it all in. Letting the silence say everything.

"What is all this?" he finally asked, his voice laced with confusion and a hint of anger.

I didn't answer right away. I stood there, arms crossed, letting him soak in the mess he had created, both in the room and in our lives. His eyes jumped from the ruined Jordans to the shredded clothes, then back to me, like he was trying to make sense of it.

"Oh, you don't know?" I said, my voice thick with sarcasm. "Let me help you out. The kitchen? Tiffany?"

His face changed. His mouth opened like he wanted to explain, but nothing came. For a split second, I saw something in his eyes. Guilt. Fear. But it didn't matter. The damage was done.
He stood there in stunned silence, his jaw clenching as he looked from me to the mess on the floor. I could see the realization hitting him. We were over.

When I finally walked away, leaving him standing in the wreckage of his choices, I felt a strange sense of release. I wasn't done feeling the hurt, but I was done feeling him.
At the doorway, I turned back one last time.

"Get out," I said. My voice didn't waver, and my eyes didn't leave his.

He hesitated for a moment, like he wanted to speak or maybe rewind time. But there was nothing left to say. Without another word, he walked out the door and to the one place he always ran to when things got hard: his mother.

CHAPTER 36

A Reset

"Every day is a chance to begin again. Don't focus on the failures of yesterday, start today with positive thoughts and expectations."

— Catherine Pulsifer

It took weeks before I could even look at him without feeling sick to my stomach. But eventually, I let him come by to see the girls. We barely spoke. Just a few words here and there when he came to pick them up or drop them off. Nothing personal. Nothing about us. He was still their father, and I wasn't going to punish them because of what he did

His betrayal hurt, but I had survived worse. My focus stayed on the girls. Their laughter. Their growth. Their need for me.

And then, slowly, he started trying to find his way back in. It wasn't through some grand gesture or apology. Just little things. A question here. A memory there. A few extra minutes at the door when he dropped off the girls.

"I messed up," he said one evening, his voice low. "I know I don't deserve another chance, but I don't want lose you. Or our family"

He swore it was a mistake. Just one time. That it didn't mean anything and he would do better. And maybe part of me wanted to believe that. This was the man I had married. The one who stood beside me when it felt like I was in it alone. I wasn't sure if I believed in him the same way anymore, but I guess I hadn't completely let go either.

I didn't let him back in that night or the next. It took a lot of time, but eventually, I started to soften. I told myself it was for the girls. For our family. For the vows we made. But deep down, I know it was also for me. For the part of me still hoping he could be the man he once was. The man I had promised to love for better or worse.

As much as I wanted to turn him away, I couldn't help but wonder if this was one of those worse moments we were supposed to fight through.

I didn't know, but I was willing to try. Willing to give us one more chance to figure it out.

What became clear almost immediately was that staying where we were would only pull us back under. There was too much noise. Too many eyes. Too many reminders of what we had just been through. And too much Wilma. Too much of my mother too.

We needed distance. A reset.

"We could go to Green Bay," Noah said one night as we sat on the couch, surrounded by the wreckage we were trying to rebuild. "It's far, but it aint too far. Close enough if we need to come back."

It wasn't a bad idea. He had stayed there before when he didn't have anywhere else to go, so he was familiar with it. It was also just a few hours away.

Still close enough to visit family, but far enough to give us some real space.

I didn't know if a new city could fix us, but I knew staying where we were would break us.

CHAPTER 37

Same Old Same Old

"If you don't learn from history, you are doomed to repeat it."

— Winston Churchill

The apartment in DePere was perfect. We had two bedrooms, a long hallway the girls ran up and down, a balcony and even a fireplace. There was also a master bedroom with a full bathroom. I didn't even know what a master bedroom was, but it was beautiful.

Down the street was a full shopping plaza, not just a store or two but everything. A grocery store. Banks. Restaurants. You could walk to just about anything you needed, and the area was peaceful. Everything was clean, quiet, and well-kept.

It was honestly better than I expected.

Noah worked the closing shift at the Burger King right down the street and brought home food every night. Whoppers, chicken sandwiches, fries, those little apple pies they made fresh. Noah loved basketball, so when he wasn't working, he'd head to the court to shoot around. There were literally no issues. Bills were manageable, the girls were happy, and for the first time in a long time, there was nothing wrong. Nothing to even argue about. Just months of pure peace.

We should have moved here a long time ago.

One afternoon, I was in the kitchen washing dishes when Noah came up behind me, wrapped his arms around my waist, and said he was going to the store.

"You need anything?" he asked.

I shook my head. "No, I'm good."

He kissed me on the neck, grabbed his wallet and keys, and headed out the door.

The girls were napping, and I sat down with a book. A couple hours later, I heard them stirring in the back room, and that's when I realized how much time had passed.

Noah still wasn't back.

At first, I figured maybe he ran into someone or stopped to eat. But the longer it went, the harder it was to ignore. I called his phone. No answer. I sent a text. Nothing.

By midnight, I was pacing the living room, glancing at the door every few minutes, Willing it to open.

When the sun came up the next morning and he still wasn't home, panic set in. I hadn't slept. I couldn't eat. I just sat there, staring at my phone, calling and texting over and over again.

"Where are you?"

"Are you okay?"

"Please call me."

The longer I waited, the more frantic the messages got. But the silence never changed.

Two days passed. I was feeding the girls, playing with them, listening to their stories but having no idea what they were talking about. I moved through the day on autopilot, just trying to keep it together. And all the while, my mind ran through every worst-case scenario. What if he'd been mugged? What if he got hit by a car? What if he was hurt somewhere and couldn't reach his phone? I kept seeing him in a ditch, phone shattered, waiting for help that wasn't coming.

By the third day, I couldn't take it anymore. I called the police and filed a missing person report.

I had already called his mother and his sisters. None of them had heard from him. My voice cracked as I gave the officer his description.

"He's about six feet tall, medium build, brown eyes. He left to go to the store a few days ago and never came back."

"Does he have any history of disappearing?" the officer asked.
"No," I said, my heart sinking. "He wouldn't just leave. He has kids. A family."

But the way he looked at me, the way the questions kept coming, it didn't feel like concern. It felt like judgment. Like the very story I was giving was dismissed as unreal before I could even finish it.

A man says he is going to the store and never comes back is the kind of thing you see on TV shows, not you expect to be living through. To him it was suspicious.

But I didn't care what that detective thought. He didn't live in this house. He didn't see the girls asking where their father was. He didn't know the way my heart jumped every time the phone rang. He didn't need to believe me. He just needed to find my husband.

By the second week of him not doing so, my mind was spinning. What if someone had done something to him? Noah was kind, but he was too trusting. What if he let his guard down with the wrong people?

The girls asked about him constantly.

"When is Daddy coming home?"

I swallowed the lump in my throat and told them I didn't know. I didn't want to lie to them. I honestly didn't know. I didn't know if he was coming back, or if I was supposed to start preparing for the possibility that he wouldn't.

I replayed every conversation we'd had before he left, searching for anything I might have missed. Some clue. Some warning. But nothing came. Just silence.

The door stayed closed. The phone stayed quiet. And I sat there, afraid that the longer it went, the less likely he was to ever walk through that door again.

I started checking my phone constantly, even when it hadn't buzzed. Any time it lit up, I'd stop what I was doing and stare at the screen like I could will it to be him. Days kept passing, and I couldn't tell if I was holding onto hope or just refusing to let go of it.

Then the phone rang, and I nearly jumped out of my skin. It was the detective handling Noah's case. My heart was pounding as I answered.

"We found him," he said.

Relief rushed through me. My knees went weak, and for a second, I thought I might cry. He was alive. He was okay.

But then the detective kept talking.

"We've spoken to him. He's fine."

Fine?

The relief turned to confusion. Then heat.

"What do you mean, fine?" I asked, my voice shaking. "Where has he been?"

There was a pause.

"He's been staying with friends. He seems to be doing well."

Doing well.

I hadn't slept. I hadn't eaten. I was dragging myself through each day trying to keep it together for the girls, and he was just out there, doing well.

I hung up the phone and stood in the quiet, trying to make sense of it. How could he do this? How could he walk away from us and act like we didn't exist?

I didn't know what to do with that information. So, I just sat with it until, days later, Noah walked back through the door.

I was in the kitchen, trying to figure out what to make for dinner, when I heard the front door creak open. I froze, my heart racing. I turned, and there he was, standing in the doorway, quiet and disheveled, holding a bag of takeout like it explained where he had been.

"Noah?" I said, my voice sharper than I intended. "Where the hell have you been?"

He avoided my eyes, shifting awkwardly from foot to foot.

"I'm sorry," he mumbled, barely above a whisper. "I didn't mean for it to go this way."

"That's it?" I snapped. "I filed a missing person report. I've been losing sleep, imagining you dead in a ditch somewhere, and all you can say is 'sorry'?"

He sighed and finally looked at me. His eyes were red, like he hadn't been sleeping much either.

"I needed a break," he said, his voice cracking. "I'm too young for this, Marla. Two kids, a house, a marriage. I never got to just live. To hang out with friends, to be stupid. To have fun. I didn't know how to handle it all."

I stared at him, my anger simmering just beneath the surface.

"So you just left?" My voice shook, though I couldn't tell if it was from rage or heartbreak. "You left me here with two kids, no explanation, no help, nothing. Do you have any idea what you put us through?"

His shoulders slumped. He rubbed the back of his neck like a child caught in a lie.

"I know I messed up," he said. "I wasn't thinking. I just... I didn't know what else to do. Everything felt like too much, and I panicked."

I wanted to scream at him, to throw every bit of my pain in his face. But when I looked at him, I didn't just see guilt. I saw fear. Shame. Regret. He wasn't trying to dodge what he did.

I took a deep breath, trying to steady myself. "Well, while you were out pulling disappearing acts," I said, my voice flat, "I found out I'm pregnant."

His eyes shot up. "Pregnant?" he repeated, like he couldn't believe what he'd just heard.

"Yeah, Noah. Pregnant." I crossed my arms. "So, if two kids and a wife were too much, now might be a good time to head back out that door."

He sank into a chair and buried his face in his hands. "I didn't know. I didn't mean to leave you like that. I didn't mean to leave them."

He kept talking. Apologizing. Promising to do better. Promising to be better. It took everything in me not to walk away right then and there. But I stayed, listening as he poured his heart out.

I heard the regret in his voice. The fear in his words. And as much as I wanted to stay angry, I understood. We were young. Neither of us ever really got to live. We met in high school, and before we even graduated, we already had a place, a child, a marriage, and a custody battle.

He had stood by me through all of it. Helping me fight for Rayna. Watching his own life unravel in the process. He was my husband. He didn't leave when it got hard for me. I wasn't going to leave now that it was hard for him.

CHAPTER 38

A Father's Dream

"A father is a man who expects his son to be as good a man as he meant to be."

— Frank A. Clark

Noah was home. He was sorry.

He kissed the girls goodnight. He took out the trash. He was trying.

But I couldn't forget that he said two kids and a wife already felt like too much.

And now there would be three.

Three kids and a wife.

If two already had him ready to walk away, what was a third going to do?

I wasn't sure if he could handle it.

I wasn't even sure if we could.

But then we found out it was a boy.

A boy changed everything.

A boy was a dream come true.

A boy put us on cloud nine.

A boy wasn't just another baby. A boy meant possibility. A boy meant legacy. The one who would carry Noah's name, his blood, his footsteps.

A son felt like a second chance to get it right.

Noah was ecstatic. A boy. His boy. He'd always loved basketball and dreamed of going to the NBA when he was younger, but life had other plans. Now, he saw this baby as his second chance. He was already talking about the lessons he'd teach him, the drills they'd practice together, and how he'd make sure Noah Jr. didn't make the same mistakes he had.

"He's going to be a NBA star," Noah would say with a grin. "Better than Jordan."

His excitement was infectious. We couldn't wait to meet our son. Every little kick brought more laughter. Every ultrasound made it feel more real. I was finally getting the boy I'd always dreamed of, and Noah was getting the chance to share something he loved with someone who could carry his name.

One second, we were floating. The next, I was gripping the cold metal bedrails in a hospital room.

I had come in for some spotting, trying to convince myself it was nothing. But the moment they began the exam, I could tell something was off.

The doctors' voices dropped low, their faces too careful, their movements too controlled. It wasn't the quiet of reassurance. It was the kind of silence that told me something was terribly, irreversibly wrong.

An incompetent cervix. That's what they called it.

A clinical term for when the cervix starts to open before the baby is ready. Before there's any real chance of survival.

What it really meant was that my body had betrayed me. Again.

And because of that, I was losing my son. My baby boy.

I didn't even realize I was delivering. They were still examining me when suddenly they said he was coming. I must have pushed, but I don't remember. My body moved without me.

And then he was here.

Baby Noah.

Still enclosed in the amniotic sac.

Like he hadn't been born at all.

The fluid was clear, the membrane unbroken—like a thin veil between life and loss.

He floated there, perfectly still.

Tiny hands. Tiny feet. Every detail of him complete.

He looked untouched. Preserved. As if the sac was still protecting him, still trying to keep him safe.

He didn't look gone.

He looked like he was waiting.

Like if they could do something, maybe everything would be okay.

But they couldn't.

And I couldn't.

My heart begged them to try.

To pause everything.

To undo this moment.

"Can't you do something?" I asked the doctors, my voice cracking through sobs. "Can't you put him back? Can't you incubate him or... or something?"

They exchanged glances. One of them stepped forward, her voice low and full of sorrow.

"I'm so sorry. He's too early. His lungs aren't developed enough. There's nothing we can do."

Her words shattered me. Too early. Not developed. Nothing they could do.

Noah stood beside me, his hand gripping mine as if he could hold me together by sheer force.

But he couldn't.

Baby Noah was gone.

How could this have happened again? First Angel, now Noah Jr. I was shattered. I cried until my chest ached, until it felt like there was nothing left inside me but an unbearable hollow.

Noah was there, holding me through the worst of it, trying to be strong for both of us. His tears fell freely as I sobbed into his chest.

He stayed by my side, refusing to let go, even when I screamed and cried and begged for the pain to stop. Sometimes, I pushed him away, yelled at him to leave me alone.

But he didn't.

He'd just sit there quietly, letting me fall apart, and when I was ready, he'd pull me back into his arms. "I've got you," he'd say, over and over, as if repeating it enough times could make it true.

But no amount of comfort could fill the empty space where my son should have been. That emptiness had a voice, and it whispered cruel things to me in the dark hours of the night.

This is your fault. Your body failed him.

The words echoed in my mind so much I started to believe them.

And then, the whispers turned outward. Sometimes, I blamed Noah. I never said it out loud, but in my mind, I replayed every event that had led us here. *If he hadn't disappeared... if he hadn't left me stressed out and trying to carry everything on my own... maybe Baby Noah would still be here.*

I would look at him sometimes and feel a flash of anger so sharp it took my breath away. He'd sit there, trying his best to comfort me, and all I could think was, *Where were you when I needed you most? Where were you when he needed you most?* It wasn't fair, and I knew it. But grief isn't fair. It twists and bends reality until you don't recognize yourself.

Losing Noah Jr. reopened old wounds I had spent years stitching shut. Angel. The first baby I lost this way. I had barely survived that heartbreak, and now here I was again, holding the memory of a child I would never get to raise. It felt like the universe was punishing me, testing how much I could take before I broke completely.

"Why does this keep happening?" I sobbed one night, curled up on the couch with Noah. "What did I do to deserve this?"

"You didn't do anything," he said, his voice steady but heavy with emotion. "This isn't your fault, Marla. None of it is your fault."

But I didn't believe him. How could I? The pain was too raw, too consuming. I replayed every moment of both pregnancies, searching for what I could have done differently. Maybe if I'd been calmer, healthier, stronger, my babies would still be here. But none of that mattered. It didn't change the fact that Baby Noah was gone. It didn't change the fact that we were two people surrounded by broken pieces, grieving the same child and trying to move forward in different ways.

For Noah, moving forward seemed to mean having sex constantly, as if physical closeness could fill the void left by our son. It was mechanical, predictable, and anything but comforting.

Every time, it was the same. Right hand at my lower back. Left hand touching a breast. His movements so rehearsed it felt like I was watching the same bad rerun on repeat. I hated it. I wanted to scream, to shove him away, to tell him it wasn't helping. But I didn't. I just laid there, waiting for it to be over. I could see he was trying, in his own misguided way, to show love and support.

It wasn't long before I found out I was pregnant again, three months at best. Grief hadn't even finished hollowing me out before I was staring at the two pink lines on the bathroom counter. My emotions were a tangled mess of disbelief, fear, and something I couldn't quite name.

This should have been a moment of joy, but it wasn't. I wasn't ready. My body wasn't ready. My heart wasn't ready. How could I be happy about this pregnancy when I was still mourning Baby Noah?

The doctors were optimistic. This time, they would monitor me closely and perform a cerclage at 12 weeks to prevent my cervix from opening prematurely. I started seeing a specialist who reassured me at every appointment that everything was under control. But even with their confidence, I couldn't shake the anxiety, the feeling that something would go wrong again.

When I found out it was a girl, my emotions twisted in ways I didn't expect. I wasn't disappointed, but I wasn't excited either.

After losing Baby Noah, I had been holding on to the idea of having a boy. But it wasn't a boy. It was a girl. And while I knew I would love her, I needed time to let go of the story I had written in my head and make room for a new one.

When Noah found out it was a girl, his reaction was less subtle. The disappointment was written all over his face, in the way his shoulders slumped and his smile faltered. "A girl, huh?" he said, forcing a grin that was more of a frown. "Well, I guess that's good, too."

He had been so excited about having a son, someone he could teach basketball to and share his dreams with. It was clear that this wasn't what he'd hoped for, and while he tried to hide it, the truth was obvious. I didn't say anything at the time. What could I say? I was still sorting through my own complicated feelings about this baby.

Despite the tension and the undercurrent of grief that still lingered, we occasionally found moments where we felt like us again. One evening, I sat on Noah's lap while he played a video game, leaning against him as the sound of buttons clicking filled the room. The girls were on the floor, sprawled out with crayons and coloring books, giggling as they watched their dad play.

Then the house phone rang. I sighed and got up to answer it, thinking it was nothing important. "Hello?" I said.

"Hi… um, is Noah there?" a woman's voice replied. She sounded young but unsure, her words hesitating like she wasn't entirely confident about making the call. "Who's calling?" I asked, more out of curiosity than concern.

"It's Ashley," she said. Her voice had a nervous edge, but nothing about it raised any alarms for me. I shrugged and handed the phone to Noah. "It's for you," I said, settling back onto his lap as he took the call.

The conversation didn't last long. Just a few ohs, ahs, and a "Yeah, I haven't talked to him in a while." Nothing about his tone felt strange. No shift in his body. No hesitation in his voice. When the call ended, he handed the phone back to me without explanation and went right back to his game.

I shifted off his lap and settled into the couch beside him, one hand resting on my belly. I didn't think twice about the call. Nothing about it stood out. No red flags. No reason to question anything.

There were other things on my mind.

By then, I was already on bedrest. The doctors had placed a cerclage in my cervix to keep it from opening too soon, and I was under strict orders to stay off my feet. No work. No lifting. No unnecessary movement. I stayed mostly on the couch, managing what I could from where I was. I counted kicks. I counted days. I tried not to count everything that could go wrong.

Even though life wasn't perfect, we made it work. Noah did what he could. I did what I had to.

For the first time in a while, it felt like we were on solid ground.

CHAPTER 39

The Edge of the Balcony

"Sometimes you just have to jump off the cliff without knowing where you will land."

— Zainab Salbi

It was a typical day, but all morning, a nagging thought kept creeping into my mind. Check the mail. It wasn't just a passing idea. It kept coming back every time I tried to relax. At first, I ignored it. The mailbox wasn't far, but I was tired, and walking all the way there felt like more effort than it was worth. I thought about asking Noah to check it for me, but something held me back. I couldn't explain why. So I let it go.

Still, the feeling wouldn't go away.

Technically, I was supposed to be on bedrest. But the girls were getting restless, and we had library movies to return. I figured a short drive wouldn't hurt. Just there and back. I told myself it would be quick, easy, and harmless.

Being cooped up all day was wearing on me anyway, and the thought of getting out for even a few minutes felt like relief. As we walked past the mailbox on our way to the car, that nagging thought from earlier returned. Stronger this time.

Check the mail.

I hesitated, then opened it and pulled out a small stack of envelopes. Flyers. Credit card offers. The usual junk. But one envelope stood out.

It looked official. The return address said it was from the state.

My stomach tightened. For a second, I thought it was another ticket that needed to be paid. Noah had a heavy foot, and ever since we used our tax return on that used car, the tickets had started piling up. I figured it was just another fine we'd have to scrape together money for.

I didn't stop walking. I carried the stack with me as I got the girls buckled into their car seats. Then I slid into the driver's seat and shut the door.

I sat there for a moment, envelope in hand. It didn't feel like a ticket. It felt heavy.

I opened it and began to read.

The words blurred together at first, my mind refusing to process them. My breath caught in my throat.

I read the letter again, slower this time, praying I had misunderstood. But no matter how many times I read it, the words didn't change.

Noah was being sued for child support by Ashley. The same Ashley who had called our house weeks ago. She had listed him as the father. And she had named her son after him. Not directly, but close enough to make it undeniable.

Each word sank deeper than the last. A son. A child I knew nothing about. It wasn't just the betrayal. It was the fact that he had carried this secret while I carried our baby. That he had said nothing. That he had let me sit on his lap, let our girls color at his feet, let our life feel whole while another life he had created waited in the shadows of ours.

I sat there in the car, the girls chatting happily in the back, completely oblivious to the storm building inside me. My hands trembled as I clutched the letter, my mind racing. How could he? How could he have done this to me, to us? We had just lost our son, and now I was finding out he had another. One he never even told me about.

It was too much. The betrayal, the lies, the timing. All of it crashed down at once. I wasn't just angry. I was livid. My vision blurred with tears, but they weren't from sadness. This was rage. Raw, unfiltered rage.

I wasn't going to wait for explanations. I wasn't going to sit in silence and hope the truth came out on its own. I needed answers. And I needed them now.

I took the girls calmly back upstairs, the letter clutched tightly in my hand. I opened the door to our apartment and heard the familiar sound of a basketball bouncing down the hallway. Noah was playing, casually shooting into the makeshift hoop we had set up. He looked so carefree, so at ease, and it only fueled the fire burning inside me.

"Rayna," I said, my voice steady and composed, "take Alyra and go to your room and play." Rayna glanced at me, sensing something wasn't right, but she didn't question it. She took Alyra by the hand and led her into their room, closing the door behind them.

Noah must have sensed the shift in the air because he stopped dribbling the ball and turned to face me, his expression a mix of confusion and unease. "What's going on?" he asked.

I didn't answer. Instead, I walked into the kitchen, opened the drawer, and pulled out the biggest knife I could find. When I turned back to face him, his eyes widened in disbelief.

"You're being sued for child support!?" I yelled, my voice shaking with fury. "You have a baby? A son? After I lost mine?!"

Noah froze, the basketball slipping from his hands. "What? Marla, I can explain." His voice cracked, but I wasn't in the mood for explanations.

"Explain what?" I screamed. "Explain how you fathered a son with some bitch while I was carrying our child? Explain how you let me lose him while you had another behind my back?"

"What exactly would you like to explain?" I screamed, raising the knife ready to end it all right then and there.

His eyes went wide and he turned and ran full speed toward the bedroom.

I didn't even blink. I stormed after him, my feet pounding the floor, the knife still in my grip. He barely got the door closed before I reached it, but it didn't matter. I raised my leg and kicked with strength I didn't even know I had.

The frame cracked. The lock gave way. The door flew open.

"Marla, stop!" he yelled, his voice panicked.

But I couldn't stop. I didn't want to stop.

All I could think about was putting that knife in his chest the same way he'd put it in mine.

I stood in the splintered doorway, knife in hand, ready.

In that moment, whatever I felt for him died. And he was about to follow.

I took a step forward, but he turned and ran.

I was right behind him.

As I passed the kitchen, I grabbed a second knife off the counter and hurled it with everything I had. It slammed into the wall just inches from where he had been a second before. He ducked behind the island, peeking out, eyes wild with fear.

"Marla, please!" he yelled. "You're pregnant! Think about the baby!"

Oh, I was thinking about the baby. The one he had with Ashley.

I snatched another knife and threw it just as hard. It clattered against the cabinet behind him, missing again, but not by much. He ducked back behind the counter.

"Marla, please, stop!" he cried out, his voice cracking. "Just let me explain!"

But I didn't want explanations. I didn't want apologies.

I was going to kill him. That was it. That was all.

Driven by sheer panic, Noah ran to the balcony, his eyes wide with terror. I followed without hesitation, the knife still clenched tightly in my hand.

I was still coming, footsteps closing in.

He looked back at me, desperation written all over his face. He had just watched me kick down the door, pregnant and furious, and he understood there was no reasoning with me. Not then. Not like that.

He was almost out of time.

He climbed over the railing and jumped.

I hoped he broke every bone in his body.

Unbelievable.

Child support.

Ashley.

A son.

CHAPTER 40

Unspoken Bonds

"Forgiveness is the fragrance that the violet sheds on the heel that has crushed it."

— Mark Twain

For better or worse. For richer, for poorer. In sickness and in health. To love and to cherish, till death do us part.

That's what I stood there and promised. Eyes locked on his, hand in his hand. In front of all our friends and family. In front of God. I made a promise.

But no one tells you what worse might really look like. I should have left him.

After the letter. After the knife. After chasing him through our apartment, screaming like I had lost my mind. After watching him jump off a second-story balcony just to get away from me.

Any reasonable person would have walked away.

But sometime after midnight, he came back. Crying. Begging. Pleading. He was so sorry. So, so sorry.

He said he never meant to hurt me. That it happened during his break, when he needed space. He told me he knew about the pregnancy, but he wasn't sure if the baby was his.

Still, he said he couldn't leave me like this. Not while I was pregnant. Not when the doctors had already said I needed to be on bed rest.

He said he wanted to be here this time. That he should have been there for baby Noah, and he wasn't going to make that mistake again. If for no other reason, he needed to help with the girls.

And in that moment, I didn't have the energy to argue.

My body ached. My head was pounding. I was pregnant. And we had two little girls who still needed breakfast and clean clothes and a mother who could hold it together.

So, I let him back in. He was right. I needed help with the girls. And starting over felt harder than staying.

But letting him back in didn't undo what had been done.

The silence between us wasn't peace. It was restraint. I couldn't unsee that letter. I couldn't un-know that somewhere out there, another woman had given birth to his child.

If we were going to make it work, there could be no more secrets. No more lies. No more pretending this wasn't real.

We had to face it head on.

So, I called her.

She answered on the first ring.

I introduced myself calmly. Told her who I was. She didn't hang up. Didn't get defensive.

"I didn't know he was married until after I was already pregnant," she said. Her voice was soft, unsure, but not malicious. She wasn't trying to start anything. She was just telling the truth.

And honestly, I believed her.

She didn't owe me loyalty. Noah did.

We made plans to come see the baby the next day.

When we pulled up, she was already standing in the doorway, rocking him in her arms. Noel. A tiny, sleepy boy, barely aware of the damage his existence had caused.

I stayed back while Noah stepped forward.

He held him carefully, like he didn't want to break him. His face flickered with a mixture of awe and guilt.

There was no denying it. Noel was his.

It was perfect, wasn't it?

Noah and Noel.

And as I stood there watching them, Noah holding the son he had with another woman, I didn't know what hurt more.

Seeing him with the baby he created without me.

Or standing there accepting that this was part of my life now, whether I wanted it to be or not.

Ashley's voice broke through my thoughts. She asked if I wanted to hold him. I hesitated. My hands were steady, but inside, I wasn't. I didn't know how it would feel to hold the baby who had come from something so painful.

Before I could answer, she stepped forward and gently placed him in my arms.

It felt like a peace offering. A quiet acknowledgment of everything we both knew but couldn't say.
I sat down slowly, easing into a rocking chair with him pressed against my chest.

He was warm. Quiet. His little breath rising and falling like the world had never shaken.

And for a moment, it felt like I was holding baby Noah. Like somehow, through all the pain and betrayal, I had been given another chance to feel something that was taken from me too soon.

Noel was innocent. Just like baby Noah had been.

I couldn't blame him. And I couldn't blame Ashley. She hadn't known. She hadn't lied.

In that moment, something softened in me.

And without even meaning to, Noel found a place in my heart. From then on, we stayed in touch with Ashley.

Noel became a part of our life. Whenever she needed extra help, we'd take him for the weekend. Sometimes even longer.
It wasn't something we planned. None of this was. But somehow, we adjusted.

He actually fit faster than I imagined. He was quiet, easygoing, and the girls adored him. Alyra would come look at him like he was her baby doll. Rayna took on the role of helper, bringing diapers and singing lullabies in her little off-key voice.

And while we were settling into this new version of our life, Wilma called.
After years of skipping rent and working the system, no one would help her. She asked us to take Frankie.

I had always thought of Frankie like a little sister. She was Wilma's youngest daughter, sweet and wide-eyed, and completely devoted to her big brother.

Wilma acted like it was no big deal. "Just for a little while. Until I get back on my feet."

She was a liar and a user and definitely not my favorite person, but Frankie didn't deserve to be caught up in her mother's mess. And if I was already opening my heart to someone else's child, what was one more?

I looked down at my swollen belly, thinking about the bed rest and no-stress orders I was under. But what could I say?

We couldn't let Frankie suffer. She was Noah's baby sister.
Noah drove down to get her. It seemed like she only came with the clothes on her back. But we adjusted.

It actually helped having another set of hands around the house. After school, Frankie played with the girls and kept them entertained when I needed to rest.

She quickly became part of our little family. She and Rayna bonded like sisters. Alyra lit up whenever Frankie walked into the room.

And just like that, our house expanded again.
But the space didn't.

We were still in a two-bedroom apartment, barely enough room to breathe. Beds lined the walls. Toys spilled into the hallway. Every inch was claimed, and every day felt louder than the one before.

After Abigail was born, just a few months later, it really felt like they were closing in. The girls bickered over space, over toys, over who got to sit closest to me. The living room doubled as a bedroom. The kitchen felt like a tightrope.
So when we found the duplex, it felt like a blessing.

Three bedrooms. A finished basement. A two-car garage. Room to stretch out, and to breathe again.

There was an upstairs and a downstairs, a real dining room where I pictured family dinners, and a backyard big enough for the kids to run around, we could even put a swing set out there.

The girls fell in love with it right away. Rayna and Alyra raced up and down the stairs, squealing as they picked their room. Frankie was just as excited. She finally had a space to call her own.

For all of us, it was a new beginning.

CHAPTER 41

They're My Family

"You can love them, forgive them, want good things for them… but still move on without them."

— Mandy Hale

For the first few months in the new house, life felt calm. Not perfect, but peaceful. We had space. The girls had their rooms.

Frankie had slipped right into our family like she had always belonged. She helped Alyra find her shoes in the mornings, taught Rayna how to fold her clothes, and made everyone laugh with her goofy impressions. If Noel cried, she was the first to pick up a toy to distract him. She didn't have to be asked. She just jumped in. She didn't feel like a guest. She felt like ours.

Even the little things started to feel easier. We'd finish dinner and clean up together. Sometimes I'd sit on the couch and just breathe. No screaming, no tension, just the sound of kids laughing in the distance and Noah nearby. I could feel myself softening again.

Then I found out I was pregnant. Again.

Rayna was six, Alyra was about to turn three, Noel was only thirteen months, and Abigail was eight months. I had already been pregnant twice in the last year, and now here we were, adding another to the mix.

I was still waking up in the middle of the night, juggling bottles, diapers, school drop-offs, and the endless hum of little voices needing something. Every day felt like a fight to keep up, to make sure each child felt seen and loved.

I was tired. My body hadn't even had a chance to recover. It didn't feel like mine anymore. It felt like my life had turned into this never-ending loop of pregnancy, baby, toddler, and then right back to pregnant again.

Noah, was thrilled. "It's another boy, I just know it," he said, grinning like it was the best news in the world. I let him believe that. Let him have his joy. I smiled. I nodded. I even believed it a little myself. We were at peace.

But peace never lasted long in my world. Carey called.

At first, it seemed harmless. She said she wanted to visit for a little while. I didn't mind. Family visits were normal, and Carey and I had never had any real issues. She was loud, yes, and a little overbearing, but nothing I couldn't handle. I figured it might even be good for Frankie to see more of her family.

So of course, we said yes.

But what started as a visit quickly turned into something else.

Carey hadn't just come for a few days. Before I knew it, she was practically living in our house with her daughter. And if that wasn't enough, her boyfriend showed up too.

Suddenly, our beautiful, spacious home didn't feel so spacious. It wasn't just the number of people. It was the noise. The movement. The overwhelming presence of them all. The energy was different. Carey and her boyfriend drank and argued, sometimes late into the night. Her daughter ran wild. Her boyfriend laid around all day, stretched out on the couch like he paid bills. He didn't work, didn't help, didn't offer so much as a thank you. He just existed, in my space.

I tried to be understanding. I tried to be patient. I tried. I really did. But it wasn't long before I couldn't take it anymore.
One evening, after stepping over a pile of toys Carey's daughter had left in the hallway, I finally snapped.

"This isn't what we agreed to," I said to Noah, my voice tight with frustration. "This is our home. Not a shelter for every single person in your family."

"They're my family," he said, shrugging like it was no big deal. "They need help right now. It's temporary."

"Temporary?" I repeated, the word bitter in my mouth. "Like Frankie's temporary? Because nothing about this feels temporary. It feels like they've moved in."

"They're going through a hard time," he said. "We've got the space, don't we?"

I stared at him.

His casual tone infuriated me. I wanted to scream, to make him see what I saw. Our house wasn't just full. It was being taken over. But Noah didn't get it, or maybe he didn't want to. All he saw was his family needing help and thought it was my job to accommodate them.

But I was already stretched thin.

I was well into my pregnancy. Abigail was still in diapers. Noel was still in diapers. We had Alyra, Rayna, and Frankie. And now Carey, her daughter, and her boyfriend? It was too much.

The kitchen lost all rhythm. I couldn't keep up with meals or cleaning. I started avoiding the living room altogether. It was loud, messy, not mine anymore. And Noah just kept shrugging, acting like it wasn't that serious.

But it was.

I had worked so hard to build a home where our kids could feel safe and stable. And now I was the stranger in it.

CHAPTER 42

Family Doesn't Mean Forever

"We cannot simultaneously set a boundary and take care of another person's feelings."

— Melody Beatti

As if things weren't bad enough, Wilma decided she wanted to visit. She kept calling, insisting she needed to come for Frankie's school open house. It made no sense. Who travels all that way just for an open house? It was ridiculous, and I wasn't having it.

"Noah, there's no room for your mom here," I said, trying to stay calm. I had told him repeatedly that she couldn't come. We were already overcrowded. I didn't want her here. I was clear. I had drawn my line.

And Noah stepped right over it.

He let her come anyway. Not because I agreed. Not because we compromised. But because she was his mom.

"She promised it would only be for two days," he told me, as if that somehow made it okay. As if my objections, my boundaries, were nothing compared to her word.

The day she arrived, I felt the tension, the intrusion, and the disruption in the air before she even stepped inside.

Wilma swept into the house like she owned it, eyes scanning every wall and corner like she was taking inventory. She had her suitcase in one hand, judgment in the other.

She didn't wait to settle in before stirring the pot. Within minutes, she was rearranging the kitchen, moving my pots, commenting on the bread I bought, asking if I needed help cooking as if I hadn't been feeding this household every day without her.

She critiqued what shows the kids were watching, questioned what they were wearing, and followed me from room to room with endless stories I didn't ask to hear.

It was supposed to have been two days. Four, five, six days passed, and she hadn't packed a thing.

By then, whatever balance we had left was gone. Carey and her boyfriend were already draining the house, but now Wilma had turned it into a full-blown circus. She and Carey started teaming up, their voices rising over mine, their opinions drowning out any sense of order I tried to maintain.

I was tired. I was pregnant. I had four kids to manage, two of them still in diapers. And instead of support, I had a woman planting herself deeper and deeper into my life while my husband stood on the sidelines.

Wilma was worse than my mother, and that was saying something. Where my mother's cruelty was overt, Wilma's was wrapped in sweetness and feigned innocence. She played the part of the doting mother and grandmother so well that people rarely saw the destruction she left in her wake until it was too late.

And now, she had turned her schemes toward us.

I could see the cracks forming in my relationship with Noah. He was caught in the middle, but instead of standing by me, he let his family take over. He didn't set boundaries; he didn't push back. It was like he didn't even see what was happening or worse, didn't care.

"They're my family," he said again, like that was supposed to be an excuse.

"And what about us, Noah? What about *our* family?" I shot back, my voice shaking with anger. "You're letting them destroy everything we've built."

But my words fell on deaf ears. He just didn't get it. He never did when it came to Wilma. Allowing her to come was the worst decision he could have made.

Her first move was as conniving as it was audacious. After I had repeatedly asked her to leave and reminded her that she had only agreed to stay for a few days to attend Frankie's open house, Wilma did what Wilma always did. She schemed.

She took her sob story to my neighbors, painting herself as a helpless victim of my cruelty. According to her, I was the villain, trying to throw her out on the street with nowhere to go. It was an act so convincing that they didn't hesitate to help her.

She had them forge my signature on her welfare application, claiming she lived with me. "I just need a little help," she must have said, tears likely glistening in her eyes. They felt so bad for her that they never questioned the consequences their "kindness" could have for me and my family. They didn't know that I had explicitly told Wilma not to use my address for anything, that I had warned her against pulling one of her schemes.

I couldn't believe it when the letter came, notifying me that my own welfare benefits were being terminated due to fraud for unreported household members. Fraud caused by her lies.

The support that helped keep my kids fed, the benefits that helped us survive, were gone. And now I was under investigation.

She had put my entire family in jeopardy. She wasn't a household member. I didn't even want her at my house at all. She was never supposed to have even been there.

I stormed into the kitchen and slapped the letter down on the table in front of Noah. My hands were trembling, the words blurring together in my mind as anger bubbled to the surface.

"Look at what your mother has done!" I hissed, the letter crumpling slightly under my grip. "We're being investigated for fraud because of her! Our entire life is under review because of her lies! We could lose everything!"

Noah stared at the paper, his face a mask of confusion and shame. His lips parted as if to say something, but the words didn't come. Finally, after a long silence, he muttered, "I'll talk to her about it."

"You'll talk to her about it?" I repeated, my voice rising with incredulity. "That's all you've got? She's destroyed our livelihood, Noah! Your mother is jeopardizing the lives of your children, and all you can say is you'll talk to her?"

My words hung in the air like a challenge, daring him to step up, to take responsibility for the mess his mother had made. But deep down, I already knew the answer. Wilma had a hold on Noah that I couldn't break. She was his mother, and that title alone seemed to excuse everything she did in his eyes.

I was done talking. Done pleading. Done tiptoeing around his mother's manipulative schemes.

"She has to go," I said, my voice cold and final.

"And if you won't tell her to leave, I'll call the police and have them remove her, but she's getting out of this house today. All of them. Carey. Her boyfriend. Her daughter. Everyone. Out."

He looked at me with tired eyes, as if I was the one causing problems. "It's not that simple," he said. "She's got nowhere to go."

"She should've thought about that before she had my name signed on these papers!" I snapped.

Noah stared at me, his face a mixture of shame and defeat. He knew I was serious, but still, he hesitated. I watched as he made his way to deliver the news, and even then, he couldn't stand up to her. "She said you have to go," he told them, avoiding the responsibility himself. Not WE said, not it's time to leave, but she said.

It was the final straw. Wilma had jeopardized everything we worked for. And Noah's failure to stand up to her sealed our fate.

CHAPTER 43

Spin Cycle

"The most dangerous woman of all is the one who refuses to rely on your sword to save her because she carries her own."

— R.H. Sin

The night Noah left, he chose his family over ours. He packed up, took Frankie, and walked out the door with them. I thought their leaving would bring me peace, maybe even relief. But I couldn't have been more wrong. His mother, Wilma, somehow managed to get into another unit absurdly close to mine. So close that our backyards touched. It felt like I was being haunted. She was two houses over, right there in plain view. I couldn't believe it. This woman who had nearly ruined my life was now settled within walking distance.

And she took full advantage. She and her kids walked back and forth like they still belonged here. They'd stop by uninvited, popping up to see the kids or asking to borrow something.

Carey, always up to something, was the worst of them. One day, she took my car without even asking and got it towed. No call. No apology. Just the keys missing and the car gone.

No matter how much I tried to shut the door, they refused to stay out.

If taking my car wasn't bad enough, I walked into the laundry room and her clothes were in my washer? I didn't care that they were still washing, I called her to come get them and come get them NOW.

She came over angry, yelling at me like I had done something to her.

"Seriously?" I said, exasperated. "You didn't even ask. You just helped yourself like this is your house. Get your stuff out my washer and get out."

She couldn't leave it alone. She kept going. Talking about how they hadn't even gone through the spin cycle yet. Then she stepped up in my face, and we were chest to chest. Carey was big, and she didn't care who she fought. She had gone toe to toe with men, she definitely didn't have no problem going at it with me.

If she thought it was gonna be easy though, she needed to think again. I was pregnant and was going to protect my baby by any means necessary.

After we got into a little wrestling match. I grabbed the pot off the stove and swung it so hard, I tried to knock her head off with it.

It didn't knock her head off, but it knocked some sense into it. She stopped, stunned, and without another word, she gathered her wet behind clothes and left.

I didn't wait for her to change her mind. I grabbed my keys and went straight to the hospital. I needed to make sure my baby was okay. Thank God he was.

But I wasn't. That fight was it for me. I was tired of being disrespected, tired of everyone taking and giving me their ass to kiss.

I was done compromising. I was done forgiving. I was done accepting bullshit in the name of love.

I was done with Noah's family. And I was done with Noah too.

I filed for divorce.

CHAPTER 44

Bridges Burned, Bridges Built

"Life is a balance between holding on and letting go."

— Rumi

I don't know the exact moment things started going in the wrong direction. Maybe it was slow, like a leak you don't notice until the floor is already warped beneath your feet. All I know is, when I met Noah, I still believed in the idea of us. Not just him and me, but the kind of "us" that could take on the world and win.

In the beginning, Noah made it easy to believe. He was steady. He was supportive. He stood by me through court dates and sleepless nights, encouraging me every time I walked into a courtroom to fight for custody of Rayna. He was my teammate, my confidant, and for a while, I thought he might even be my future.

But things changed. Or maybe I did. Or maybe we both did.

I know I wasn't always easy to love. I had trust issues rooted deep. People in my life had a way of disappearing just when I needed them most. So, I kept a wall up. I stayed guarded. I expected Noah to leave, and if I'm honest, I probably pushed him away trying to brace for the moment he did.

Still, that doesn't excuse everything he did. The lying. The cheating. The baby with someone else. Those weren't just slip-ups. They were betrayals. And I called them mistakes because it was easier than admitting I had built my life around someone who was tearing it apart.

While he was betraying me in ways I couldn't control, I was making choices of my own. Choices I thought would hold us together.

Choices that left scars just as deep. For me, those choices came with consequences. They came with a record.

By the time I met Noah, I already had one charge from the incident with the nurse. Being with him brought two more.

The first was the worthless check. We had three kids, no money, and a fridge that always seemed one day away from empty. I used one of his checks to buy groceries, convinced there'd be money in the account before it cleared. But of course, it wasn't.

When the check bounced, it didn't just overdraft my account. It overdrew my future. I thought I was walking out with groceries. What I carried instead was a criminal charge that followed me for years.

Then came the obstruction charge, the one that still makes my stomach turn when I think about it.

We had just left Racine and were on the road, snow falling steady, blanketing everything in white. The kind of cold that sinks into your bones no matter how many layers you wear. Noah was driving, and yeah, he was speeding. When the flashing lights hit behind us, I knew it was bad. But I didn't realize how bad until they ran his name. He had a warrant. Unpaid tickets. Nothing serious, but serious enough for them to take him in.

I should've stepped aside. Should've let them do their job. But I didn't. I lost it. I held on to that man like my life depended on it. Me and the officers ended up in a full-on tug of war in the snow, each one of us pulling at him like we could change what was happening. At one point, we all went down, slipping and falling in the cold, wet, snow.

That charge didn't just go on my record. It carved into my memory. A frozen moment in time that still makes me ask what exactly I was holding on to. And why?

Maybe because in my mind, losing him felt like losing everything. But looking back, I see it was me I was losing all along.

After everything with Noah, I was picking up the pieces, starting to rebuild. And that's when someone I unexpected stepped into my life

CHAPTER 45

A Familiar Stranger

"Every second a seeker can start over, for his life's mistakes are initial drafts and not the final version."

— Sri Chinmoy

I hadn't seen him in years, not since childhood. Back then, his presence had been fleeting. He would appear and disappear just as quickly, caught in a cycle of addiction and incarceration. To me, he was more myth than man, a name I knew without ever really knowing the person behind it. I had long since stopped wondering if he'd ever come back.

Besides, I had already found my father. Junior was the man who had stepped in when Howard had stepped out. Junior was the one who had been there, the one I had called "Daddy" with certainty, with love. He had filled that role without hesitation, becoming the anchor I hadn't known I needed.

So, when I ran into Howard's sister, Francine, and she said, "He'd love to hear from you," her voice was full of a warmth I couldn't return. I hadn't been looking for him. I hadn't even been thinking about him. But she handed me his number.

I took the number, but I didn't use it right away. I wasn't sure I even wanted to. What was I supposed to say to the man who had abandoned me? The man who left me to grow up feeling unwanted, unprotected, and unloved? The man who had chosen addiction over fatherhood. Who had let someone else step in and be my father. The man I had spent my whole life learning to live without.

I was furious. Furious that he had the nerve to exist on the other end of a phone number. I was mad at my aunt for even giving it to me. I didn't ask for him. Maybe I'd toss the number in a drawer.

Maybe I told myself I'd throw it away. Either way, I had no plans to call.

Life went on, as it always does. Between school, the kids, and everything else I carried, thoughts of him came and went. But that number was still there, waiting, daring me to use it. It took time. Months passed before I did. And when I called, I wasn't sure what I was expecting. An apology? An explanation? Some kind of reason that could make sense of why he had never been there?

I didn't get any of that.

What I got was his voice. Raw. Surprised. And filled with something I couldn't quite name. He sounded… happy.

Howard still had his demons. The alcohol was still there, and the drugs hadn't disappeared completely. But he was trying. He wasn't the same man who had spent my childhood in and out of jail cells.

He was older now, a little steadier. The moment he met my children, he embraced it as his second chance. A chance to be the father he never was to me and the grandfather he desperately wanted to be for them. His body was worn down by years of addiction and the weight of pancreatic cancer treatments. But you'd never know it when he was with us.

One Sunday after we reconnected, Howard invited us over for dinner. He wanted to do something special to show me and the kids that he was here, that he was trying. So after church, we headed to his house, where he had a meal waiting: fried chicken, potato salad, and rolls.

I took a bite of the potato salad and immediately knew. I did not like it. At all. It wasn't even close to good. It tasted like the literal definition of someone putting their foot in it. But when I looked up, there he was, watching me expectantly, his face lit with the kind of pride that only comes from someone putting their heart into it.

And I couldn't do it. I couldn't tell him the truth.

242

So, I smiled. "This is the best potato salad I've ever had," I told him.

From that moment on, it became our thing. Every Sunday, after church, we went to his house, and every Sunday, he had a fresh batch of potato salad waiting just for me. He looked forward to making it, pouring his heart into every spoonful, convinced he was giving me something I loved. And every Sunday, I sat at his table, eating that awful potato salad with a smile, letting him believe it was the best thing I ever tasted.

My children adored him, calling him "Grandpa" with so much love and joy that it softened the edges of my guarded heart. Every time we visited, his face would light up like they were his own personal sunshine. And truth be told, they were.

He didn't just sit back and watch them play. He joined in.

One day, I walked in to find him holding Alyra's tiny hands, swaying back and forth to some old-school R&B, his laughter filling the room as she tried to match his steps.

It was moments like those that made you forget the weight he carried, moments where his love for them overshadowed everything else. Howard didn't just provide love. He provided stability. When I decided to go back to school, he was there to offer support. He understood it wasn't just about getting a degree. It was about reclaiming a dream I had long buried.

When I was younger, I had always wanted to be a lawyer. A public defender, to be specific. I had spent so much of my life being accused of things, defending myself against unfair allegations. I wanted to be the one fighting for people who couldn't fight for themselves.

Even when I began dating again, Howard stepped in to help. He babysat the kids whenever I needed him. It didn't matter how tired or sick he felt. He was always there, offering me the support I needed.

He couldn't undo the past, but he showed up for the future. And that was something.

CHAPTER 46

The Wrong Kind of Right

"Mr. Right is coming, but he's in Africa and he's walking."

— Oprah Winfrey

Dating again wasn't easy, especially after the kind of love I had known. I didn't trust people, and I didn't trust myself. Trust felt dangerous. But having Howard in my corner made it easier to try.

He would tease me about the people I met, flashing his fake "fatherly approval" with a raised eyebrow and a smirk. What he never said out loud, but I always knew, was that he just wanted me to finally find something real. Something safe. Something that wouldn't leave me worse off than where I started.

First, there was Marshall. He came into my life during a rare night out at a club with Allie. He was charming, funny, and carried himself with a confidence that was hard to ignore. When we first met, his cologne was intoxicating. It stopped me in my tracks. I couldn't resist asking, "What are you wearing? You smell so good." He flashed a sly smile and said, "It's called Come Get Me.'" That one line summed him up perfectly. Smooth and effortlessly intriguing.

We clicked instantly. Texting and late-night phone calls in the days that followed. He was the kind of guy who could make you laugh and feel special with just a few words. But Marshall's life wasn't without its complications. He lived in Chicago, a few hours away, and shared a home with his child's mother. That was a glaring red flag.

The potential for drama was too much for me to overlook. I had my own children to think about, and I couldn't afford to invite someone else's drama into my life. While I enjoyed our

245

conversations and the brief escape he offered, I kept my distance. I couldn't take someone like Marshall seriously, no matter how good he smelled or how effortlessly he could make me smile. Some connections just aren't meant to be anything more than fleeting.

Next came Allen, the pastor's son from our local church. He was a barbershop owner who cut hair for some of the city's NFL players, but it was his role at church that initially drew me in. He played the drums in the church band, and I couldn't help but notice the way he'd glance at me during service, a subtle connection that sparked my curiosity.

Allen had a quiet confidence that was magnetic, and spending time with him was easy. He didn't fit the mold of a typical pastor's son. He drank and smoked, habits that didn't align with the image I had of someone raised in the church. Still, I wasn't looking for anything serious at the time, and neither was he. Our relationship was lighthearted, more about companionship than commitment.

My connections weren't always conventional, and I've never been one to discriminate when it came to connecting with people. That's how I ended up meeting Tamekia on a phone chat line. She lived in Virginia, and from the very beginning, the conversation just flowed. We'd talk, laugh and share stories like we had known each other forever.

One night, we were joking around about celebrity crushes and who we found attractive. I made an offhand comment about someone being fat, not thinking anything of it. But then the line went quiet. Completely still. Just silence on the other end.

"Do you have something against fat people?" she asked, her tone calm but curious.

Now I paused. I didn't have anything against bigger women, but I wasn't really attracted to them either. "No, not at all," I said. Then I got curious. "Why?" I asked. "Are you fat?"

She hesitated, then said, "Nah, I'm thick."

"Okay...so what do you look like?"

"I'm light-skinned, with long hair, and I've got a body like Kim."
Lil Kim's look was iconic. Curvy, confident, and fine as hell. At that point, it was on. We'd been talking for months and figured it was time to meet in person. Tamekia arranged to take a Greyhound bus from Virginia to Wisconsin.

The day she arrived, I stood at the bus station, heart pounding with anticipation. I was nervous and excited, wondering if she would really show up. I watched as people got off the bus one by one, still searching for the Lil' Kim look-alike I had pictured in my head. Passengers trickled out, and as the bus pulled away, I started to think she hadn't come after all.

But then, from the side, a girl wrapped in a blanket who had been standing there unnoticed spoke up.

"Are you Matrice?" she asked.

"Yeah..." I answered slowly.

"It's me. Tamekia."

Y'all. The Tamekia standing in front of me must have been looking into Snow White's stepmother's enchanted mirror when she described herself, because this wasn't the Lil' Kim I was expecting. At all.

Trying to process the disconnect and stay polite, I said, "I thought you said you had a body like Lil Kim...?"
Her face lit up. "I said Kim! Like Kim...from *The Parkers*."

I stared at her, stunned. Now, she knew *damn well* Kim from *The Parkers* was not what anyone would consider "thick." Who even thinks about Kim from *The Parkers* when describing their figure?

Plus, she wasn't even the size of that Kim!! She was more the size of Kim's mother, Nikki!

Still, I couldn't leave her stranded after she had traveled all that way. I brought her home and tried to keep things friendly, letting her know I didn't think I was into women anymore. The truth was, I just wasn't into *her.*

She stayed for a few weeks, clearly emotional about the situation. Eventually, I bought her a bus ticket back to Virginia and sent her on her way. Lesson learned: always clarify *which* Kim someone is talking about.

After that fiasco, I figured the universe owed me a harmless rebound. Or at the very least, someone who lived in the same time zone and didn't show up with emotional baggage and a suitcase.

That's when Shawn came into the picture.

I met him in the most random way, at a gas station. Allie and I were driving when he and his friend pulled up beside us, matching our speed. They kept glancing into our car, throwing looks and motions like they had something urgent to say. At first, we ignored them, but they were persistent, signaling for us to pull over.

Curious and maybe a little amused, Allie and I exchanged a glance before turning into a gas station. Because obviously, that's the safest place to meet random strangers waving their arms out of a car window. They followed and parked right next to us. The second Shawn stepped out of his car, it was like he already knew how this was going to play out.

"Y'all good?" he asked, his cocky smile hinting he was enjoying himself a little too much.

I raised an eyebrow. "We were, until you started driving like you were auditioning for Fast & Furious: Milwaukee Drift."

He laughed, and to be fair, it was a nice laugh. Deep. Easy. The kind of laugh that made you forget, momentarily, that this whole interaction was a little ridiculous.

"I'm Shawn," he said, sticking out his hand like we were at a job interview.

He stood there chatting for a few minutes. His friend talked to Allie, who was doing her best "I'm being polite but I'd rather be anywhere else" impression.

Meanwhile, Shawn and I hit a weird groove. Light flirting, playful teasing. He wasn't overly smooth, but he was funny. And sometimes, funny is better than fine.

He had that bad boy energy. Street-smart, charming, and rough around the edges. He wasn't what I'd call husband material, but I wasn't looking for a husband. I was just looking for a good time and a little distraction.

But Shawn came with his own baggage. He was a low-level drug dealer, trying to get by. I didn't condone his lifestyle, but I also saw the man behind it. Or at least, I thought I did.

CHAPTER 47

Love on the Edge

"Sometimes the person you'd take a bullet for ends up being the one behind the trigger."

—Unknown

Shawn and I spent months getting to know each other. We talked, went out, and took our time figuring out if this was something real. I wasn't in a rush to bring anyone new into my children's lives, especially not someone with Shawn's background. When he finally met them, I was surprised by how natural it felt. He and Enrique bonded almost instantly.

I will never forget how he potty trained Enrique. Shawn turned it into target practice, dropping a few Cheerios in the toilet and telling him to hit them. It was silly but it worked, and it also showed me a softer, more thoughtful side of him.

Shawn talked often about wanting to be a father and wanting his first child to be with me. I already had four children and wasn't entertaining the thought of having another one. But what I didn't know was that Shawn had already decided for both of us. He was actively trying to get me pregnant, whether I was ready or not.

Eventually, he succeeded.

I was shocked when I found out. My son was supposed to be my last baby. I was finally getting back on track, taking college classes, and working toward a better future for my kids. A new baby was the last thing I needed.

Shawn lit up when I told him. He was going to be a father, and for a while that was enough. Ultrasounds, name lists, quiet drives home. He was present. If there were problems, I didn't see them.

251

Then one afternoon, Allie and I were out running errands when we saw a familiar car. Shawn's car, the one he always drove. Without thinking, we followed it. I assumed it was him, maybe on his way to see me, or running one of his hustles. But when the car finally stopped and the driver stepped out, it wasn't Shawn. It was a young woman, visibly pregnant, her belly round and ready to pop at any moment.

I froze. My mind tried to make sense of what I was seeing. Maybe she was a cousin or a family friend. Someone borrowing his car. It never occurred to me that she could be anything more. Desperate for answers, I walked up to her and introduced myself, pretending I was curious about the car. She smiled politely, but when I asked how she knew Shawn, her face shifted. She looked confused, almost defensive.

"I'm his girlfriend," she said, her voice steady but uncertain, like she was trying to gauge my reaction. "I'm pregnant with his baby."

Her words hit like a sledgehammer. Girlfriend? Pregnant? **His** baby? My head spun. I was already showing, just as pregnant as she was. How could we both be carrying his child at the same time? How could he be with me almost every night and still manage to have a whole other life?

I turned away, my chest tight with disbelief and betrayal. He wasn't just cheating. He was building another family while planning one with me. The reality of it was too much to process, too painful to fully grasp.

That night, I confronted Shawn. There was no need for lies or excuses. He could see it in my face. I already knew.

"She was pregnant before we got serious," he tried to explain, his voice low and almost apologetic. "I didn't know how to tell you. I didn't want to lose you."

His words felt hollow. He claimed he was trying to figure out who he was going to "build a life with," as if it were a decision he could make like choosing between two cars. He promised he loved me, that he never meant to hurt me, that he only wanted to be with me.

But the damage was done.

The stress of the betrayal crushed me. My body, already fragile from my history of an incompetent cervix, couldn't handle the devastation. A few weeks later, my water broke far too early. I was rushed to the hospital, fighting back tears of fear and exhaustion.

I was forced to deliver my daughter, Asia, knowing she wouldn't survive. She was too small, too early, and there was nothing anyone could do.

Grief had swallowed me whole, and instead of giving me space, Shawn found a way to make it heavier. He tried to make things better, or at least, what he thought "better" looked like. He started bringing the baby he had with the other woman over to my house when she went to work. Maybe he thought it would help fill the emptiness, that holding his daughter might ease my pain somehow.

But it didn't. If anything, it deepened the wound. I couldn't look at that baby without thinking of Asia, without feeling the sharp sting of what could've been. Still, I let him come. I let him place that baby in my arms.

I was just going through the motions, too heartbroken to resist his determination to prove that I was the one he wanted. He showered me with promises of a better future, and in my sadness, I let myself believe him. What felt like love, or something close to it, began to blossom between us.

Shawn became a steady presence in my life, taking up more space than I ever intended. Somewhere along the way, I started putting him before everything else, even my father, Howard. My days became wrapped up in Shawn and the kids.

Even as Shawn pulled me deeper into his world, Howard was fighting to hold me to mine.

He noticed the shift. Howard had been there when I lost Asia, holding everything together when I couldn't. He'd watched my kids when I couldn't be there for them and encouraged me to keep going, to finish school, to follow through on my dream of becoming a lawyer. But after Asia, school felt like a far-off dream. I needed a break, needed to breathe, and Howard didn't understand.

Howard believed in me when I struggled to believe in myself, pushing me toward the dreams I was trying to bury. He saw potential in me even when I couldn't see past my pain. But he never approved of Shawn. He saw through the charm, the promises, and the facade I clung to. He saw the instability I refused to acknowledge.

"You can do better," he'd say, his voice sharp with frustration. His disappointment stung in ways I wasn't prepared for, especially coming from a man who was battling pancreatic cancer caused by years of drinking and drug use which he refused to stop doing.

How could he judge me when he couldn't fix his own brokenness?

Still, despite our strained relationship, I went to his house every Sunday. I sat at his small kitchen table, eating the same potato salad I pretended to love. We'd watch football while the kids played, his tired eyes lighting up as they ran around the room, filling his quiet home with laughter.

But even in those moments, there was a heaviness between us, a shared understanding of things left unsaid. He wanted me to rise above my circumstances, to be the woman he knew I could be. I wanted him to see that I was trying.

One afternoon, the kids and I went to visit him like we always did. Howard was thrilled to see his grandkids, lighting up as they ran through his small apartment, their laughter filling the air. He danced with them, his steps slower than they used to be but still full of life. He looked tired that day, though. Something about the way he moved, the way he smiled, seemed different.

As the afternoon went on, my phone buzzed. It was Shawn.

"Where are you?" his voice came through the line, sharp and insistent. "I need you to come now."

Howard must've sensed something because when I started gathering the kids to leave, "Stay a little longer," he said quietly, his voice steady but pleading. "I'll be back tomorrow, Howard. I promise." As I stood to leave, he reached out and grabbed my hand. His grip wasn't tight, but it was firm enough to make me pause.

"Stay," he said softly. His eyes, usually so full of strength, seemed tired, pleading. "Just a little longer."

I hesitated, torn between them but Shawn's words echoed in my mind. He needed me. And Howard... I'd come back tomorrow.

His eyes were filled with something I didn't understand at the time, something deeper than sadness. But I was too caught up in Shawn's latest crisis to see it. Gently, I pulled my hand away, and promised him again, "I'll be back tomorrow." He nodded slowly, disappointment etched into every line on his face.

Tomorrow never came.

That night, while I was with Shawn, arguing about something so trivial I can't even remember what it was, Howard had a heart attack. My phone was on silent, tucked away as Shawn and I yelled at each other, the fight escalating into something physical. I missed every call, every message. By the time I finally checked my phone, it was too late.

Howard was gone.

CHAPTER 48

Fractured Promises

"Some people break promises for the pleasure of breaking them."

— William Hazlitt

After Howard's passing, my world shifted in a way I couldn't fully understand at the time. His death was more than just the loss of a father. It meant losing a protector, a believer, someone who stood by me without question. He was sick. He was struggling.

But he still made space for me. He watched my kids while I was at school, while I was in the hospital fighting to save Asia. He never made a scene about it. Never complained. Didn't ask for recognition. He just showed up.

But I didn't always see it that way. I was too wrapped up in the mess I was in. Letting Shawn take up space in my life while my father faded right in front of me.

I kept thinking about the wasted arguments. The way I'd dismissed his advice, angry that he expected better from me when he couldn't seem to fix his own life. How could he judge me? But he wasn't judging me, he was rooting for me. He believed I could have more when I had forgotten how to believe it myself.

And I kept replaying that last moment. The way Howard held my hand. The plea in his eyes. If I had stayed a little longer… If I had just sat beside him instead of walking out that door... maybe he would've known how much he meant to me. Maybe he'd still be here.

I felt trapped in a cycle of grief and survival, each loss cutting deeper into my soul, leaving little room for healing. I kept putting my own life under review, replaying the arguments I should have let go of, the choices I wish I had made differently, and the love I never fully showed.

Shawn should've been the one helping me carry the weight, but he became the weight. He kept dragging me through his mess, and I kept letting him. He'd promise to do better, and I kept waiting for a version of him that didn't exist. I was drowning, and he was busy chasing the streets, living a life I couldn't control but couldn't seem to let go of either.

Until I was left with no choice.

I saw the pictures while scrolling, disbelief turning into rage with every post. Picture after picture of my car! My cherry-red convertible with the "Shns Grl" license plates, plastered all over social media! Like it belonged to her! Shawn had lost his cotton-picking mind! She was sprawled all across the hood of my car!

How *dare* he let someone parade around in my car. A car I'd driven through every storm, every visit to Howard's, every trip to the hospital. A car that symbolized how much I'd invested in him, in *us*.

Her smug smile burned into my memory, the way she leaned back like she had conquered something.

Then there was *him*. Shawn. The same man who had whispered promises of forever, who begged me to believe in *us*, now resting his head comfortably in her lap. It was like seeing my entire life mocked in a single frame.

I felt the rage hit before the heartbreak. It surged through me, white-hot, obliterating every ounce of sadness I'd been drowning in since losing Howard and Asia. I couldn't cry anymore. I was done crying. All I could see was red. The same red as my car. The same red as the fire burning inside me.
I snatched my phone and started calling Shawn, over and over desperate for an explanation. A*ny* explanation. Voicemail.

Again.

Voicemail.

I dialed with trembling hands, my breath coming in sharp gasps. After everything I had been through, losing Howard, losing Asia, all the sacrifices I'd made to be by his side?

Each unanswered call was like gasoline poured on an already raging inferno. Since he wanted to play games, and ignore my calls, I could play games too. What one person won't do another one will. He didn't want to answer, I knew who would.

"911, what's your emergency?"

"Officer, I would like to report a crime."

I reported every detail I knew about his drug operation, his hustles, his habits, where he stayed, what he drove. He thought he could live two lives without consequences.

Not this time.

By the next morning, Shawn's world came crashing down the same way he had shattered mine. He called me from jail, his voice panicked, breathless, and confused. His place had been raided, and he couldn't understand how they knew so much or how they had it all. There were hours of surveillance footage, and most of it featured my car.

He never suspected me. He never knew the final tip that sealed his fate came from me. Considering they had already been watching him, he was obviously going down regardless, I just helped speed up the process.

CHAPTER 49

Fading into the Background

"It's a terrible thing, isn't it? To be invisible."

— Chuck Palahniuk

I sat in that courtroom drowning in disgust at him and shame at myself.

I was testifying for a man who had betrayed me over and over again.

Standing there, swearing to tell the truth.

The truth was, I shouldn't have been there.

I should've left him to deal with his problems on his own, the way he always left me to deal with mine.

But my loyalty wouldn't let me walk away.

He should've taken the plea deal, one year in jail, followed by supervised probation, a gift compared to the 4 years he ended up with.

After that day, everything inside me just... stopped.

Dreams I used to chase drifted so far out of reach they felt like someone else's memories.

Law School became a forgotten ambition.

My world narrowed to just my children.

They were the only faces I could still trust, the only reason I kept moving forward.

Leaving the house became harder.

Going to a school concert, a sports game, or a parent-teacher meeting felt like paying a debt I didn't remember owing.

I showed up. I smiled. I left.

At home, it was quieter.

Safer.

No family to throw me away.
No promises of forever waiting to be broken.
No pregnancies lost to bodies that couldn't hold them.
No father reaching out one last time while I let go and walked away.

The world outside felt cruel and unforgiving, but inside those walls, nothing could touch me.

Nothing could take anything else from me.

The longer I stayed hidden, the more invisible I became, even to myself.

Days blurred into nights.
Nights blurred into months.
Seasons changed outside my window and I barely noticed.

I spent years trapped in my own world, locked behind the walls of grief, loss, and social anxiety.

Going outside felt like stepping into enemy territory. I was exposed, vulnerable, and weighed down by memories.

But isolation is a lonely place.

The walls that protected me also started to suffocate me.

One night, after the kids had gone to bed and the loneliness became too loud to ignore, I started browsing the web. I wasn't ready to step back into the world, but I was desperate for something that felt alive.

That's how I found Myspace.

It was a world where I could exist behind the safety of a screen, where I could be social without ever leaving the confines of my home.

At first, it was just something to fill the empty hours.
Scrolling through pages of strangers.
Reading profiles.
Filling empty hours without asking or giving anything more.

It felt safer than anything I had known in years.
Behind a screen, I could watch without being watched.
I could exist without having to explain myself to anyone.

So, I decided to create a profile.

Nothing flashy.

Just a real picture and a different name.

A small shield between me and a world that had already taught me how much it could hurt.

One night, I received a message.

Bold and direct, the words caught my attention before I even knew what to expect.
I stared at the screen for a long moment.

I didn't owe anyone anything.

I could have closed the laptop and returned to my carefully constructed silence.

Instead, I clicked on the profile.

It was impossible to ignore.

Bright watches. Chunky jewelry.

Sleek cars lined up behind him like trophies.

An unwavering confidence practically leapt off the screen.

Normally, a page like that would have made me scroll past without a second thought.

But something about him seemed intriguing.

Maybe it was the way he carried himself, or maybe I was just tired of feeling invisible.

He was not exactly my type.

He was heavyset, with a broad face that reminded me a little of Forest Whitaker. One eye sat slightly lower than the other.

He wouldn't have stood out in a crowd if not for the way he carried himself.

He didn't even seem to care what anyone thought of him. And somehow, that confidence made him magnetic in a way I hadn't expected.

Maybe that's what made me answer.
It was only online.

Just messages filling the quiet hours I used to spend alone.

It started simple. The conversations stretched late into the night, typing back and forth across the silence of my house.

I told myself it did not have to be more than that. Just a distraction, nothing that could break through the walls I had spent so long building to keep myself safe.

I didn't know much about him yet, but his name was Seyvn.

CHAPTER 50

Ignored Signs

"I saw the signs but loved you anyway."

— Lang Leav

Seyvn was everything I thought I needed at the time. Funny, available, uncomplicated.

His messages felt like a distraction in a life that had grown cold and monotonous.

We talked about small things that filled the empty hours. Our days. Our kids.

Seyvn had two daughters of his own. He slipped stories about them into our conversations the way a proud dad might.

It wasn't long before our late-night messages turned into phone calls that stretched until sunrise.

His voice had a way of filling the silence I had grown used to, and the loneliness did not seem so overwhelming.

Somewhere in the middle of all the calls and conversations, a kind of comfort started to grow between us.

Not love, but not nothing either.

After months of late nights and long talks, a few what-ifs started to creep in.

What if this could be something real?

What if I didn't have to be alone anymore?

We kept messaging, kept calling, and somewhere along the way, it started to feel steady.

Like maybe it could just stay that way. Safe. Distant. Easy.

But after a few more months, Seyvn suggested visiting me in person.

Part of me panicked at the thought. My home had become my fortress, a space where I could control who got close and how much of myself I had to show. Letting him in meant opening a door I wasn't sure I was ready for.

I had never planned for visits or anything else that meant being in person.

He lived in New Jersey.

I lived in Wisconsin.

We would never be able to make it work with that distance. It was never supposed to get that far.

But somehow, it already had.

I was scared and hesitant.

But after all the late nights and the quiet spaces he had filled, it felt too late to pretend he hadn't already gotten inside.

Maybe this wouldn't end the way it always seemed to.

Maybe this time would be different.

Maybe he was different.
Maybe I could be, too.

So I said yes.

The day Seyvn arrived, I was nervous.

But the moment I saw him, that nervousness faded.

He stepped out the airport with that same easy charm I had gotten used to online. A warm smile, a playful energy, and a familiarity that made it hard to believe we had never actually met in person.

From the second he slid into the passenger seat, conversation flowed like we had been doing this for years.

I was so caught up talking to him on the drive home that I missed the exit and got lost.

He smirked, accusing me of setting him up, which only made us laugh harder. By the time we got to the house, I was completely at ease.

The kids already knew about Seyvn.

I had talked to them about him, even more so when we planned his visit.

So, it wasn't awkward. He slipped right in, joking with them, asking about their favorite shows and what they liked to do for fun.

The house was already loud, already full of life, but somehow, he fit into the noise without disrupting it.

He helped with dinner, stayed up late telling stories, and watched television sprawled out on the couch while the kids played around him.

As the night wore on, he started to open up about himself. He spoke about his businesses, music producer, mechanic, other grand ideas always on the brink of success. His confidence made it all sound so real.

269

It felt like a normal visit at first. Normal enough to make me let my guard down.

But blinded by hope and longing, I only saw what I wanted to see.

We were still getting to know each other, and despite my reservations, I felt safe enough to let him into my world.

But safety built on fantasy never lasts.

One quiet evening after the kids went to bed, I sat at my computer, absentmindedly typing my ex's name into the search bar.

The pastor's son.

Not about rekindling anything, just harmless curiosity. A passing thought about what he might be up to these days.

I didn't realize Seyvn was watching from across the room.

"What are you doing?" he asked sharply, his voice cutting through the quiet.

"Just looking something up," I replied casually, closing the window.

But that was not enough.

"Give me the computer," he demanded, his eyes blazing.

Before I could move, he spun around and punched the mirror on the wall.

Glass shattered, raining down sharp warnings I didn't yet understand.

The sound jolted me, but I forced myself to stay calm.

"You need to leave," I said, my voice trembling despite how hard I tried to steady it.

He stepped closer, his chest heaving.

Then, in one swift motion, he lunged for the laptop.

Fear surged through me.

I bolted for the door, ran to my car, and locked myself inside.

My hands fumbled over my phone, dialing 911 through shaking fingers and blurred tears.

He banged on the window, shouting. Apologies, anger, and desperation all tangled together.

The police came, their flashing lights slicing through the night.

They separated us and asked questions.

I played it down.

"It's fine. We just had a disagreement. He's leaving in the morning."

And he did leave, but not for long.

The mirror was broken, but I convinced myself we were not.

I mistook his apology for sincerity. His outburst for passion.

I also blamed myself.
He had traveled all the way from New Jersey to see me.

And there I was, searching for another man.

It felt like a betrayal.

I convinced myself that if the roles were reversed, maybe I would have reacted the same way.

He was sorry. I was sorry.

We both promised to do better.

It was not a warning sign to me.

It was a mistake.

One we could fix.

At least, that was what I thought.

Distance made it easy to overlook the cracks I had seen up close.

Easy to cling to the fantasy instead of the reality.

After Seyvn's first visit, things seemed to settle. We fell back into long distance life, talking late into the night, making plans, and sharing stories.

But cracks don't disappear just because you stop looking at them.

They grow.

And grow they did when Seyvn called one night, "I need to come back to Green Bay for a while."

CHAPTER 51

The Missing Piece

"I don't think your missing pieces ever fit inside you again once they go missing."

— John Green

Seyvn's voice on the other end of the line sounded tight, almost frantic.

"I'm in trouble," he said, and I could hear the panic he was trying to hold back. He told me things had gotten out of hand after his daughter acted up at school. In the heat of the moment, he popped her with a rolled-up magazine, not thinking much of it at the time. Just a quick reaction. Something he probably thought wasn't a big deal.

But it was.

Somewhere between anger, hurt, and whatever else was swirling inside her, his daughter yanked one of her cornrows clean out of her scalp.

She wore her hair in long, thick braids that framed her little face. And now there was this big, raw patch sitting right at the front of her head.

When she walked into school the next morning, the teachers noticed right away.

Of course they did.

There was no way to hide it, no slicked-back ponytail or cover-up could make it disappear.

I don't know what she tried to say, if she even tried to explain at all. Maybe she made up a story. Maybe she just stayed quiet.

But it didn't matter. The missing braid told a story all by itself.

The teachers had no choice. They were mandatory reporters.

One look and it was already too late.

Before Seyvn even finished telling me what happened, I already knew.

This was not going to blow over.

By the time Seyvn found out how bad things were, Child Protective Services was involved, and the wheels were turning faster than he could keep up with. He tried explaining, tried pleading his case, but no amount of talking could undo what the teachers had seen.

Child Protective Services acted fast.

They placed the girls with their mother and allowed her to stay in

Seyvn's house, as long as he agreed to leave.

Just like that, he was banned from his own home.

His world crumbled overnight.

He felt powerless, furious at the system, and drowning in guilt.

In his mind, he had only been trying to discipline his daughter, trying to correct her before the world could.

But now, that same world was calling him a danger.

When he called me, it was not just for comfort anymore.
It was for refuge.

He had nowhere to go. He had a strained relationship with his mother and his grandma lived in senior citizen housing.

He had no one else to turn to.

His desperation pulled at something deep inside me.

Despite the uneasiness I still carried from our rocky first visit, I couldn't turn him away.

I could hear the helplessness in his voice, the way it cracked when he said he had nowhere to go.

I knew that feeling too well, and maybe some part of me wanted to save him the way no one had saved me.

"Come to Green Bay," I said, trying to sound steadier than I felt. "We'll figure it out."

Looking back, I wonder what I was really offering him.

A safe place.

A second chance.

Or maybe I just wanted to feel like I was doing something right.

Either way, I opened my door.

And my world.

I knew taking him in would not bring his daughters back right away.

It would not undo the choices he had made.

But at the very least, I could give him somewhere to land while he figured out his next move.

I tried to make it as bearable as I could.

I bought him a Yamaha keyboard and set up a small studio in the finished basement, thinking maybe if he had something to focus on, it would keep him from spiraling any further.

Music had always been his thing.

Maybe it could hold him together while everything else around him was falling apart.

At the time, it felt like the right thing to do. A way to lift him out of the darkness he was trapped in. What I didn't realize was how much deeper that darkness would reach, or how quickly it would consume everything around us.

At first, things seemed manageable. He settled in, spending hours in the basement making beats on his keyboard. Music was his escape, and seeing him in his element made me hopeful that maybe, he was no longer just getting through the day, but actually showing up for it.

The kids liked him there too.

He had a playful, easygoing side that made him fun to be around. For a little while, it felt like we had carved out a small pocket of peace.

But the cracks started to show.

At first, it was little things.

Long silences when he got lost in his head.

Flashes of frustration over things that shouldn't have mattered.

A misplaced toy.

The kids laughing too loudly upstairs.

Moments when his whole body seemed to stiffen, like he was holding something back.

He never exploded.

He flickered.

A sigh.

A forced smile.

A muttered excuse about being stressed or missing his girls. And just like that, he would smooth it over, as if nothing had happened.

I told myself it was understandable.

He was grieving the loss of his family, and I knew what it felt like to lose people you love. I thought if I could be patient enough, kind enough, steady enough, maybe it would pass. I thought I could be his refuge.

But even as I tried to be patient, little things started to bother me.

Seyvn's cleanliness, or lack of it, was something I noticed almost immediately after he moved in. At first, I brushed it off as him adjusting to a new environment, maybe even being a little depressed after losing custody of his girls. But as time went on, it became clear that cleanliness just wasn't his priority.

He would leave messes everywhere. Dirty dishes not put in the sink, clothes left on the floor, and trash he would forget to throw out. I was constantly picking up after him, hoping it was just a temporary adjustment. It wasn't.

The little things added up fast. He used my razor without asking, a small but invasive violation that made my skin crawl. Worse, one day I noticed my toothbrush wasn't the way I left it. Suspicious, I asked if he had touched it for some reason. At first, he denied it, but eventually, he admitted he had used it because he couldn't find his. No apology. No recognition of how disgusting that was. Just a shrug, like it was nothing.

But the worst part was that he didn't shower regularly. Days would pass before he would finally wash up, and even then it felt like he only did it because I insisted, not because he cared and no matter how much I tried to overlook it, it changed the way I looked at him. It made him unattractive to me.

But he was dealing with a lot, from having to leave his home to being separated from his daughters. I knew depressed people sometimes have trouble doing even the basics, so I tried not to stress him too much about it.

Plus, things could get tense with him sometimes, but it was never anything that set off alarm bells. One night, after a long, tiring day, we had a disagreement about something small, something I can't even remember now. What I do remember is the way his attitude shifted. His voice got sharper. His body stiffened. And then, just like before, he punched the wall.

It wasn't fear that froze me. It was surprise. Not at what he did, but that it was happening again.

He apologized right away, brushing it off like it was nothing.

Blamed it on stress, on being tired, on everything he had been carrying.

And honestly, it was easy to believe him.

At the time, it didn't seem like something to be afraid of.

It felt like a man who was hurting, trying to hold too much inside.

Over time, some of that weight seemed to lift. When the case with

Child Protective Services closed, Seyvn was allowed to return home. His children's mother had secured her own place, and there was no longer any reason for him to stay in Green Bay.

A part of me was relieved to see him go.

CHAPTER 52

Down and Dirty

"I learned long ago, never to wrestle with a pig. You get dirty, and besides, the pig likes it."

— George Bernard Shaw

Once Seyvn went back to New Jersey, things should have ended. We kept in touch, but only sporadically through occasional texts and a phone call every now and then. It felt like the distance would do what I hadn't yet: close the chapter for good.

Then one afternoon, while the girls were at school, I was cleaning their room. As I reached under the pillow to straighten the sheets, I noticed Rayna's journal tucked just beneath it. I didn't mean to read it, but the book fell open and there it was, written in her neat little handwriting:

"I miss Seyvn so much. I wish he didn't have to leave."

That one line stopped me cold. I hadn't known how much he meant to her. I hadn't realized he was still here in ways I hadn't seen.

Rayna wasn't one to warm up to people easily. She was guarded, careful with her trust. Seeing how much she missed him caught me off guard. My son adored him too and knowing that Seyvn had connected with my children made me reconsider ending things.

Maybe there was more to this than I had let myself believe.

So, we kept talking. The phone calls got longer. We talked late into the night, laughing, reminiscing, imagining what life could look like if we just started over. He sounded different. Calmer. More surer of what he wanted. He talked about the future like it was still possible for us.

Eventually, he asked me to visit. Just a few days, he said. Nothing big. Just a chance to be around each other again and figure out what we still had. I agreed.

It would be my first time flying. I was nervous, but curious. Maybe this would bring the clarity I needed. Maybe it would finally give us answers.

So I boarded that flight with hope, with a heart willing to believe in second chances, completely unaware of what was waiting for me on the other side.

I wasn't just showing up with hope. I was showing up with help. I brought thousands of dollars in cash, planning to help him catch up on his house payments. His home was in foreclosure after everything with Child Protective Services, and I wanted to ease his burden and show him he wasn't alone.

But life had other plans.

After getting off the plane, I headed straight to the airport bathroom. In my hurry, I set my wallet on the toilet paper holder before steadying myself into a half-squat over the toilet, too focused on avoiding contact with anything else to give it a second thought. When I finished, I flushed, washed my hands, checked myself in the mirror, and walked out.

It wasn't until we were halfway to his house that my stomach clenched. My wallet. My heart pounded as I turned to Seyvn, barely getting the words out before he whipped the car around.

We sped back, my mind racing faster than the tires on the pavement. By the time I reached the bathroom, I was frantic, throwing open stall doors like a lunatic, praying to see it sitting right where I left it. But my wallet was gone.

Clutching onto one last shred of hope, I made my way to the airport's lost and found, my heart pounding with every step. And then, against all odds, they had it. My wallet. But as soon as I opened it, a cold wave of realization hit me. The cash was gone.

Thousands of dollars, vanished in an instant.

My stomach twisted. My hands trembled. It wasn't just money. It was Seyvn's chance to keep his house from foreclosure. It was stability, survival, the only real safety net he had left. And now, it was gone.

I turned to Seyvn, but there was nothing to say. He looked as defeated as I felt, the weight of it pressing down on both of us. We stood there, silent, disappointed.

Still, I told myself to move forward. Money could be replaced. I had made the trip for a reason, and I wasn't going to let one setback ruin it.

On the drive to his house, we talked. We listened to music. He wasn't even worried about the money. He said we'd figure something else out. His reaction surprised me. It wasn't what I expected. Maybe he really had been working on himself.

That gave me a little hope.

When we arrived at his house, the first thing I noticed was how it sat by itself. No sidewalks. No stores. No neighbors close by. Just a house sitting in the middle of a wide, open stretch of land. It used to belong to his grandmother.

The yard was mostly dirt, packed down from years of four-wheelers and dirt bikes tearing through it. His friends came over all the time, riding, hanging out, fixing cars, just being outside.

The ground showed it. Tire tracks cut deep into the yard like scars.

Then there were bags.

Plastic grocery bags. Hanging from trees, in the bushes, around the yard. I didn't know what they were. I figured maybe they had bird seed in them. Rodent repellant. Or maybe trash had blown in and gotten stuck. I didn't think too much more of it.

As we walked inside the house, the smell hit me. I know cleaning had never really been his strong suit. But this wasn't just bad. It was bad, BAD.

Thick. Sour. It clung to the air, the walls, everything.

I just stood there for a second, trying to take it all in. The smell. The mess. The heat in the air that made everything feel heavier. He moved around like it was normal. Like this was just how things were.

Clothes were everywhere. Thrown in corners, stuffed in the couch, half-buried under other junk. The kitchen was worse.

The sink was overflowing with dishes, and more were scattered across the counters, on the stove, even on the floor. Some of them had food caked on so thick it looked like part of the design on the plate.

In the corner, stacked up like supplies for a storm, were huge jugs of water. Just sitting there while everything around them rotted.

The smell in there hit different. It had layers. Rotten food, old trash, something sour underneath it all. I held my breath without even realizing it.

At one point, my hand brushed against something on the counter. I don't know what it was, but it was sticky and warm, and I immediately went to wash my hands.

I turned the faucet. Nothing came out.

That was what the bottles of water on the floor were for, Seyvn told me.

There was no running water.

The toilets didn't flush. No way to wash your hands, clean up, or take a shower.

I couldn't wrap my head around it. How do you even function like this?

That's when I noticed the bags again.

There was a stack of them sitting on the couch. Plastic grocery bags. They looked brand new, like he had just grabbed them from the store. Same kind that were hanging from the trees and stuffed in the bushes outside.

They definitely weren't in any of the garbage cans around the house. I don't think any of the garbage cans around there were being used at all.

So, I asked him.

"What do you use the bags for?" I didn't know what to expect, but whatever I had imagined, it wasn't what he said next.

He told me he'd been using them as toilets. He does number two. Tie them up. Toss them into the yard for the bank to deal with when they take the house.

He said he tries to throw them as high as he can into the tree so they can't get to them.

Like that was normal. Like that made sense.

I didn't say anything. What was there to say? The words just sat between us, heavy and disgusting, like everything else in that house.

I literally just stood there, trying to process the sheer filth of it all.

The smell. The mess. The fact that he had been living this way like it was just another Tuesday.

I had traveled across states for this. For this?

I didn't have the good sense my momma should've given me. The kind that would've told me to head straight back to the airport and take my ass home.

Nobody ever taught me when to walk away.

So, I did what I came to do.

I rolled up my sleeves and got to work.

I started in the bedroom. First thing I did was open the window. I needed air. That was where I'd be sleeping, so it had to be at least somewhat clean. I picked up clothes, tossed out trash, and cleared space on the floor. I stripped the bed and put on a set of clean sheets I found in the closet. He said they had never been used.

Maybe the girl's mom left them behind. I didn't ask. I was just glad they were there.

By the time I finished, the room looked too clean. Like it didn't belong in that house.

Then I moved to the kitchen.

There were dishes everywhere. In the sink. On the counters. On the stove. On the floor. There were so many I couldn't even soak them all at once. I had to wash them in shifts, scrubbing one set while the others waited.

I opened one of the water jugs, poured it into the sink, and added bleach. My eyes started burning. My nose stung. I didn't care. I just kept going.

The counters were crusted over. The stove was stained with grease and something else I didn't want to think too hard about. I poured bleach straight onto everything and let it sit while I tackled the floor. It was sticky in some places, slick in others. Every step made a sound. The mop water turned black. I had to go over that floor about 50-11 times just to see the tile again.

Then I opened the fridge.

Slammed it shut.

Took a breath. Opened it again.

Moldy food. Leaking containers. Takeout trays from who knows when. Something fuzzy in the back I refused to identify. I grabbed a trash bag and started tossing everything. Wiped it down with bleach and slammed it again.

I scrubbed every surface, washed dishes, and did whatever it took to make that house feel like something other than a biohazard. I wasn't holding back. I used the water. I used the bleach. And if we ran out, he was going to get more. Period.

He should've done all this a long time ago.

Then I moved to the living room.

Same story. Clothes everywhere. Dishes shoved between the couch cushions, sitting on the floor, stacked on the TV stand. I grabbed a trash bag and just started moving. Picked up what I could, stuffed it in. Grabbed the plates and carried them back to the kitchen.

I wiped down whatever surfaces I could find. Some of the stains had been there so long I stopped trying to figure out what they were. I just kept scrubbing.

The last thing left was the rug.

I figured it'd be the easy part. Just vacuum it and be done for the day.

But the moment the vacuum came on, I saw them.

Maggots.

Lots of them, writhing beneath the fabric like they belonged there more than I did.

I gasped, stumbling back, my stomach twisting in revulsion.
Seyvn didn't even flinch. He acted like they were just bread crumbs growing out of the rug. He grabbed it and dragged it outside, tossing it right out there with all the other nasty shit.

I stood there, frozen. Trying to breathe through my nose. Trying not to cry.

It wasn't just the filth that got to me. It was how unfazed he was by it all. No embarrassment. Just another day.

I kept telling myself that maybe cleaning his home would help shift something in him too. That if I could just get the house in order, maybe the rest of his life would follow.

But looking back, I knew better. The mess wasn't the issue.

Maybe it was a reflection of who he was. And no amount of scrubbing could have changed that.

Thankfully, there was a gas station just down the street where I could go to the bathroom when I needed to. And I had my YMCA membership to shower.

I could clean the house. Scrub the floors. Dump the dishes. Even face the maggots, though barely.

But I wasn't going to stop being me.

I wasn't sleeping in filth. And I definitely wasn't using bags for a bathroom.

CHAPTER 53

A Night Out, A Lifetime In

"Sometimes it's the smallest decisions that can change your life forever."

— Keri Russell

While staying at Seyvn's house, I met Tonya. She was the girlfriend of one of his friends. Loud, sharp, and unbothered. Her laugh had weight to it, like someone who had seen too much to take anything too seriously.

We connected easily.

One afternoon, we decided to take a trip to Atlantic City. I just wanted to see the lights and have fun.

Tonya and I had an amazing time. We walked the boardwalk, laughing, taking pictures, and eating greasy fries drowned in ketchup.

We stayed until the lights came on and the boardwalk started to glow against the night sky. Neither of us wanted to leave.
But we couldn't stay forever.

As we pulled into Seyvn's driveway, I noticed the house lights were off. I figured he wasn't home yet and thought nothing of it.

But as soon as I stepped out of the car, the front door creaked open. And there he was, standing in the doorway, his face hidden in the shadows behind him.

His eyes locked onto me with an intensity that made my skin prickle. Before I could say anything, he stormed toward the car, his voice already raised. "Where the hell have you been?"

Tonya, sensing the shift in the atmosphere, quickly muttered, "I'll wait in the car." Her presence felt like a lifeline, but I couldn't let her get caught in whatever this was about to become.

"We went to Atlantic City," I said, forcing my voice to stay steady. "It was just a day trip."

His face twisted with something between disbelief and rage. His eyes raked over my outfit, a simple pair of black cotton shorts and shirt. "You think you can walk around like that? Looking like a damn...!" His words burned, dripping with venom.

He barely paused before turning his anger toward Tonya, still seated in the driver's seat. "And you!" he spat. "Why would you have her out here acting like you!?"

Tonya's eyes widened, but she stayed silent, gripping the steering wheel. I opened my mouth to speak, to try to explain, but Seyvn wasn't listening.

Suddenly, he turned and marched toward the house. "You wanna be out running the streets?" he yelled. "Fine!"

One by one, he started throwing my belongings out of the house. Clothes, shoes, bags. Anything he could grab. He hurled them toward the driveway, some hitting the side of Tonya's rental car with a sickening thud. My hands shook as I silently prayed he wouldn't damage the car.

"We need to go," I whispered, grabbing what I could from the lawn.

Before I could even reach the passenger side, Seyvn charged toward me, his face contorted with rage. "You think you can just leave?" I hurried in the car and Tonya got out there as fast as she could! As we sped down the street, headlights appeared in the rearview mirror. Seyvn's car, closing in fast. He was chasing us.

My heart pounded in my chest, every instinct screaming at me to get away. I told Tonya to drive faster, to head somewhere where we might find help or at least lose him in traffic.

Suddenly, flashing blue and red lights lit up the night. A police cruiser pulled us over, cutting off our escape. My stomach dropped. This could go one of two ways, and I wasn't sure which was worse.

When the officer approached, Seyvn was right behind him, already weaving a tangled web of lies. "I was just trying to stop her from coming back to my house!" he yelled, his voice desperate but rehearsed.

The officer turned to me and Tonya, his expression unreadable. "Ma'am, what's going on here?"

I hesitated, my pulse still racing. My mind screamed to tell the truth, to say he was dangerous and unstable, but fear kept my lips sealed.

"We had an argument," I managed. "I was leaving, and he... followed us."

The officer didn't need further explanation. He told us to go ahead while he stayed with Seyvn to make sure we weren't followed.
We drove off, hearts pounding, hands shaking. Free. At least for the night.

Tonya drove me back to her place, her expression tight with concern but her voice steady, offering comfort I didn't even know I needed. My hands trembled as I tried to steady my breath, to slow everything down. She told me to stay, said I'd be safe. I didn't argue.

I sat on the edge of her couch, numb, replaying everything in my head. The screaming. The chase. The cop. And now this. I felt foolish for letting things spiral the way they had. Ashamed that I hadn't seen it coming, even though I knew I couldn't have.

Later that night, I went into her bathroom just to be alone. I don't know what made me take the test she had sitting on the sink. Maybe it was instinct, or maybe I just needed to rule something out. But the moment I saw those two lines, the floor seemed to drop beneath me.

I gripped the edge of the sink and stared at the test, hoping my eyes were wrong. They weren't.

I was pregnant.

And just like that, fear, guilt, and confusion hit me all at once. My chest tightened. My vision blurred. How could this be happening now, after everything? After the fight, the yelling, the chaos?

I sat on the bathroom floor, knees pulled to my chest, and tried to catch my breath. My mind spun with questions. I blamed myself.

Maybe if I hadn't gone to Atlantic City. Maybe if I had stayed in the house like I was supposed to. Maybe if I hadn't let Tonya talk me into having fun. I told myself I came to New Jersey for Seyvn, not for some spontaneous girls' trip. Maybe if I'd done things differently, he wouldn't have exploded like he did.

I barely spoke for the rest of the night. Tonya didn't push. She let me sit in the silence, only breaking it to ask if I needed anything or to remind me that I could stay as long as I needed.

That night on her couch, I couldn't stop thinking about my kids. Four of them, waiting for me back home. I was supposed to be gone for a few days, help Seyvn, and head back to my real life. Instead, I was here, trying to figure out how this one decision was going to touch everything I had worked so hard to protect.

I didn't know what I was going to do. I just knew I had to figure it out. Fast.

CHAPTER 54

Knock Knock

"The doors will be opened to those who are bold enough to knock."

— Tony Gaskins

Tonya's place felt like a safe haven. Her apartment was small but familiar, the kind of space where things just felt normal. Seyvn didn't know where she lived, which gave me a fragile sense of security.

We spent the days running errands, watching movies, cooking random meals. Just doing regular stuff. But every now and then, I'd drift off in my thoughts, trying to figure out what this pregnancy meant and how the hell I was going to deal with it.

Tonya never asked questions. She just gave me room to breathe. I was still sorting through all of it when someone knocked at the door one afternoon. It wasn't frantic or threatening, but steady and uncertain.

Tonya peeked through the peephole and turned to me, her face a mix of surprise and concern.

"It's Dallas," she whispered. Dallas was Seyvn's closest friend, the one who was always lingering in the background but rarely saying much. He was shorter, a little stocky, with rich chocolate skin that gleamed under the right light. His long hair was usually pulled back, emphasizing his striking light brown eyes.

Where Seyvn commanded attention with flashy bravado, Dallas was the opposite. Quiet, steady, and observant.

It was clear he admired Seyvn, maybe even envied him, chasing after his larger-than-life persona like a kid trying to keep up with his older brother.

I froze. My first thought was that Seyvn had sent him. My second was that Seyvn might be right behind him.

Tonya looked at me, waiting.

I stepped closer to the door, trying to listen, trying to feel what might be on the other side besides Dallas. It was quiet.

I didn't hear another voice. I didn't feel a presence. Just stillness. I hesitated, then gave a small nod for her to open it.

Dallas stepped inside slowly, his hands slightly raised like he came in peace.

I folded my arms. "Why are you here, Dallas?"

He looked around once, then back at me. "I'm not here to start anything. I just... wanted to check on you."

There was a pause. He shifted his weight.

"I'm not trying to speak against him," he said carefully, "but Seyvn's got a history. That's why his daughter's mother left."

He looked down for a beat.

"I should've said something sooner," he added, almost like he was talking to himself. "But I didn't think it would come to all this."

He looked up again. "I don't really know what to say."

His honesty landed harder than I expected. "I didn't know..." My voice cracked, and I hated how small I sounded.
Dallas took a hesitant step closer. "You didn't deserve any of this." His gaze was steady, sincere.

Before I realized it, I was crying. Quiet tears that had been building for days. Maybe it was the pregnancy. Maybe it was the way he threw my things, the bags in the yard, the police, the fear, the confusion.

Dallas stepped closer, hesitating just a moment before gently pulling me into a tight embrace. I didn't resist. I didn't even think.

I just let myself lean into him.

It didn't make sense. I didn't really know him. He didn't really know me. And somehow, he still showed up.

His arms were firm and steady, and for a few seconds, it was exactly what I needed. I let myself rest there, just long enough to feel something that wasn't fear or shame or confusion.

"I'm so sorry," he whispered.

I pulled back, wiping a stray tear. "It's not your fault."

When he turned to leave, he paused at the door.

"Thank you for coming," I said quietly.

He gave a small nod.

"I'll check on you again before you head out," he said.

Then, like he already knew what I was thinking, he added, "I won't tell him where you are. I swear."

True to his word, Dallas came back. Not to pry or ask questions, just to check in like he said he would. And somehow, his presence didn't feel out of place.

The four of us me, Tonya, her boyfriend Marcus, Dallas, and I were hanging out in Tonya's living room. Music playing, snacks on the table, something light on the TV that no one was really watching. The energy felt easy. Tonya and Marcus were joking back and forth while Dallas and I mostly listened, chiming in here and there.

For a little while, I forgot why I was there, laughing at Marcus's jokes and listening to Dallas quietly chime in with surprisingly sharp wit. Tonya was playing DJ, scrolling through her phone and switching tracks, filling the room with music that made the space feel safe.

We even talked about the pregnancy. Nothing heavy. Just small comments and playful side conversations, like it was something simple instead of everything it actually was.

Tonya and Marcus started going back and forth about a video game, half-playing, half-arguing over who was better. Dallas and I watched, laughing when one of them lost.

Then came the knock.

It wasn't loud. Just firm. Steady. The kind of knock that makes people stop talking.

And we did.

Tonya muted the music, exchanging a quick glance with Marcus. My stomach twisted as I watched Dallas shift uncomfortably, his usually calm demeanor replaced with something tense and unreadable.

The knock came again, louder this time. Determined.
Tonya slowly rose from the couch, motioning for Marcus to stay put. She moved toward the door with quiet caution, peeking through the curtain covering the small front window.

Her shoulders tensed. She turned to me, her expression unreadable but serious.

"It's Seyvn."

The air left the room.

Marcus stood, fists clenched at his sides. Dallas didn't move. He just stared at me, like he was silently calculating every possible outcome.

I didn't need to hear anything else. I jumped up and slipped down the hallway, heart racing, feet moving before my mind caught up.

I made it to the bathroom, closed the door, and locked it. My hands were shaking as I backed up against the wall, trying to breathe. I didn't want to see him. Didn't want him to see me.

From inside, I could hear everything.

"What are you doing here?" Tonya asked, her voice clear and steady.

"I came to get her," Seyvn said. His tone wasn't loud, but it was firm. Unshaken. Like he had already decided how this was going to go.

"She doesn't want to see you. You need to leave."

The pause stretched.

Then his voice came back, a little tighter. "Open the door, I just want to talk to her."

He tried again, smaller this time. "Please."

My pulse raced. Every second felt stretched, charged with the possibility of violence. Then, unexpectedly, Dallas spoke up.

"Let me talk to him," he offered quietly, already moving toward the door before anyone could stop him.

Dallas eased the front door open just enough to slide outside, leaving us inside to listen in tense silence. I strained to catch bits of their conversation. Dallas was calm, measured. He talked to Seyvn like a brother, telling him he just needed to cool off, that this wasn't the way to handle things.

But Seyvn was determined. "I'm not leaving until I talk to her," he declared. His voice trembled, not with anger but with desperation.

Minutes passed like hours. Then I heard Seyvn's voice again, closer now. He'd somehow talked his way inside.

He was calling for me, his voice breaking with something almost like regret. I pressed my back against the cold bathroom wall, silently willing him to leave. But I knew he wouldn't until he saw me.

A soft knock came at the bathroom door, followed by his muffled voice. "Please...I'm so sorry. Just talk to me."

His words came faster, desperate now. "I love you. I miss you. I can't let you leave like this...not with us on bad terms. Please."

I felt trapped. This wasn't even my house, and I didn't want to impose on Tonya any more than I already had. Seyvn wasn't leaving until I faced him.

Taking a shaky breath, I unlocked the door and stepped out, my heart pounding. "I'm pregnant," I blurted.

He froze, then his face crumpled. In an instant, his arms were around me, pulling me into a fierce, trembling hug. "I'm so sorry," he whispered, his voice breaking. "I messed up...I was scared...I thought I lost you."

His tears soaked my shoulder as he begged for another chance. "Let's just talk...please," he pleaded.

Against every warning, every gut instinct, I nodded. We stepped outside into the cool night air, leaving the others inside. He spoke with a raw sincerity that shattered my defenses, weaving words of regret and love so skillfully that, I believed him.

I thought about the baby growing inside me, about the future I didn't want to face alone. Maybe he really was sorry. Maybe we could fix this.

Despite Tonya's whispered warnings and Dallas's silent plea in his eyes, I walked back to his car.

Back to him.

I didn't want to cause more drama at Tonya's place. She had opened her door to me, no questions asked. And after everything, she didn't deserve to be caught in the middle.

But going with him wasn't as hard as I thought it would be.

When we got back to his house, it was still clean.

The water jugs I'd used were sitting where I left them, only now they were full again.

He picked up dinner that night, nothing fancy but thoughtful. He was calm, affectionate, and seemed like he genuinely wanted to do better.

Things were going so well that he convinced me to extend my stay another week. I had spent a few days at Tonya's, and in my mind, it felt like I owed him that much. He rubbed my feet, made me laugh, and jumped on video calls with my kids like he had always been part of their lives.

His charm came back in full force, and for a little while, I let myself believe it. Maybe things really could be different. Maybe the baby we were expecting would bring out the best in him.

Then one evening, he brought up Dallas.

He mentioned it casually, just a passing comment about him being at Tonya's. His tone was light, like he was just making conversation.

"Why was Dallas there?" he asked.

I glanced up from the shirt I was folding. "Marcus is his friend too. We were all just hanging out."

He gave a short nod and looked away, but something about the pause that followed didn't sit right with me. It wasn't tense, but it stayed with me longer than it should have.

A few days later, the door slammed hard enough to rattle the walls as Seyvn stormed inside, his face twisted in anger. Dallas's girlfriend, upset that he had been at Tonya's house, planted the idea in Seyvn's paranoid mind that Dallas and I had slept together.

That lie was all it took to set him off.

"You think I'm stupid?" he yelled, pacing the small room. "You think I don't know what happened?"

I was stunned. "Nothing happened! Dallas came to check on me because you were acting crazy Seyvn!"

But logic didn't matter once the idea was in his head. In that moment, I was already guilty.

"You think I didn't see how y'all looked at each other?" he pressed, voice rising with every word. "Why else would he be there?"

I tried to explain. I didn't even know Dallas like that. His accusations became cruel and personal, leaving me reeling. It felt

302

like my loyalty, my truth, my very character as a woman were suddenly under review, and no amount of explaining seemed enough.

Before I could say another word, Seyvn grabbed his phone and called Dallas, demanding he come over immediately. Dallas lived just around the block, so it didn't take long.

He walked in cautiously, already aware of the mess he was stepping into. His girlfriend had made the same accusations to him, and it didn't take much to connect the dots. His normally cool, laid-back expression hardened as he met Seyvn's furious gaze.

"You got something you wanna tell me?" Seyvn growled.

Dallas sighed, clearly fed up. "What do you think happened?"

"You were at Tonya's house while I wasn't there. Why?"

Dallas squared his shoulders, exasperation etched into every word.

"Man, this girl came all the way down here from Timbuktu to be with you, and you was tripping. One of us had to make sure she was good. That's all it was."

Seyvn's fists clenched at his sides, still unconvinced. "Why should I believe that?"

Dallas let out a short, bitter laugh. "Man, she's not even my type. You know I don't like big girls. You really think I'd do that to you? I was being a friend because you couldn't be."

Seyvn didn't respond, but his jaw tightened, his face stuck somewhere between anger and realization. He knew Dallas was telling the truth.

After a long silence, he turned away and muttered, "Man, whatever."

Dallas lingered for just a second, glancing at me with something between sympathy and disappointment. He didn't say a word. Just shook his head, like the moment already said everything for him.

He turned and walked out.

For a moment, the room was silent. I didn't say anything, not wanting to set Seyvn off again. But slowly, the energy in him changed. His anger faded. His posture slumped, and his voice dropped.

"I don't want to lose you," he said. "I know I mess up, but I'm trying."

I understood where he was coming from. Dallas had come to Tonya's house and didn't tell him. And it was Dallas's girlfriend who brought Seyvn over there that day, who saw Dallas's car and lit the match. Maybe Dallas and I could've handled it differently. Maybe we should have said something sooner. I didn't think it was that deep, but to Seyvn, it was.

Before I could respond, he dropped to his knees and wrapped his arms around my waist, pressing his face into me like he didn't know what else to do. His voice cracked as he whispered, "We're having a baby. I don't want to mess this up."

But he hadn't messed up alone. We both had. And we could both find a way to fix it.

Chapter 55

Showing Up

"You don't have a right to the cards you believe you should have been dealt. You have an obligation to play the hell out of the ones you're holding."

— Cheryl Strayed

When I got back home, I was relieved to see my kids but caught off guard to find Wilma and Carey there too. Allie had been watching the kids while I was gone, but she conveniently forgot to mention that her mother and sister had shown up to "help."

Their help usually came with strings or drama. Still, I didn't want to cause a scene. They were my children's family, and even if I didn't love the surprise, I wasn't trying to keep them from their grandkids, nieces, or nephew. I just wished someone had told me they were coming, especially since I wasn't even home when they showed up. But boundaries had always been a foreign concept to them.

Eventually, they packed up and left, and for the first time two weeks, I could finally breathe. At least a little.

The reality of my pregnancy settled back over me, heavier than ever. Seyvn and I were on decent terms, but that didn't change the fact that I was now pregnant with my fifth child. I didn't believe in termination, so that was never an option, but raising another baby felt overwhelming.

I kept thinking about how it all started. Back on Myspace, where life was simple and filtered and full of possibility. That version of our story felt like it belonged to someone else.

Seyvn was still trying. He called often, talking about plans and the baby, and about starting over somewhere new.

At first, it felt like wishful thinking. But the more we talked, the more it started to sound possible. I wanted to believe him. Not just for me, but for the kids. For the life growing inside me. For the chance to build something better.

Then he showed up.

He drove all the way from New Jersey to Green Bay to be there when his daughter was born. He made it just in time. His presence surprised me. It calmed something in me, though I wasn't sure if it was because he truly cared about me or because he genuinely wanted to be a father. Maybe it was both.

Watching him hold her with such care, seeing the way his eyes softened when he looked at her brought out the version of him I had hoped existed.

The one who meant what he said.

The one who could love her the way she deserved.

No matter what had gone wrong between us, I couldn't deny him the chance to be her dad. He showed up when it mattered. And that meant something.

That's when the idea of starting over didn't just seem possible, it started to feel necessary. We needed neutral ground. A place untouched by everything we had already been through. Not Wisconsin. Not New Jersey. Somewhere new.

And that's how Delaware came into the picture.

The plan moved fast. Too fast. Before I had time to second-guess it, I had already transferred my housing voucher, started packing, and committed to the move. I didn't give myself time to think about what might go wrong.

I sold everything I could, the couches, beds, dining table. Whatever didn't sell, we left behind. If it didn't fit in the pickup truck, it didn't come. We moved with almost nothing but the clothes on our backs.

I kept telling myself it was fine. We'd rebuy it all when we got there. A couch is just a couch. A bed is just a bed. As long as we had the money, we could piece everything back together.

The 16-hour drive stretched endlessly ahead of us. At first, it felt like a clean slate, like we were putting real miles between ourselves and everything that had gone wrong. But somewhere along the way, the excitement started to thin out, replaced by an unease I couldn't shake. It sat heavy in my chest, unspoken, as if my body knew something my mind refused to accept.

Even before we crossed state lines, life kept throwing up warning signs. Some subtle. Some loud. But I ignored them all, convincing myself that once we got there, everything would fall into place. I had to believe that. Otherwise, what were we doing?

We arrived in Delaware without a plan. No apartment lined up. No family waiting to take us in. Our only option was a budget hotel on the outskirts of town.

We spent nearly a month in that tiny, worn-out room, and it felt like a lifetime. Every morning, I woke up to the stale scent of old carpet and cleaning chemicals that couldn't mask years of use. The walls were so thin we could hear entire conversations from the neighboring rooms: arguments, crying babies, even someone's late-night TV marathons.

Eventually, luck or something close to it showed up. We found a house through a Craigslist ad. The landlord wasn't someone I would normally trust, but beggars couldn't be choosers. The lease was only for a year, and after so long in the hotel, having four walls and a front door we could call our own felt like a win.

It was a four-bedroom, two-bath home with a small kitchen, dining room, living room, and an unfinished basement. It was older, with creaky floors and worn fixtures, but it had charm. More importantly, it had space. The front and back yards stretched wide, giving the kids room to run and play.

We found furniture through Craigslist also, surprisingly nice pieces considering most of it was free. A sturdy dining table, a cozy sectional, and even beds for the kids.

Bit by bit, the house felt like home. We hung family photos on the walls, added colorful curtains, and let the kids' artwork take over the refrigerator door.

Seyvn seemed more settled. He smiled more, played with the kids in the yard, and pitched in on house projects. There was a lightness in him I hadn't seen before, like he was finally building the life he'd always wanted. He found work as a mechanic, fixing cars with the same skill and precision he used to repair electronics.

Encouraged by his potential, I helped him start a small repair business out of the house. He had a gift for bringing broken TVs, game consoles, and old radios back to life, and clients started coming through word of mouth. For a while, it felt like we were really getting our fresh start. The tension and uncertainty that had followed us for so long began to fade, replaced by something steady.

For me, I still didn't care to go out much. The world felt unpredictable. But the library was steady. Quiet. Safe. I never minded going there.

Delaware had more libraries than I could count, and each book was filled with new adventures waiting to be discovered. The kids and I made it a tradition to visit as many libraries as we could. They looked forward to the reading circles and craft sessions. I looked forward to escaping into someone else's story, even if only for a little while.

At home, I made sure the kids stayed busy with more than just TV. Weekdays were filled with science kits, art projects, and homemade scavenger hunts. Weekends were for music. We'd blast the stereo, play dress-up, and dance until we couldn't breathe from laughing. We'd gather around the old gaming console and take turns playing Rock Band.

That first Christmas in Delaware came faster than I expected, and money was tighter than ever. I searched Craigslist for secondhand gifts, hoping to piece together something special. Seyvn was determined to make sure the kids had a magical holiday, even if it meant taking chances. More than once, he walked out of stores with things he hadn't paid for, brushing it off like it was no big deal.

I didn't agree with it. I hated that he put himself at risk. But I also understood the heart behind it. He was trying to give them something we couldn't afford. It didn't make it right, but in a world that had taken so much from us, it was hard not to see the love in it, even if it came wrapped in risk.

Marla Matrice Murphy

CHAPTER 56

Daddy's House

"We do what we have to do, so we can do what we want to do."

— James Baldwin

Seyvn's daughters, Sevannah and Nyla, had recently started spending weekends with us. They blended in easily with the rest of the kids, with dress-up clothes scattered everywhere, loud laughter echoing through the halls, the occasional sibling rivalry, and our living room transformed into a stage for impromptu performances. For a while, it felt like everything was working.

The house had finally quieted after another chaotic weekend. In the bathroom, steam clung to the walls as Alyra knelt by the tub, helping Sevannah wash up. They giggled about something only they understood, their laughter spilling out like sisters who had known each other forever.

Then Alyra's expression shifted. She noticed hair growing in a place she hadn't seen before, and curiosity got the better of her.
She reached out and touched it.

That single moment unraveled everything.

The next week, Sevannah told the school, setting off the mandatory reporting requirements. The same rules that had once wreaked havoc on Seyvn's life were now threatening to wreak it on mine.

When they asked Sevannah where she was when she was touched, she said, "Daddy's house."

And technically, that meant my house.

I wasn't scared of CPS. I was scared of losing my Section 8 voucher. Delaware's housing rules were strict. If a man lived with you while you were on Section 8, he had to be legally married to you and listed on the voucher. Seyvn had already been staying with us, especially after losing his home in New Jersey. If the state found out, they could terminate my housing assistance, and just like that, we'd have nowhere to go.

I didn't see a way out. The only way to protect our home, and keep our kids safe, was to make it official.

We had to get married.

We had a simple courthouse ceremony. Seyvn was ecstatic, grinning like the Cheshire cat. He whistled and sang the whole way there as if this was the moment he had been waiting his entire life for.

I, on the other hand, felt trapped. This wasn't how I imagined getting married for the second time. There was no love story. No grand gesture. Just a government form that needed to be signed. But I told myself it was the right thing to do. We had a daughter together. The kids needed stability. It was what it was.

But even as I forced a smile for the courthouse clerk, a voice in the back of my mind whispered: *DON'T DO IT!*

For a little while, I thought I had made the right choice.

But the peace didn't last.

Less than a week after CPS closed the case, Seyvn decided Alyra needed to be punished for "causing" the investigation. I heard him yelling, his voice sharp and heavy, rattling through the walls. I stayed in the other room.

I told myself he wouldn't hurt her. He yelled, he slammed things, but he had never crossed that line before. Maybe part of me believed that since we were married now, he was her father too, and fathers disciplined their children.

Whatever the reason, I stayed where I was. I didn't protect her the way I should have.

I should have left right then. Packed up my kids and never looked back. But I didn't. I told myself it was just a mistake, a moment of bad judgment. Yelling never hurt anyone. Maybe some yelling would scare her enough not to repeat what she had done.

And when nothing else happened, I convinced myself it was over.

Life seemed to settle into a manageable rhythm. We never spoke about what happened with Alyra. We just moved on, like it hadn't happened at all.

Before long, Sevannah and Nyla were back on the weekends. The girls slipped into their usual routines, playing dress-up, putting on little performances, and laughing like nothing had changed, with the understanding that everyone would keep their hands to themselves.

No exceptions.

CHAPTER 57

Deliberate

"When someone shows you who they are, believe them the first time."

— Maya Angelou

I thought the worst had passed, but really, it was just shifting into a different form.

Seyvn worked long hours as a mechanic, built his electronics business on the side, and spent whatever free time he had working on his music.

One evening, I decided to surprise him by making his favorite meal: shrimp Alfredo. I wasn't much of a cook, but I wanted to do something nice. I picked out what I thought were the right shrimp, feeling proud of myself for the effort.

When he walked in and saw the package on the counter, his face twisted in disgust.

"What are these," he snapped, his voice sharp enough to cut glass.

Confused, I stammered, "I thought these were the shrimp you liked."

"You thought what? That you'd get the cheapest thing you could find? You can't even do something so simple."

I stood there, stunned, my heart pounding. Before I could explain, his anger exploded. Words like 'worthless' and 'stupid' filled the room, searing into my chest.

Then, he hawked and spit right in my face.
Not once, but twice.

Deliberate and degrading.

I froze, humiliation and fury battling inside me. My breath caught in my throat as disbelief and disgust crashed over me. My face burned, not from the spit but from the sheer violation of it.

I stumbled back.

Without thinking, I rushed to the kitchen sink and turned the faucet on full blast. I plunged my face beneath the stream of cold water, scrubbing hard, as if I could wash away more than what he had done.

Behind me, Seyvn paced, muttering something I couldn't hear over the rushing water and the pounding of my heart. For a moment, I let the coldness numb me, offering a fleeting escape from the reality I'd have to face as soon as I lifted my head.

When I finally straightened, droplets clung to my face like unspoken tears. I caught a glimpse of my reflection in the window above the sink. Wet, quiet, and barely recognizable.

And still, I faced him.

I turned slowly, my face still damp, my fists clenched at my sides. He stood a few feet away, his chest rising and falling. The wildness in his face was already shifting, softening into something more familiar.

"I didn't mean it," Seyvn muttered, his voice low, almost pleading. "You know how stressed I've been... It just happened."

The room felt too small, the air too thick. He stepped closer, his hands reaching out hesitantly. "You know I love you... I just lost control."

The weight of those words pressed against my chest. Love shouldn't feel like this.

This wasn't the first time he'd lost control. Just the first time it had looked like this.

"I'm not doing this," I whispered, more to myself than to him.

His expression hardened for a split second before softening again, his voice smoothing into something almost gentle. "We have a family... you can't just throw that away."

It was always about the family, about making it work. But at what cost?

My fingers trembled as I wiped lingering water from my face and nodded, not because I believed him, but because I didn't know what else to do.

Seyvn was apologetic. He cooked. Cleaned. Played with the kids.

The days went on.

On the surface, everything looked fine.

But nothing about it felt that way. No matter how clean the house looked, I could still feel the spit on my skin

CHAPTER 58

I Love You More

"There is no such thing as a perfect parent. So just be a real one."

— Sue Atkins

The one thing I could always count on was my children.

They were my purpose, my balance, the reason I kept pushing forward when everything else felt like it was falling apart.

The girls were my light, my laughter, and my joy, but Enrique, my only son, carried something more. He wasn't just my child; he was my heart outside of my body, he was the air in my lungs, the blood in my veins, a living, breathing embodiment of a love so fierce it felt like my heart might burst. Enrique was a miracle, a prayer answered after the pregnancy with Noah Jr. ended in heartbreak.

Pregnancy with Enrique wasn't easy either. Noah's family only added to the stress. I'll never forget the day I had to swing that pot at his sister's head to protect myself and my unborn son. That moment symbolized everything I'd been through to keep him safe, even before he was born. From the very beginning, I was willing to fight for him. Literally.

When Enrique finally arrived, he was everything I'd dreamed of and more. I was overwhelmed by love for him. I didn't know how it was possible to love someone so much, so fully. He was my Momma's Boy, my pride, my everything.

From the time he could talk, we shared a bond that was as unshakable as it was unique. And that's how our game, I Love You More, was born.
It always started the same way. I'd scoop him up in my arms and say, "I love you, Momma's Boy."

319

And without fail, he'd smile that mischievous smile of his and reply, "I love you more."

I'd let out an exaggerated gasp, staggering back like I'd been struck by lightning, one hand clutching my chest. "No!" I'd cry, shaking my head with theatrical despair. "Impossible! I love you more!" And just like that, the showdown began.

"No, I love you more!" he'd counter, his little voice full of determination.

The back-and-forth would go on until it escalated into tickle fights, wrestling matches, or full-on chases around the house. The girls loved it, too. They'd join in, cheering for Enrique or me, laughing so hard they'd be clutching their sides.

One day, Enrique decided to up the ante. He was on a wrestling kick, pretending to be one of the members of D-Generation X. He crouched low, arms wide, yelling, "You can't beat me!" like he was in the middle of a WWF match. He tried to pull a wrestling move on me, grabbing my arm and giggling so hard he could barely keep his balance.

"You think you're stronger than me?" I teased, scooping him up effortlessly.

"Yep! I love you more!" he yelled, wiggling in my arms like he was trying to escape.

The girls ran behind us, shrieking with laughter, their voices ringing out in playful excitement as they jumped and squealed, caught up in the moment.

I carried him into the kitchen, all of us laughing uncontrollably. Then, in a stroke of pure silliness, I opened the freezer. "If you don't admit that I love you more, I'm putting you in this freezer!" I said, holding him over it like he was a sack of potatoes.

320

Enrique squealed with delight. "Nooooo! You can't do that!" he laughed, his little legs kicking in the air.

"Oh, yes, I can!" I said, laughing so hard I could barely hold him up. "Well, I guess into the freezer you go!" "Admit it! I love you more!"

"Okay, okay!" he finally yelled, giggling so hard he was practically out of breath. "You win! You love me more!"

I set him down gently, "That's what I thought," I said triumphantly. "Mommy always wins."

Enrique grinned up at me, "Next time, I'm going to win," he declared, already plotting his next move.

We both knew he wouldn't. He never could. And that was the beauty of it, the game wasn't about winning or losing. It was about love.

The girls clapped and cheered, and for a moment, the house was filled with pure, unfiltered joy. It was one of those rare times when nothing else mattered. Just me and my children. No stress. No fear. Not even the world outside.

All that mattered was us.

CHAPTER 59

Unforgivable Acts

"There are things that can never be undone, things that can never be forgiven."

— Cassandra Clare

Even in the happiest moments with my children, like playing I Love You More with Enrique or chasing the girls around the house, there was sometimes a shift when Seyvn was around.

Most of the time, he joined in, laughing with the kids or teasing me about how I let them win too easily. But every now and then, his energy would change the room without him saying a word.

I learned to read it quickly, adjusting the conversation or redirecting the kids if I thought something might set him off. He would get irritated over small things, such as a misplaced tool or the kids being a little too loud, but it never went further than a grumble or a mutter under his breath. I told myself it was

just stress from work. Everyone has bad days, right?

At first, those days were rare. But they started coming more often.

One night, I went upstairs to check on Lilly, her tiny breaths steady and peaceful in her crib. The house was quiet except for the low hum of the television.

Seyvn sat on the edge of the bed, scrolling through his phone. We started talking about Nyla's upcoming birthday. It was an ordinary conversation until I mentioned the wrong date. Before I even realized he had moved, he was standing in front of me.

His hand hit me hard. My head snapped to the side, heat spreading across my cheek as blood filled my mouth. The world tilted, and for a second, everything went white.

Before I could steady myself, my foot caught on a shirt thrown across the floor. I went down hard, the slap of skin against hardwood echoing as the impact jolted every bone in my body.

Agony shot through my lower back, ripping a scream from my throat before I could stop it. My vision blurred as I registered the searing pain radiating from my tailbone. I couldn't move. I couldn't breathe. I couldn't process what had just happened.

Blood dripped steadily from my nose. My ears still rang from the blow, but through the haze of pain and shock, I could hear the sound of his heavy breathing.

He stood there, fists clenched, jaw tight, eyes blazing with something I couldn't recognize. Something cold and terrifying.

Then, without a word, he turned and walked out, leaving me crumpled on the floor, sobbing and gasping for air.

This was the first time he'd ever hit me.

As I lay there, barely able to move, my mind racing with a thousand fragmented thoughts. How did we get here? How did I get here?

For what felt like forever, I stayed on that cold, hard floor, in too much pain to move. My face throbbed with every heartbeat, and the sharp ache in my back settled into a relentless, burning reminder of what had just happened.

Eventually, I went to the bathroom, gripping the sink for balance. Blood smeared across the porcelain as I washed my face, each splash of water like ice on fire. I stared at my reflection. Swollen, bruised, and defeated. A stranger stared back.
But I couldn't stay stuck in that moment. I had kids who needed me. I wiped away the blood, forcing myself to stand straighter, even

as every inch of my body protested. I couldn't let them see me like this.

By the time Seyvn returned, hours later, I was in bed, pretending to be asleep. He slipped in beside me like nothing had happened, like we were still normal, still okay.

But nothing was okay. And deep down, I knew it never would be again. After that night, I knew I had to leave. I couldn't stay after what he'd done. I thought I had timed everything perfectly. He was supposed to be at work for hours, long enough for me to pack, load the kids into the car, and be gone before he even realized what was happening. Every movement felt like I was defusing a ticking bomb. Silent, precise, desperate.

With shaking hands, I stuffed clothes into bags, grabbed diapers, a few toys, and important papers. My heart pounded like a war drum as I strapped the kids into the car, my eyes constantly scanning the street for his car. No sign of him. Not yet.

I slid into the driver's seat, breathless but hopeful.

I turned the key. Nothing.

"No, no, no!" I whispered frantically, twisting the key again. Still nothing.

My stomach clenched. I checked the gas gauge. Full. I tried the ignition once more, praying for a miracle. The car stayed silent.

Before I could process what was happening, headlights appeared at the end of the driveway. My heart stopped.

He was home.
How did he know? How could he possibly know?
Within seconds, he was out of the car and storming toward me. I scrambled for my phone and dialed 911, begging the dispatcher for help. The officers arrived quickly, and two squad cars pulled up.

"What seems to be the problem?" one officer asked, eyes shifting between Seyvn and me.

"The car won't start," I said, my voice trembling.

Calm as ever, "There's no gas," he said smoothly. "She must've run it dry."

"That's not true," I snapped, my voice rising. "The tank is full. He did something to the car!"

The officers frowned and checked the gas gauge, then asked me to try the ignition. The engine stubbornly refused to turn over.

One officer sighed, clearly impatient. "Ma'am, there's no sign of tampering. Without proof that a crime has been committed, there's nothing we can do."

I stared at them in disbelief as they walked back to their cars. Seyvn gave them a friendly nod, thanked them, and even promised he'd "take care of it."

As the police pulled away, his face darkened. "Going somewhere?" he sneered.

I backed up slowly, but there was nowhere to run. Somehow, he'd trapped me without saying a word or making a move.

My chest tightened as the police cars disappeared down the street, taking with them the only sliver of hope I had left. The air felt suffocating, thick with the weight of helplessness.

Seyvn's eyes stayed locked on mine, daring me to try something, anything. But I was frozen. My hands trembled at my sides, fists clenched with frustration, anger, and fear tangled into one unbearable knot.

"You're not going anywhere," he said, voice calm and steady, almost conversational, like we were discussing dinner plans.

I hated how collected he looked, how sure of himself. Like he knew he'd won. And in that moment, he had.

"Y'all, get out the car and go back inside," he instructed smoothly, not even glancing their way. The kids hesitated, eyes shifting from me to him, uncertainty etched across their faces. Rayna clutched her baby sister tightly against her chest, shielding her like a protective wall. I forced a nod, blinking back tears as they slowly got out and walked toward the house. My heart clenched as I watched them disappear through the front door, leaving me alone with him.

The car door creaked as he leaned against it, arms crossed, watching me with quiet satisfaction. He didn't yell, didn't raise a hand. The silence was worse. It was the cold certainty that no matter what I did, no matter how hard I tried, he would always be one step ahead.

I felt the fight drain out of me, replaced by a hollow ache in my chest. This wasn't just a bad moment or a rough patch. This was my reality. And for the first time, I truly understood that leaving wouldn't be as simple as packing a bag and turning a key.

He pushed off the car with an eerie casualness. "Better come inside," he said, his tone almost gentle. "The kids need you."

He walked toward the house without looking back, fully expecting me to follow, and I did. My legs moving on autopilot, my mind screaming at me to run even as I stepped through that familiar doorway.

The sound of the door closing behind me said it all. I wasn't getting out.

Not yet. In the days after the failed escape, I convinced myself it had been a fluke. A moment of anger that wouldn't happen again. He hadn't hit me during the last fight, and I clung to that as proof things weren't as bad as they seemed. Maybe things could get better if I was more careful.

He was definitely good with the kids. He played with them, fixed their toys, and taught Enrique how to work on cars, taking him under his wing like a proud father. I watched them bond and told myself this version of him was the real one.

So, I tried harder. I cooked, kept the house clean, made sure the kids were quiet when he came home. I moved carefully, anticipating his needs before he even asked, convinced that if I could just be perfect, we could live the dream we once talked about instead of the nightmare it had become.

CHAPTER 60

"You Called My Father?"

"A father is a man who expects his son to be as good a man as he meant to be."

— Frank A. Clark

The house was quiet, a stillness hanging in the air that felt both peaceful and foreboding. Seyvn had left earlier, saying he was going to help his father fix up a house and would be back in a few hours. I should have known that was a lie. He had taken a shower, which he rarely did without prompting. And he definitely wasn't dressed for working on a house.

But I didn't care where he went. His leaving felt like a reprieve, a temporary escape from the constant tension. The kids and I enjoyed the quiet. We watched movies, listened to music, danced, and cooked. It was actually a good day.

Things changed as I put the kids to bed. I went to make Lilly's nightly bottle and realized we didn't have enough formula. She was down to her last bit, and both he and my car were gone. He wasn't answering his phone.

The only person I could think to call was his father. Maybe Seyvn really was with him. My fingers hovered over the screen, unsure, but I couldn't let my daughter go hungry.

When the line connected, his father's voice was gruff.

"Hello?"

I swallowed hard. "Hi, it's Matrice... um... is Seyvn with you?"
There was a pause on the other end. "Seyvn? No... why would he be here?"

329

Panic surged in my chest. "I thought... he said he was working with you today."

His father exhaled sharply. "I haven't seen him," his father finally said, confusion creeping into his tone. "What's going on?"

I swallowed hard, my heart pounding. "It's nothing," I said. "I just...thought he might be there. Thanks."

I ended the call and sat on the edge of the bed, cradling my face in my hands. The room felt colder, the silence heavier. He wasn't with his father. He wasn't working. He'd lied. Where was he... and with who?

I gave the baby a jar of food and a bottle with apple juice and water, hoping it would be enough to help her sleep. It wasn't ideal, but it was all I had. She finally dozed off, and I eventually drifted off too.

Sometime during the night, I heard his boots on the stairs. Each step was slow and heavy. The bedroom door creaked open, and even before I saw him, I could feel the tension enter the room.

"You called my father," he said, his voice low and cold.

I didn't answer. I just got up and started walking toward the bathroom, hoping to avoid him, hoping to avoid whatever was coming.

But I didn't make it far.

His fist slammed into my lower back, pain shooting up my spine. I stumbled forward, gasping, before he threw me onto the bed.

The mattress broke my fall, but not the violence. He came at me fast, his fists landing with force and fury.

My only thought, through the haze of agony, was that I should've known better.

"You think you're slick?" he spat, towering over me like a predator savoring its kill. "You think you can go behind my back and tell people my business? Make them think I can't handle my own family?"

I choked on a sob, every breath a struggle as sharp, searing pain spread through my back that was barely recovered from the broken tailbone. My voice cracked as I whispered, "I just... I needed milk... for the baby."

The mention of our daughter made him pause, his jaw tightening. For a fleeting second, I thought he might stop. But hope was dangerous, and I knew better by now.

He knelt down, his face inches from mine, eyes burning with unhinged fury. His hand shot out, gripping my jaw in a vice-like hold, forcing me to meet his gaze.

"You think I don't know what you're trying to do? Make me look weak?" His voice was low and venomous, each word dripping with malice.

I tried to shake my head, but his grip was iron. "I swear... I didn't..."

"You don't make decisions around here," he hissed, bending down so his face was inches from mine. His breath was hot and bitter, laced with rage. "You don't call nobody without my say-so. You hear me?"

I nodded weakly, my entire body trembling. The baby's cries echoed faintly from her crib, cutting through the suffocating tension. He heard her too, his head snapping toward the sound.

His expression changed, just barely, but enough for me to see that twisted version of love he claimed to have for our daughter. He turned abruptly, storming toward the crib in the corner of our room. Lilly stirred, letting out a soft whimper, unaware of the chaos she'd unknowingly quieted. He reached into the crib, gently adjusting her blanket with hands that had been so violent just moments before.

Without another word, he stormed out of the room. I heard him grab his keys from the counter and storm out. I prayed he would never come back while I lay there, shaking and gasping for air, my hand clutching my bruised ribs. The baby's cries grew a little louder. Drawing strength from her, I forced myself up, every movement sending fiery bolts of pain through my body.

I stumbled toward her crib, biting back sobs as I scooped her up, holding her tight against my chest. Her small warmth was the only comfort I could cling to.

The front door creaked open barely thirty minutes after he'd stormed out. I froze, still sitting on the bed where I was holding the baby with shaky hands. My heart pounded as his heavy footsteps echoed through the house, stopping just outside the bedroom door.

He stepped inside, holding a plastic grocery bag like nothing had happened. His expression was calm, a complete contrast to the rage he had unleashed earlier.

"I got the milk," he said flatly, tossing the bag onto the bed.

Without another glance in my direction, Seyvn turned and walked down the hall to his makeshift studio. Seconds later, the deep thrum of bass-filled beats spilled from behind the closed door, vibrating through the walls like a living, breathing thing. Music was his escape, his way of forgetting.

Relief flooded through me, though it was quickly replaced by a familiar, suffocating dread. I grabbed the formula, mixed a fresh bottle, and gently fed the baby until her soft, contented breaths told me she was asleep.

I laid her down carefully, adjusting the blanket around her tiny form, and allowed myself one fragile moment of stillness. My body ached from the earlier blows, but the emotional bruises left me breathless.

I sat on the edge of the bed, staring at the darkened window as each beat from his studio cruelly counted down the seconds of a life that no longer felt like mine.

The music stopped abruptly, leaving behind a deafening silence. Heavy footsteps followed, growing louder, closer. I straightened up, heart pounding as the door creaked open.

He stepped inside, his presence thick, filling the space before he even spoke. He walked past me, peeling off his pants as he moved toward the bed. The mattress sank under his weight as he sat down, rubbing his hands over his face, exhaling like he was releasing tension.

Then his eyes lifted to mine.

"Come lay down," he murmured, his voice deceptively soft.

Every instinct screamed at me to move away, to put space between us. But where would I go? With the car disabled and nowhere safe to turn, I was trapped.

Slowly, carefully, I slid down onto the mattress beside him, my body stiff, my breathing shallow.

He wasted no time. His arm wrapped around me, pulling me in with a grip that felt more like a restraint than affection. His breath was steady, almost peaceful, as though holding me erased everything that had happened earlier.

For him, maybe it did.

For me, it never would.

I stared at the ceiling, my mind racing with plans I couldn't yet piece together. His arm felt like a steel band across my waist, anchoring me in place.

I couldn't move, couldn't risk waking him. His arm tightened instinctively even in sleep, as if he sensed my thoughts of escape.

I tried to will myself into numbness, to block out the sharp ache in my ribs, the bruises blossoming beneath my skin.

In that stillness, I allowed myself one dangerous thought. A promise I didn't dare speak aloud.

One day...

CHAPTER 61

Even this

"If you're going through hell, keep going."
— Winston Churchill

Dawn crept in slowly, brushing faint light through the worn blinds. He stirred beside me, his fingers twitching before tightening their hold once more. A silent reminder of control, even in sleep. I stayed frozen, heart pounding, until his breathing deepened again.

At some point, exhaustion must have taken over. The alarm's piercing beep cut through the fragile stillness, yanking me from restless sleep. My body ached, bruises throbbing beneath the thin blanket, but there was no time to think about that. The day had already started, and I had to move.

I slipped out of bed slowly, glancing back to make sure he was still asleep. His face was relaxed, peaceful in a way that almost made last night feel like a twisted dream.

The baby stirred in her crib, letting out a soft whimper before settling again. I adjusted her blanket, pressing a gentle kiss on her tiny forehead. Stay asleep a little longer, my perfect princess.

I grabbed my scarf from the dresser, fingers trembling as I wrapped it carefully around my neck, wincing as the fabric brushed against tender, bruised skin. The dark blotches bloomed like ink stains across my collarbone, impossible to hide completely but easy enough to explain away. At least to them.

I tiptoed down the narrow stairs, every creak of the old wood making my heart pound. Don't wake him. Not yet.

The hallway was dim, the soft hum of the furnace the only sound.

I paused at each of their doors, listening for any sign that last night's chaos had seeped into their dreams. Silence. Maybe they slept through it.

I headed into the kitchen, setting a pot of water on the stove for oatmeal. It was warm, filling, and familiar. They didn't always like the free breakfast at school, so I made sure they had something good before they left.

I stirred the oatmeal slowly, letting its warmth seep into my aching hands. The familiar rhythm steadied me. Stir, scoop, sprinkle the brown sugar on top, just the way they liked it.

Footsteps padded softly across the worn linoleum. My oldest appeared first, rubbing her eyes with small, determined fists. "Morning, Mommy," she murmured, voice still thick with dreams.

"Good morning, Sunshine." I kissed her forehead, breathing in the familiar scent of coconut oil and sleep. "Go wake your brother and sisters for me, okay?"

She nodded, already turning toward the hall. A few minutes later, they came shuffling in one by one, small faces still creased from pillows, yawning but ready to start another day. My boy, always the last to emerge, but quick with a sleepy smile that melted every jagged edge inside me.

I set the bowls on the table, watching them climb into their usual spots. Their small hands gripped spoons as they ate, feet swinging beneath the table. The soft clinks of metal against ceramic filled the quiet room, blending with the soft hum of the refrigerator.

I leaned against the counter, letting myself linger just a moment, watching them. Memorizing the curve of their smiles, the way they nudged each other playfully, completely unaware that I was barely holding myself up.

Please... let them never make the choices I made.

I prayed they would be stronger than I'd been. That they'd know they were worth more than just surviving, more than hiding bruises beneath scarves and forcing smiles that never reached their eyes. Even though everything I did, every compromise, every night spent biting back tears, was for them. I just hoped they never had to do the same.

They scraped the last of the oatmeal from their bowls and carried them to the sink, clattering them in with a practiced ease that tugged at my heart. My oldest reached for the dish rag without being asked, wiping the table like she always did.

I felt a familiar tightness in my chest. Not from fear this time, but from love so fierce it felt like both a blessing and a curse.

They deserved more. They deserved everything.

And Seyvn... he loved them too. He wasn't always the monster I feared in the dark. To them, he was still the man who played silly games, taught them how to ride bikes, and lifted them high on his shoulders like they were invincible.

They loved him. God, they loved him.

How could I take them away from the only father they'd ever really known? How could I rip that from them? And Lilly... my perfect princess... didn't she deserve her father too? Hadn't they lost enough?

"Y'all ready?" I called out, forcing brightness into my voice. "The bus won't wait!"

They lined up by the door, tugging on jackets and backpacks. One by one, I kissed their warm cheeks, holding on just a second longer than usual.

"Be good," I whispered, voice hitching despite my best efforts. "I love you."

They repeated it with a laugh, slipping through the front door into the crisp morning air. Then my boy paused, turning back with that familiar spark in his eyes.

"I love you more, Mommy."

A sharp ache radiated from my bruised ribs, but I pushed the pain down, locking it away where he'd never see. He could never know.

I couldn't help but smile, the weight on my chest easing just a little. I reached out, giving his side a playful tickle like always. "Take it back before I kick your butt," I teased, like I always did. Keeping my voice light, steady. Normal.

He laughed, squirming away. "Okay, okay! I take it back!"

"Good." I playfully pushed his head one last time, holding on to that fleeting moment of joy despite the burning throb beneath my scarf. He shot me one last grin before racing toward the bus stop where his sisters waited, backpacks bouncing against small shoulders.

I stood by the door, watching them until the bus's brakes hissed and its doors swallowed them up.

The house felt impossibly quiet once the bus rumbled down the street, leaving behind a stillness that pressed in from every side. I stood by the window a moment longer, watching until they were completely out of sight.

The sound of footsteps thudding down the stairs, broke the stillness. My stomach twisted. He was awake.

"Hey, babe," he greeted easily, flashing that disarming smile, the same one that had once made me believe in something better.

"Did the kids get off okay?"

"Yeah," I answered, forcing a smile that felt like glass in my throat. "They're good."

"Cool." He plopped down on the sagging couch, grabbing the remote. The familiar anime intro blasted through the room as he leaned back, completely at ease.

"You gonna make breakfast?" he asked, not looking away from the screen.

I bit the inside of my cheek until I tasted copper. Say yes. Don't make him wait.

"Yeah," I managed. "What do you want?"

"Fried pancakes and cheese eggs. You know how I like 'em."

"Okay." I turned back to the kitchen, breathing through the sharp pain radiating from my lower back.

As the skillet hissed and the smell of butter filled the air, I let my mind drift to my babies. I could still hear my boy's laughter echoing in my mind: "I love you more, Mommy."

For the kids, I'd endure anything.

Even this.

CHAPTER 62

Gone

"Nothing you do for children is ever wasted. They seem not to notice us, hovering, averting our eyes, and they seldom offer thanks, but what we do for them is never wasted."

— Garrison Keillor

I should have known better than to hope for a quiet afternoon. His anger never needed a reason. That day it found one. No milk for the cereal.

He paced the kitchen, slamming cabinets, muttering curses under his breath. I kept my head down, scrubbing the already-clean counter, hoping he'd run out of steam. But he didn't.

"I can't stand this place!" he snapped, his voice sharp. "You don't ever have what we need. I'm sick of it!"

I clenched the edge of the sink. Breathe. Stay calm.

"You could always leave." The words slipped out before I could stop them, my voice betraying me with a shaky edge.

His head snapped up, eyes narrowing dangerously. "What did you just say?"

I lifted my chin, forcing the words past the knot in my throat.

"You can leave. No one's keeping you here."

Before I could move, he crossed the space in two quick strides and slapped me across the face so hard I saw lightning. An audible, sharp gasp followed my own. I turned and saw my daughter's best friend frozen in the doorway, eyes wide, lip trembling, her whole body locked in place.

Whatever safety she thought existed here was gone.

I pressed my fingers to my burning cheek, swallowing down the rage, the shame, the unbearable ache of knowing she'd never forget what she saw. This had to end. I was done.

A few weeks later, after he came home from work, I made my move. He walked in like he always did, tossing the truck keys carelessly onto the kitchen counter before heading upstairs to the music room, his usual routine after a long shift. He didn't even glance my way. I hadn't heard the hood close, hadn't heard any tools clanking outside. He hadn't disabled the truck.

I knew he'd be up there for a while. He always was, messing around with his music, lost in his own world.

It was the opening I'd been praying for.

I moved quickly but carefully, heart pounding like a drum in my chest. Diapers, bottles, and formula. Essentials only. We didn't need much. Just enough to keep the kids safe until we could figure out what came next.

I cradled the baby in one arm while guiding the others toward the door, trying to keep my voice steady. "Come on, you guys, be quiet and let's go."

They obeyed without question, sensing the urgency beneath my calm tone. We reached the truck and I opened the passenger door and started buckling the baby into her car seat, while the other kids got in their own seats. Almost there. Almost free.

I was so focused on what I was doing, buckling the baby securely into her car seat and double-checking the straps, that I didn't hear the screen door open. I didn't hear the heavy boots crunching across the gravel or the snap of twigs underfoot. My mind was locked on the task at hand. Get them in. Get them safe. Get them out.

I closed the truck door gently, moving toward the back to help the older kids in, my mind locked on the next step. Almost there... almost free.

Then, movement. Too fast. Too close.

Before I could react, he was there.

He scooped my son into his arms in one swift, calculated motion. Not rough or violent. Gentle, almost lovingly. My boy didn't resist, didn't understand the danger coiling around him like a trap.

He just smiled up at Seyvn, trusting and innocent, like nothing was wrong. Like he was safe.

"Come on, boy," Seyvn said smoothly, his voice low and steady. "Let's go do man stuff."

"Seyvn, no!" I gasped, rushing toward them. "Don't do this. He's just a baby!"

He turned slowly, his face twisted with something dark and cruel.

"You wanna leave?" his voice low and steady. "Fine. But not with my son."

And just like that..... They were gone.

Straight into the woods, his figure disappearing into the dense shadows with my son cradled tightly against his chest.

I stumbled after them, legs buckling beneath me. But I couldn't stop.

Panic surged, sharp and suffocating, tearing through my chest. He took my son. He took my baby.

Not to hurt him. To hurt me. At least I didn't think he would. I hoped he wouldn't.

He knew I would never leave without my son.

I ran into the house, chest heaving, heart pounding like a drum in my ears. Get the phone. Call 911.

My fingers trembled as I snatched the phone off the counter, frantically punching the numbers. My breath came in sharp, broken gasps as the line connected.

"911, what's your emergency?"

"He took my son. He kidnapped my son!" I choked out, voice shredded from screaming. "Please, send someone. He ran into the woods with my son."

The dispatcher's voice was steady. Too steady. Detached, like this was just another call.

"Who took your son, ma'am?"

"Seyvn! My Husband! He grabbed him and ran!"

"Is the child in immediate danger?"
Immediate danger?

"He took my baby!" I cried, fists clenching in my hair. "He's just a baby!"

"Ma'am, I need you to calm down so I can send help."

Calm down? How could I calm down when my world was gone?

The flashing lights cast eerie red and blue shadows across the dark yard as two patrol cars pulled into the driveway. Their sirens were off. Silent. Cautious. They stepped out slowly, hands resting lightly on their belts. Not urgent. Not ready.

I ran toward them, nearly collapsing in the dirt, voice ragged and broken.

"He took my son. He ran into the woods. You have to go after them. Please!"

The officers exchanged a glance. Calm. Indifferent. Impersonal. One stepped forward, notebook in hand. "Who took your son, ma'am?"

"Seyvn. My Husband. I was trying to leave, to escape him and he grabbed my son and ran."

The officer scribbled something down, still maddeningly calm.

"How old is the child?"

"He's five. Just a baby. Can you do something?! Please."

The second officer asked evenly, "Do you have a custody order?"

I stared at him, stunned into silence for a moment. A custody order?

"No! He's my son! I'm his mother! He kidnapped him!"

They didn't flinch. Didn't soften.

"Ma'am, without a custody order," the first officer said slowly, like he was explaining something simple, "this sounds like a domestic issue."

Domestic. Issue.

The words punched through me hollowing out my chest. How could they say that?

"He's not his biological father! They aren't even related," I screamed, voice cracking. "He has no right. He took my son. You can't just do nothing."

The officer sighed, almost wearily. "Unless the child is in immediate danger, there's not much we can do."

Not much they could do.

Nothing.

How would we know if he's not in immediate danger when he's not even here.

I collapsed to my knees, the earth cold and unyielding beneath me.

My hands clawed at the dirt, helpless sobs ripping from my chest.

They weren't going to help.

Somewhere out there, in the dark, in the cold, he had my baby.

Not because he loved him.

But because he hated me.

He knew I would never leave without my boy.

And... he was right.

The flashing lights faded into the darkness as the patrol cars disappeared down the road. The night air clawed at my skin as I stumbled back toward the house, barely aware of my shaking legs carrying me forward.

The other kids were back inside, their small faces pressed anxiously against the front window. They hadn't seen everything, but they had seen enough.

I forced myself to steady. To be Mommy again. Strong. In control.

I wiped my face with trembling hands, swallowing the bitter taste of helplessness. They couldn't see me break. Not now.

I threw the door open and gathered them into my arms, holding them so tightly I could feel their little hearts pounding against mine. Too fast. Just like mine.

"Where's Enrique?" Rayna whispered, her voice trembling.

I choked back a sob, forcing a smile. "He's... he's coming back," I managed. "Everything's going to be okay."

The hours dragged on in unbearable silence. I paced the house like a caged animal, ears straining for any sound, any sign. Every creak of the old floorboards made me jump, hope rising only to crash again into empty stillness.

Images flashed through my mind. My son's small face disappearing into the woods. His trusting eyes looking up at Seyvn. He had never seen the danger.

But I had.

I could still hear Seyvn's venomous voice echoing in my head. "You wanna leave? Fine. But you're not taking my son."

The back door creaked open, cutting through the silence like a blade. My breath hitched. My body locked in place as heavy footsteps echoed through the house.

And then.

"Mommy?"

I rushed into the kitchen, knees nearly buckling beneath me.

There he was.

Momma's Boy. Small, tired, but safe. His face lit up with that same innocent, trusting smile that always melted every sharp edge inside me. He ran toward me, arms wide, and I caught him, holding him so tightly I thought we might fuse together.

He smelled like the night air and French fries.

"I got a Happy Meal," he announced proudly, holding up the toy like a trophy. His cheeks sticky with ketchup.

Tears stung my eyes, hot and relentless, but I forced a shaky smile.

"That's great, baby," I whispered, pressing a kiss against his cheek.

Thank you, God. Thank you.

Behind him, Seyvn stood in the doorway.

"Did you think I wouldn't bring him back?" he asked smoothly.

His voice was low, almost mocking.

I said nothing. I couldn't. There was nothing left to say. I had already screamed, already begged. None of it mattered.

My son tugged on my hand, oblivious. Already chattering about the toy he got with his meal, completely untouched by the nightmare that had swallowed me whole.

To him, nothing was ever wrong.

I held his small, warm hand in mine, committing the feel of it to memory, afraid of how close I had come to losing it.

"Let's get you cleaned up for bed," I whispered, my voice cracking.

He nodded happily, bouncing toward the bathroom as if this was just another ordinary night.

When the house finally settled into uneasy stillness, I sat alone on the edge of my bed, shaking hands pressed against my face. Silent tears traced burning paths down my cheeks.

He had taken my son to control me, to punish me, to erase whatever fight I had left. To make me afraid to breathe without his permission.

And it worked.

Marla Matrice Murphy

CHAPTER 63

No Sudden Moves

"Silence is a source of great strength."

— Lao Tzu

After he took my son, I resigned. Arguing made things worse. Leaving wasn't safe. So, I stopped trying. I moved quietly. I kept the house calm. I made things look normal, even when nothing was.

And for a while, it worked.

Time passed.

Lilly was becoming such a big girl. Her tiny legs had grown stronger, steadier. She was taking her first wobbly steps now, always determined, always curious.

I remember the exact moment she took that first step.

She was standing by the edge of the TV stand, her chubby fingers gripping the edge as she eyed the space between her and Seyvn.

He crouched a few feet away, arms open wide, grinning like she was his whole world.

"Come on, pretty girl," he coaxed, his voice soft and warm, the way it used to be when things were good.

She hesitated for a moment, her little brows furrowed in fierce concentration, and then she let go.

One shaky step.

Then another.

"You're doing it!" Seyvn laughed, his voice lit with genuine joy.

"Come on, baby! You got this!"

Her face broke into the biggest smile, pride shining brighter than anything I'd ever seen. She wobbled but didn't fall, stumbling right into his waiting arms with a burst of glee.

He scooped her up, laughing, spinning, covering her face with kisses. "That's my girl!"

I watched them, heart aching in ways I couldn't even begin to explain. For a few precious seconds, it was just love. No fear. No tension. Just them.

And for a moment, it almost felt normal....

CHAPTER 64

Father's Day

"It is easier for a father to have children than for children to have a real father."

— Pope John XXIII

Father's Day began as a celebration of love, family, and the purest kind of joy.

The house was alive with excitement. The kids had spent the weekend practicing their surprise for Seyvn, a choreographed song and dance they put together themselves. They poured their hearts into it, each one taking a part in the song, singing and dancing while sharing all the reasons they loved him.

His daughters, Sevannah and Nyla, joined in, their voices blending with Alyra's as they laughed and giggled through every practice. Lilly toddled around happily, her tiny hands clapping along as if she were part of the performance.

I sat back with my camera, capturing every precious moment. Watching them work so hard, so full of excitement and love, filled my chest with warmth. Their faces glowed with pride as they nailed each part of the routine, their laughter filling the house.

It was pure. It was beautiful. It was everything a family should be.

While the kids were in the living room practicing, I was cooking.

The kitchen was filled with the smell of baked turkey wings smothered in gravy. The baked macaroni and cheese bubbled in the oven, its edges crispy just the way he liked it. A carrot cake cooled on the counter, frosting swirled in soft peaks on top. I wanted the dinner to be just as special as the day the kids had worked so hard to create.

When Seyvn walked through the door after work, the kids swarmed him, their voices a chorus of "Happy Father's Day!" He smiled, his face softening as he hugged each of them.

"Daddy, you have to see our video!" Alyra said, her eyes wide with excitement.

Sevannah and Nyla chimed in, practically bouncing with anticipation.

"Alright, alright," he said with a chuckle. "Let me change first, and I'll be right down."

As Seyvn headed upstairs, I stayed behind, checking on the food and stirring the gravy to make sure everything was just right. The kids were gathered in the living room, buzzing with excitement.

"I have to grab my laptop," I told them. "I'll put the SD card in and get it set up on the TV so your dad can see it."

Alyra, beaming with pride, nodded enthusiastically. She'd worked so hard on this presentation, organizing her siblings and pouring her heart into making this day special. Her joy was infectious, and even Lilly clapped her little hands as if she understood the moment's importance.

Within the next half-hour or so, I went upstairs, Lilly balanced on my hip and Alyra walking eagerly beside me. Both of them were happy, excited, and innocent.

When I walked into the bedroom, Seyvn was sitting on the bed with my laptop open on his lap. I didn't think much of it at first. I reached for the computer, my mind focused on getting everything set up for the kids.

"I need the laptop," I said lightly, smiling, ready to take it and head back downstairs.

But he didn't move. His face was twisted in a way I hadn't seen in a long time. Cold. Furious.

"What's this?" he spat, his voice low and venomous.

I froze, confused. "What do you mean? I need to…"

Before I could finish, he punched me in the face with a force that nearly blinded me. The room spun as pain exploded across my cheek and temple, the suddenness of it leaving me stunned.

"What the hell is this?!" he screamed, shoving the laptop toward me.

I realized then what he'd found. The messages I'd sent to Thomas, my childhood friend, more like a cousin really. Someone I'd confided in because I had no one else. I had written to him about my distress, about wanting to take my kids and leave Delaware to go back to Wisconsin.

I'd forgotten to log out of Facebook.

Alyra gasped beside me, her happy excitement replaced by a look of pure terror. Her wide, innocent eyes darted between me and Seyvn as she clutched her little hands together, frozen in place.

Give the baby to Alyra," Seyvn growled, his voice laced with rage.

"No," I said, holding Lilly tighter. "No, I won't."

"Give her the baby!" he shouted, stepping closer, his fists clenched.

Seyvn didn't care. His rage was a tidal wave, drowning out everything else. He head-butted me, the sharp crack of his forehead against mine sending a fresh wave of pain through my skull.

Alyra's voice broke through, trembling and small. "Mommy... please..."

"No!" I cried, tears streaming down my face.

Alyra was crying now, begging me to give her the baby. "Mommy, please! Just give her to me!"

I looked into Alyra's eyes, and my heart broke into a thousand pieces. She was pleading with me, her voice trembling, her hands shaking. Lilly was still in my arms, screaming, her cries piercing through the chaos. I clung to her like a lifeline, my safety net, the one thing that kept Seyvn from unleashing everything on me.

But Seyvn didn't stop. He didn't care that I was holding his child, didn't care that Lilly was screaming, didn't even consider the possibility that his blind rage could harm her. He head-butted me again, harder this time, and I saw stars. My vision blurred, my knees buckled, but I didn't fall. I couldn't.

Alyra stood frozen, tears streaming down her face. Her terror was palpable, etched into her every movement.

"Give her the baby!" Seyvn screamed, his voice thunderous and filled with fury.

"No," I whispered hoarsely, shaking my head even as my body trembled.

Alyra begged me again, her voice cracking, barely audible through her sobs. "Mommy, please. Please give her to me."

I looked into her tear-filled eyes, knowing she didn't understand the full weight of what she was asking. "Alyra," I whispered, barely able to form the words, "if I give her to you, he's going to kill me."

Her face crumpled, and I saw her small shoulders shake. Maybe she wanted the baby to protect her sister, or maybe she just wanted me to stop getting hit. Maybe she thought she could save us both.

Another head-butt came, and this time I staggered back, barely able to keep my grip on Lilly as pain exploded through my skull. My strength was fading, and with it, my ability to protect both of them.

Seyvn screamed at Alyra. "Take the baby! Go downstairs!"

My heart shattered into pieces I didn't know how to put back together. I couldn't protect them, and I couldn't risk Lilly getting hurt. Trembling, tears streaming down my face, I handed Lilly to Alyra.

"Take her," I whispered, my voice shaking. "Take her and go. Don't come back up here."

Alyra backed away, clutching Lilly tightly, her hands trembling but strong enough to hold her sister. Her wide, terrified eyes locked onto mine for a moment before she turned and fled, carrying Lilly out of the room.

I watched them disappear, knowing it might be the last time I ever saw them.

Then Seyvn turned all his fury on me.

He punched me relentlessly, each blow landing harder than the last. I stumbled backward, my legs giving out beneath me as the force of his fists sent me crashing to the floor. I curled into a ball, arms wrapped tightly around my head and torso, desperately trying to protect myself.

But it wasn't enough.

He kicked me with his boots, each strike landing with brutal force. My ribs, my back, my legs. Every part of me felt the relentless assault. The pain was overwhelming, radiating through my body with every kick.

I screamed for my life, my voice raw and desperate, echoing through the house. "Stop! Please, stop!" I sobbed, the words tumbling out between agonized cries.

He didn't stop.

He was twice my size, maybe even triple, and there was nothing I could do to stop him. Every kick, every punch landed with a rage that made one thing clear. He didn't just want to hurt me. He wanted to end me.

Lying there, screaming for my life, I couldn't muffle the sounds this time. My screams weren't just for me. They were for anyone who could hear them, anyone who might come and save me before it was too late.

But Seyvn wasn't satisfied.

Even as I lay curled on the floor, screaming and begging him to stop, it wasn't enough for him. His rage demanded more.

He pulled me up of the floor as if I weighed nothing. I tried to fight him off, clawing at his hands, twisting my body to break free, but he was too strong. So much stronger than me. He slammed me onto the bed.

He straddled me, pinning my arms to my sides, his full weight pressing down on my chest. I fought to stop him, thrashing beneath him, but it was no use.

"Stop! Please, stop!" I sobbed, but my voice was drowned out by the blood roaring in my ears and his furious shouts.

There was no shielding my face, no protecting myself from what was coming. I was utterly defenseless, pinned like prey beneath a predator.

Helplessness washed over me in a tidal wave of terror. There was nothing I could do. Nothing.

I knew I was mere seconds away from dying.

He raised his fist, and I watched as his eyes darkened, his face contorted with unrelenting rage. His fist hovered in the air, trembling with the force of his anger, and I knew this was it. He was going to pound my face until I was unrecognizable. Until there was nothing left.

I tried to turn my head, to move anything, but it was useless. I was completely at his mercy. And he had none.

I closed my eyes, tears streaming down my face, my thoughts racing to my children. Alyra, who begged me to give her the baby, who stood there petrified, too young to understand why I hadn't let go sooner. Lilly, whose cries had pierced the air, unaware of the danger surrounding her. All I could think was, they can't lose me. Please, God, don't let them lose me.

I tried to scream, but the weight on my chest made it impossible. My voice came out in broken gasps, a desperate cry for help that no one could hear.

Then… there was a knock at the door.

"New Castle County Police Department!"

The sound cut through the room like the only thing standing between me and a body bag, freezing Seyvn in place. For a moment, his fist hovered in the air, the rage in his eyes dimming just enough for me to see something else. Recognition.

He got off me, slowly, his movements deliberate and controlled. As he stood, I gasped for air, the first real breath I'd taken in what felt like an eternity. My chest heaved, my body trembling uncontrollably, but I was alive.

He unlocked the door and opened it, his voice suddenly calm, smooth. "She attacked me," he told the officers, gesturing toward me like I was the aggressor.

But one look at me, bloodied, broken, barely able to move, was all it took for them to see the truth.

"Turn around, hands behind your back," the officer commanded, stepping forward to cuff him.

Seyvn complied at first, stepping out of the room with the officer and walking a short way down the hallway. His movements were slow and calculated, his voice eerily calm as he responded to the commands.

But then something changed.

Maybe he remembered that he hadn't finished what he started. Maybe the rage was too consuming to be contained. Whatever it was, he suddenly tried to pull away from the officer, yanking his arm free as he turned back toward the room.

In a flash, Seyvn rushed down the hallway, dragging the officer with him, his eyes wild with determination. His voice boomed, unintelligible in its fury, as he barreled toward the door, intent on getting back to me.

My heart seized in my chest as I realized what was happening. He wasn't done. He was coming back to finish.

With every ounce of strength I had left, I stumbled to the door, my body screaming in protest as I pushed it shut. My hands fumbled with the lock, my breath coming in ragged gasps as I twisted it into place just in time.

I pressed my battered body against the door, bracing myself, knowing it was the only thing standing between me and Seyvn's unstoppable rage. I could hear the scuffle outside. The officer shouted commands, the sound of heavy boots on the floor, and Seyvn's furious voice echoing down the hallway.

He banged against the door once, twice, before more officers arrived. Their voices grew louder, and I heard the unmistakable sound of a struggle as they finally managed to subdue him.

I collapsed against the door, my body giving out as the last shreds of strength drained from me my body trembling and broken, every breath sharp and agonizing. My vision blurred, my heartbeat thundered in my ears, and the pain was a cruel reminder of how close I'd come to losing everything.

But I was still alive.

Barely.

CHAPTER 65

A Call for Help

"Courage is not the absence of fear, but the ability to act in spite of it."

– Mark Twain

I didn't know it then, but in the living room, Rayna had heard everything. My screams cut through the house, slipping past walls and closed doors until they reached her. The other kids huddled together, crying and confused, but Rayna didn't join them.

She picked up the phone. Her hands must have been shaking as she dialed, her heart pounding loud enough to drown out everything else. Yet when the dispatcher answered, her voice unwavering.

"My mommy is screaming, he's hurting her. Please hurry!"

I can only imagine the strength it took to say those words. To push past fear, past the instinct to freeze, and do what even some adults struggle to do. What even I have struggled to do. Act.

The dispatcher asked questions, and she answered them, her voice unsteady but firm. She gave our address, described the sounds, held onto her courage when the weight of it all should have been too much for a child.

But it wasn't for Rayna. She saved my life.

When I was released from the hospital, the only thing on my mind was getting to my children. The neighbors who had taken them in during my absence greeted me with warm but worried smiles. Their kindness was a blessing in one of the worst moments of my life.

But I wasn't the only one waiting to see my children. Child Protective Services were waiting also.

Their presence felt overwhelming, an uninvited intrusion into my life at its most vulnerable. The caseworker explained that my hospitalization and the police call triggered a mandatory investigation. They wanted to know everything.

They had to make sure my kids were safe.

They began by explaining the stringent sight and sound laws. To Child Protective Services, the fact that they'd heard the screaming, seen the bruises, and police were called due to violence was enough to put their emotional well-being at risk.

The caseworker started with me. Her tone was sharp but wrapped in professionalism. "Have the children ever been caught in the middle of a physical altercation? Have they been hit before? Have they expressed fear of him?"

I gave them as little information as possible, just enough to satisfy their curiosity and get them out of my life. I knew from experience that nothing good came from Child Protective Services being involved. Thankfully, my children didn't know much.

When they spoke to Rayna, she answered carefully, sharing that she had heard loud noises and seen me upset at times. Beyond that, she had little to tell them. The younger kids were even less aware. I had worked so hard to shield them from the worst of it, to make sure they didn't see the horrors that unfolded behind closed doors.

In that moment, I was grateful for how little they knew.

The caseworker reviewed the situation and presented me with a safety plan. I agreed without hesitation, signing a promise to stay away from Seyvn and protect the kids from any further contact with him. These were easy decisions for me. I had no intention of letting Seyvn near me or my children ever again.

Child Protective Services' presence was unnerving. My children were my world, and every choice I made was for them.

Yet strangers had stepped into my home, pulling those choices apart and putting my role as a mother under review. They were, for the moment, satisfied with the steps I had taken, and their involvement passed like a storm, sudden and unsettling.

They didn't require me to stay in a shelter, but I was still terrified and knew I needed a safe space to figure out my next steps. One of the officers who had helped me gave me a card with the shelter's information and told me to call when I was ready.

So, I packed up the kids and made the call to the domestic violence shelter. When I explained my situation, they did not hesitate to help. They assured me the location would remain confidential and that we would be safe there.

Walking into the shelter brought both relief and heartbreak. Relief came from knowing Seyvn couldn't find us here. Heartbreak came from realizing how far my life had spiraled, that this was now our reality. The staff welcomed us warmly, showing me and the kids to a small room, we would call home for the next few weeks. The room was plain, with two twin bunk beds pushed against the walls and a small dresser in the corner. The air smelled faintly of cleaning supplies, and the walls were bare except for a small window that let in a sliver of afternoon light.

The kids clung to me at first, their eyes darting around the unfamiliar space, but eventually they loosened their grip and began to settle.

At the shelter, the fog in my mind began to clear, but the fear never left. If anything, it sharpened. Seyvn was still in custody, his bail set at one hundred thousand, but numbers didn't comfort me. Numbers could change. Someone could help him. He could find a way. And if he got out, he would come for me. I was sure of it.

Even with locked doors and security measures, I felt exposed. I kept imagining him just beyond the shelter walls, waiting. Every creak in the hallway made me look up. Every unfamiliar voice made my chest tighten. While the kids played with donated toys in the common area, I sat nearby, pretending to read while my mind ran through every way he might find us.

Wisconsin became more than an idea. It was the only place I could breathe without looking over my shoulder.

It wasn't because there was comfort waiting for me in Wisconsin. There wasn't. When I'd been admitted to the hospital, the staff had called my mother as my emergency contact in case I didn't survive. We hadn't spoken much since I left for Delaware, but the news had shaken her. She wanted her grandchildren there. I didn't know what would happen once I arrived, but I knew what would happen if I stayed.

We didn't have the best relationship, and I never would have told her or anyone about the abuse from Seyvn. It was too embarrassing, too hard to admit. Still, she cared about her grandchildren. She always wanted to know how they were doing, and I knew if I went back to Wisconsin, she would help, if for no other reason than to talk about me later with her sisters and mine.

That was enough for me. Plus, it would only be temporary. I could transfer my Section 8 back to Wisconsin, though I'd likely have to wait for a place to open up. We were still on welfare, and Abigail's disability benefits would help too, though Seyvn had drained most of it for years. But this time, it would be different.

This time, it would be ours like it was before I even met that crazy psycho.

But in order to get there I needed money. I needed it fast. And I needed to be gone before he had the chance to walk free. I didn't have every detail worked out. I didn't need to. All I knew was that we had to get there.

That's when I turned to Seyvn's electronics.

He had built his business on pallets of high-end items, sourcing them from auctions and closeouts. It was a lucrative setup, but not without its cost. The money he used to buy those pallets didn't come from hard work or savings. It came from the benefits we received. Welfare. Abigail's disability checks. Even the household money meant for the kids' needs. All of it flowed through his hands to fund his next big find.

For Seyvn, the thrill wasn't just in selling the items; it was in the discovery. He loved opening those pallets, sifting through the headphones, TVs, and gaming systems like he was uncovering buried treasure. And when he sold them, he pocketed the profits, deciding how much went toward the household and how much went into his own pocket.

But now, those pallets were my salvation.

I didn't care about the thrill. I didn't care about their worth. I only cared about how fast I could sell them and how much money I could get. I listed the items on Craigslist, pricing them so low it was almost painful. Beats by Dre headphones for less than half of what they were worth. Sony TVs that should've sold for hundreds, gone for a fraction of that.

I wasn't looking to make a profit. I was looking for a way out.

Each time I handed over an item to a buyer, I felt a small flicker of hope. Every dollar brought me closer to Wisconsin, closer to safety, closer to a life where Seyvn couldn't control anymore.

The desperation drove me to work relentlessly. I wasn't just selling electronics; I was dismantling Seyvn's power over me piece by piece. And for the first time in years, I felt like I was finally in control.

The biggest sale came when I decided to list the twin-turbo engine.

Unlike the pallets, the engine wasn't part of Seyvn's business. It was his personal treasure, a prized possession he had dreamed of installing in his Z350. He'd spent months obsessing over the perfect model, looking over forums, researching specs, and finally saving up to buy it. That engine wasn't just a piece of machinery to him. It was his pride, his identity, the centerpiece of his vision for his car.

But to me, it was a reminder of everything he'd taken from us. Every dollar he'd saved for that engine came from somewhere: the benefits we received, the money meant for groceries, for bills, for the kids. For me.

It was more than just an engine. It was a symbol of his selfishness, his control, and his indifference to what our family really needed.

That's why I didn't hesitate.

I listed it for just $500, even though it was worth thousands. I needed the money, and I needed it fast.

My hand trembled on the mouse as I posted the listing, all I could think about was what he'd do when he found out. I had to stop and remind myself: He's in jail. You're safe right now.

But the memories didn't care. The memory struck me like a freight train, dragging me back into that room, to that night. I could still feel the searing pain from the head-butt, the way my skull had cracked against his with a force that left me dizzy and disoriented. My body remembered too. My ribs still ached from the kicks. My broken pinky throbbed beneath the splint, a constant reminder of what he did.

I could feel his weight pressing me into the bed, suffocating and inescapable, my arms pinned helplessly at my sides. I was trapped, defenseless. His face was inches from mine, contorted with rage.

I couldn't block the blows. I couldn't stop what was coming. I could only stare up at him, screaming for my life, knowing he wouldn't stop until there was nothing left of me.

And then the knock.

That single, sharp knock on the door followed by "New Castle County Police" cut through everything, halting the fists I had been bracing for. It was the sound that saved me from death's door.

I shook off the memory, grounding myself back in the present. He wasn't here. He was in jail. And by the time he got out, I planned to be long gone.

The engine sold within hours.

I had barely posted the ad when the calls started coming in. By the end of the day, a father and son were at the house, their truck rumbling in the driveway as they stepped out, wide-eyed at the deal they had just landed.

"This is the best deal I've ever seen," the father said, shaking his head in disbelief.

The son, barely old enough to drive, was already inspecting the engine, his hands moving carefully over the surface as if it were made of gold. "It's perfect," he said, grinning from ear to ear.

They had brought a small crane to lift the engine into the truck bed, their excitement evident as they worked together to secure it. The father glanced at me more than once, his expression curious, but he didn't ask why I was letting it go for so little. Maybe he thought I didn't know its worth. Or maybe one look at me told him everything he needed to know.

Either way, I forced a smile, nodding along to their chatter, my mind miles away. They weren't just taking an engine. They were helping me reclaim my freedom.

As they drove away, waving their thanks, I stood rooted in place for a moment, watching their taillights disappear into the distance.

My chest felt heavy, my breaths shallow. Every sale brought me closer to Wisconsin, but it also reminded me how precarious this escape was.

By the time I finally had enough money for Wisconsin, I felt a small surge of relief. It wasn't much, but it was enough to set the plan in motion.

Four days before we were set to leave, I packed up the kids and left the shelter to return to the house one last time. It was time to clean it out and prepare for the move.

The house was cold and hollow when we stepped inside, finally showing itself for what it had always been. Not a home. Just a chapter I was ready to slam shut.

CHAPTER 66

The Last Thing I Expected

"This was the last thing I expected. You destroy my life and then feed me some inspirational philosophy."

– Richelle Mead, Last Sacrifice

We spent that first day packing what little we would take, stacking boxes and bags by the door. The kids helped where they could, their excitement buzzing in the air as they asked questions about the new place and arguing over who got to sit by the window. Just like when we left Wisconsin, I sold everything that wouldn't come with us, like the beds, the couches, the dining table. One by one, people carried away pieces of the life we were leaving behind.

Two days before we were set to leave, I called Seyvn's grandmother. She had always been kind to me, and I felt like I owed her a goodbye.

"We're leaving," I told her, keeping my voice steady. "In two days, we're going to Wisconsin."

There was a pause on the other end of the line, long enough for my chest to tighten.

"What if he gets out?" she asked, her voice soft, almost hesitant.

"He won't," I said, steady and sure. "The bond is too high. There's no way he can get that kind of money before we're gone."

She hummed in acknowledgment, though something in her tone felt heavier than usual. "I'm glad you're getting out of there," she said after a moment. "It's the right thing to do. For you and the kids."

"I'll miss them," she added, her voice tender.

"You can always call," I offered. "And I'll make sure they know how much you love them."

"I'd like that," she said, but there was a note of something I couldn't place. Sadness, maybe.

"Thank you for everything," I said, ready to end the call and focus on the final preparations.

"Take care of yourself," she said, her voice soft. "And be safe."

When I hung up, I didn't think twice about her tone or her words.

To me, it had just been a goodbye.

I had no idea what was coming next.

But the next day, the kids and I worked tirelessly to finish clearing out the house. The once-cluttered space was now stripped down to its bones, with boxes and bags lined up neatly by the door. The kids, excited about the move, darted around helping where they could, their laughter filling the hollow rooms.

The sun was beginning to set as we lined up the last of what we'd take with us. I looked around the empty house, feeling a strange mix of emotions. Relief. Hope. And a lingering sadness for what had been lost within these walls.

That evening, I decided we needed a little celebration. We'd made it this far, and tomorrow, we'd be on the road to Wisconsin. It felt like the first step toward reclaiming our lives.

"Who wants ice cream?" I asked, smiling at the kids as they sat on the floor, eating their dinner off paper plates.

Their faces lit up, and they jumped to their feet, shouting, "Me!"

We piled into the truck and drove to a small ice cream shop. The kids picked their favorites. We laughed together as we sat outside, sticky and happy, savoring the moment.

For the first time in what felt like forever, we were a family without fear.

That night, we returned to the house from our little celebration. The kids, still giggling and sticky from ice cream and popsicles, tumbled out of the truck one by one, their laughter lifting the weight that had been crushing me for weeks.

I lingered behind, helping Alyra with her oversized popsicle, the kind so big it was almost comical in her small hands. She was determined to finish it, even though it was too much for one sitting.

As we approached the house, the familiar exhaustion began to creep in. We were so close. Just one more night, and we'd be gone.

And then I saw him.

Seyvn was walking up the driveway.

For a moment, the world seemed to tilt, my brain struggling to make sense of what my eyes were seeing. He wasn't supposed to be here. He wasn't supposed to be anywhere near us.

Before I could react, Alyra let out a scream so piercing it seemed to split the night in half. The sound jolted me, but it wasn't just her scream. It was the look on her face.

Terror. Pure, unfiltered terror.

She clutched her popsicle like it was the only thing keeping her attached to reality, her small frame trembling as she stared at the man who had caused so much pain.

My heart shattered.

Every instinct screamed at me to grab her, to run, to yell for help, to do something. Anything. But I didn't.

I opened my arms.

I opened my arms to the man who had broken my nose, shattered my finger, and left my body a bruised and battered canvas of his rage. My casted hand, the visible evidence of what he'd done, reached out as if to welcome him back.

And I hugged him.

His boyish grin spread across his face, lighting up like he had just come home from a long trip. His arms wrapped around me tightly, pulling me close as he said, "I'm home! I missed y'all so much."

I wanted to throw up.

How was this possible? How was he standing here, smiling, like none of it had happened? Like he hadn't come within seconds of killing me?

I forced myself to smile back, swallowing the bile that rose in my throat. I couldn't let him see the devastation inside me. I couldn't risk doing anything that might set him off.

All the hope I had built over the past few weeks drained out of me in that instant. My escape plan, the life I had envisioned for my kids and me, evaporated in the shadow of his presence.

If it weren't for my children, I would've preferred to die.
As he stood there, his grin unwavering, I swallowed my anger and tried to stay calm. My heart was pounding so hard I was sure he could hear it, but I forced my voice to stay even.

"You shouldn't be here," I said, careful to keep my tone soft, as if I were on his side. "There's a restraining order, Seyvn. If someone sees you, you could get in serious trouble."

He laughed. A light, almost dismissive sound that made my skin crawl. "What trouble?" he said, brushing it off like I had made a joke. "I'm here with my family. No one's going to care about some piece of paper."

I clenched my jaw, forcing myself to stay composed. "But they might," I pressed gently, trying to appeal to his self-interest. "What if the neighbors call the police? You just got out. You don't want to risk going back in, right?" His grin faltered slightly, but only for a moment. "No one's calling the cops," he said confidently.

The words had barely left his mouth when I saw it. A police car, rolling past the house, slow and deliberate. Not in a rush, not with sirens blaring, but with the kind of presence that said they weren't just passing through. They were looking for something. Or someone.

Alyra's scream had likely sent someone reaching for the phone. It was too sharp, too raw, too loud to be ignored.

My breath caught in my throat. For a fleeting moment, hope surged in my chest. They had to notice. They had to stop. They had to see him standing here, violating the order, violating the lifetime PFA. My heart screamed for them to notice, to stop, to come save us. I stared at the car, willing the officers to turn their heads, to see him.

But they didn't.

They drove on, disappearing down the street as if nothing were wrong.
I silently begged them to turn around, to pull over, to save us.

But the car kept moving, disappearing into the darkness without a second glance.

I felt my stomach drop, the disappointment was soul-crushing, a sharp, bitter sting that left me hollow. I felt my knees threaten to give out beneath me, but I stayed upright, staring at Seyvn as he turned his grin back on me.

"See? Nothing to worry about," he said smugly, completely oblivious to the storm raging inside me.

I forced a tight smile, trying to keep the desperation from spilling over. "You really shouldn't be here," I tried again, my voice quieter now, almost pleading. "You know the order. Please, Seyvn, just go. This isn't safe for you."

But he didn't move.

Instead, he stepped closer, his face softening with that boyish charm that used to make me melt. "I missed you," he said, his tone gentle now, like he actually believed we were a happy family again. "I missed the kids. I just want to be with y'all."

I bit back the words I wanted to scream at him. We didn't miss you! We don't want you here! Leave us alone!

But I couldn't say that. Not now.

"You could get in trouble," I tried again, desperation creeping into my voice. "You know the bond conditions. If someone calls…"

"I missed you," he said, cutting me off again. His tone was softer this time, almost tender, like he believed those words could erase everything that had happened. "I'm home now."

Home.

The word twisted in my chest, sharp and cruel. This wasn't a home. It had never been a home.

I bit my lip, nodding slowly as if I agreed. "I understand," I said again, hating the way the words sounded, hating how powerless they made me feel.

Seyvn motioned toward the house, his grin unwavering. "Let's go inside," he said, as casually as if he hadn't just turned my entire world upside down.

I hesitated, my feet refusing to move. Every fiber of my being screamed to stay outside, to stay in the open where someone, anyone, might see us. But I knew better. He wasn't going to leave, and resisting him could only make things worse.

"Sure," I murmured, my voice barely above a whisper. I followed him inside, my body stiff and my mind racing.

The kids were huddled together on the floor, their frozen treats forgotten as they watched us with wide, anxious eyes. Alyra clutched Lilly tightly, her protective instincts kicking in even as her fear showed in the way her hands shook.

Seyvn looked around the room, his grin never faltering, even as he took in the bare walls and empty spaces. "Where's all the stuff?" he asked, his voice light, almost teasing. "Didn't realize I was coming home to a minimalist lifestyle."

I forced a small laugh, my heart pounding as I tried to choose my words carefully. "I didn't know what I was going to do without you here," I said, keeping my tone casual. "I figured it would be easier to just move back home with my mom. I started packing everything up and selling some things to make the transition easier."

He chuckled, shaking his head as if I'd said something ridiculous.

"Back to Wisconsin?" he asked, still grinning. "You were really going to leave all this behind?"

I nodded, swallowing the lump in my throat. "I didn't think I could stay here without you," I said softly, the story sliding out easily. "I wasn't sure how to make it work on my own."

To my surprise, he didn't question me further. He didn't ask about the twin-turbo engine, the electronics, or even the cars that were now missing from the driveway. He didn't seem to care at all.

Instead, he spread his arms wide, his grin growing even bigger. "Well, I'm back now," he said, his tone full of boyish excitement. "And that's all that matters. We're a family again."

My stomach turned at his words, at the way he said them like they were some kind of gift, like he'd forgotten that he was the reason we were in this situation in the first place.

For a moment, I allowed myself to hope that maybe jail had changed him. Maybe he'd come back different. Maybe this version of Seyvn, the one who didn't seem angry or violent, was who he'd stay.

But deep down, I knew better.

I nodded anyway, forcing a smile as I said, "Right. That's all that matters."

"How did you get out?" I asked.

Seyvn looked at me, his boyish grin returning like he hadn't just disrupted every plan I had so carefully made. "My grandmother paid my bond," he said simply, as if it were no big deal.

His words hit me like a physical blow.

"She paid your bond?" I repeated, my voice barely above a whisper.

He nodded, oblivious to the rage bubbling just beneath the surface of my carefully composed expression.

His grandmother. She had known. She had known he was getting out, and she hadn't said a word to me.

I wanted to scream, to cry, to demand answers, but I knew better. Instead, I nodded again, swallowing the fury and devastation that threatened to consume me.

"That's nice of her," I said evenly, though the words tasted bitter.

I turned to the kids, with that forced tight smile. "It's late," I said, my voice trembling slightly. "Why don't you all go lay the blankets out in one of the rooms and get ready for bed?"

They hesitated, their eyes darting between me and Seyvn. Alyra was the first to move, gently tugging Lilly toward the empty bedrooms. Rayna, Enrique and Abigail followed, their bodies tense as they turned the corner without a word.

CHAPTER 67

Return to Sender

"Any negativity that comes to you today should be returned to sender."
— Thema Davis

After sending the kids to their makeshift beds, I stood in the empty living room for a moment, staring at the packed boxes lining the walls.

Everything was ready.

Or it had been.

"We should go upstairs," Seyvn said, his voice light.

I nodded, saying nothing. My body moved on autopilot as I followed him. Each step up the stairs felt heavier than the last, dread curling in the pit of my stomach.

The bedroom was stripped bare, just like the rest of the house. No bed, no furniture. Just the shadows of a life I wanted to forget. Seyvn didn't seem to notice or care. He shut the door behind us and turned to me, his grin still plastered across his face, like we were newlyweds on their first night back together.

"I missed you," he said, his voice low and playful.

I didn't respond.

He moved closer, his hands finding my waist. I froze. Every nerve in my body yelled at me to pull away, to scream, to do anything. But once again, I didn't.

"We've got some catching up to do," he murmured, his lips brushing against my neck.

I stayed still, my mind begging me to pull away, to speak, to stop him. But I didn't.

Seyvn's fingers tugged at the hem of my shirt, lifting it over my head with deliberate care. His movements were steady, almost reverent, like he was trying to show me that this was different, that he was different.

"Let me take care of you," he said softly, his voice dripping with a sincerity that made me want to vomit.

I didn't resist as he unfastened my pants, his hands brushing against my skin as he slid them down. Piece by piece, he undressed me, his touch firm yet oddly gentle, as though he believed he was giving me something I needed.

But I didn't need this.

I needed him to leave.

I was stripped down to nothing, the cool air brushed against my bruised skin, and all I could think about was how exposed I felt. Not just physically, but emotionally.

I swallowed hard, my throat dry as I forced myself to stay still. This wasn't love. It wasn't even passion. To me, it felt like control. Like he was reclaiming his place, and what I wanted didn't matter at all.

He guided me to the floor, his hands firm but not rough, as though he was trying to convince me this was tender, this was different. The bare hardwood pressed against my back, cold and unforgiving, just like the reality I was trying to escape. There wasn't even a blanket to shield me from the chill or from him.

He leaned over me, his weight familiar in the worst way, his grin still plastered across his face. "Let me show you how much I've missed you," he said, his voice soft, almost coaxing.

I nodded numbly, my body moving only because I didn't see another option.

He lowered his face between my legs, his tongue tracing over me, dipping inside me, sucking on me like his life depended on it. Like he had something to prove.

Seyvn didn't believe in giving pleasure, not like this. He'd always been about taking, about control. But now, he seemed determined to convince me that he could be different. As if this act, this single act, could rewrite the countless ways he had been cruel to me.

I lay there, motionless, as his mouth moved with a fervor that felt almost desperate. His tongue, his lips, his entire focus was on me, as though he thought this performance could erase the damage he had done.

I wanted to recoil, to shove him away, but my body stayed frozen. Each movement he made sent a wave of disgust rippling through me. My skin crawled, not just from his touch, but from the memory of his fists, the weight of his body pinning me, the sound of his voice spitting venom and threats as he tried to snuff me out.

I felt detached, like I was watching it all happen to someone else.

My splinted and wrapped hand lay awkwardly at my side, a reminder of everything I had endured, and yet he seemed oblivious to the pain he had caused, both physical and emotional.

As he kissed his way back up my body, his lips lingering on my stomach, my chest, my neck, I lay frozen beneath him. His movements were slow and deliberate, as though he thought he was building intimacy, reconnecting. But every kiss felt like a brand, each one igniting a deeper disgust inside me.

When he positioned himself between my legs, my entire body tensed. I wanted anything but this. Despite what he had just done, despite the performance he thought would soften me, I was still dry, my body refusing to yield to him.

Seyvn didn't hesitate. He used his hand to guide himself, pressing against me, and my body betrayed me, responding with just enough wetness to let him in. The feeling made me want to scream, to claw my way out of my skin and run as far away from him as I could.

When he entered me, the dam broke. Silent tears slid down my face, hot with shame.

As he moved over me, his weight pressing down, I couldn't stop the memories from flooding back. The last time he'd been on top of me. The way he'd pinned my arms. The way his fists had threatened to break every piece of me.

I was still sore from the beating, my ribs aching with every shallow breath. My hand throbbed under his grip, and yet he acted like none of it mattered.

Seyvn must have seen the tears, but he didn't stop. If anything, he probably thought I was crying out of love, overwhelmed by the connection he imagined we were sharing.

But love was the furthest thing from my mind.

With every movement, the hate inside me grew.

Hate for him. For his obliviousness. For his cruelty disguised as affection. For believing this could ever make things right.

But even more, I hated myself. For letting it happen. For being too weak to stop it. For not fighting harder to keep him out of my life, my body, my soul.

When he finally finished, he let out a deep, satisfied sigh and rolled off me, pulling me into his arms like we were a couple in love. His grip was firm, not harsh but possessive, as though he were ensuring I couldn't slip away in the middle of the night.

"I told you I missed this," he murmured, his voice soft and full of pride.

I didn't respond.

I stared at the ceiling, my tears slowing but not stopping. The ceiling blurred through the sheen of moisture in my eyes. I locked everything away, burying the rage, the shame, the despair under a cold, unyielding mask.

By the time he finally fell asleep, I felt like every part of me had been stripped away.

I turned my back to him, curling into myself, my body aching. Not just from the bruises and broken bones, but from the unbearable weight of what had just happened. His arm draped heavily over me, pinning me to the floor like an anchor.

Tears slid silently down my face, soaking into the hardwood beneath me, but my mind wasn't focused on him anymore. It drifted downstairs, to the kids.

What were they thinking?

Chapter 68

Not Yet

"We must accept finite disappointment but never lose infinite hope."
— Martin Luther King Jr.

I hadn't slept, but morning came anyway.

The sunlight creeping through the windows felt like an accusation, illuminating all the shame and disappointment I was trying to hide. Seyvn stirred beside me, stretching with a satisfied groan, his arm still draped over me like a chain I couldn't break.

When his eyes opened, his grin was already there, as though the night before had been nothing more than a blissful reunion. "Good morning," he said, his voice cheerful, oblivious.

"Morning," I mumbled, forcing myself to sit up, every muscle screaming in protest. I moved slowly, carefully, pretending to stretch as I slipped out from under his arm.

I hurriedly got dressed and made my way downstairs, each step heavy with the weight of what was waiting for me.

The kids were already awake, sitting together in a quiet cluster, their faces a mix of hope and worry. Rayna's eyes found mine immediately, her gaze searching for answers.

"Mommy," she whispered, her voice barely audible. "Are we still leaving today?"

I knelt in front of her, forcing myself to meet her eyes despite the shame and defeat that threatened to swallow me whole. "Not likely," I admitted, my voice breaking. "I don't think it's going to happen today."

Her face fell, but she didn't cry. None of them did. They just sat there, silent and still, their small shoulders bearing a weight they shouldn't have to carry.

"I'm sorry," I said softly, looking at each of them in turn. "I'm so sorry. But we will leave. Maybe not today, but soon."

They nodded, their trust in me unwavering despite everything. That trust was both a gift and a burden, and I clung to it as I stood, trying to steel myself for what had to come next.

Even if it wasn't going to be that day, I had to find a way to move forward.

Seyvn might have thrown a wrench into my plans, but he couldn't derail them completely. I had already come too far.

The boxes by the door were still packed. The movers could be rescheduled. The money I'd scraped together was still there, waiting for its purpose.

I couldn't lose sight of the goal. I wouldn't.

Every action I took that day was calculated, deliberate. I acted as though nothing had changed, as though the move wasn't looming over me like a fragile dream about to shatter. I let Seyvn see what he wanted to see: a woman who was still tied to him, too scared to leave, too defeated to try.

But inside, I was already strategizing. I knew it wouldn't be easy, and I knew it wouldn't be immediate, but I also knew one thing for certain: we weren't staying.

The movers came and went that morning. I told them we weren't ready yet, plastering on a polite smile as I sent them away, even though every fiber of my being wanted to beg them to stay and load the truck as quickly as possible. But with Seyvn there, looming in the background, it wasn't an option.

The boxes by the door sat untouched, a silent reminder of how close we'd come.

Since there was nothing left to sleep on, we went out later that day to buy air mattresses.

It wasn't a decision I made lightly. Spending the little money I had on something temporary felt like a betrayal of my plans, but the kids needed somewhere to sleep, even if it was only for a few days.

As we walked through the store, the kids picked out the mattresses, their excitement over something new a sharp contrast to the barrier I faced. I let them chatter and smile, forcing myself to join in as best I could.

"It won't be for long," I said softly, mostly to myself, as I put the air mattresses into the cart.

Rayna, ever perceptive, looked up at me, her big brown eyes filled with a quiet understanding. She didn't say anything, but the slight nod she gave was enough to let me know she believed me.

And I had to believe it too.

The mattresses were inflated that evening, spread out across the empty living room where the kids quickly made themselves at home. Their laughter and energy filled the space, momentarily pushing back the darkness that had settled over me.

Seyvn sat nearby, still wearing that same boyish grin, talking about how nice it was to have the family together again. I nodded along, pretending to listen, but my mind was mapping out the next steps, calculating how to finish what I'd started.

I hatched a plan, one that I thought would finally allow us to leave. The restraining order was still in place, and Seyvn's very presence in the house was a violation. If I could just get the police to enforce it, maybe, just maybe, they'd keep him long enough for me to make our escape.

So, I started calling the police, anonymously. Every time I managed to leave the house, I would make the call, my voice low and steady as I reported his presence. "There's a man violating a restraining order at this address," I'd say, hanging up before they could ask too many questions.

When the officers arrived, I'd act surprised, confused even, playing the part of the supportive partner. "Seyvn?" I'd ask, feigning ignorance.

Every time, they took him away. And every time, within an hour he was right back.

They kept him just long enough to process him and release him, as if the restraining order was nothing more than a suggestion. The cycle felt endless, each arrest a fleeting victory that dissolved as soon as he walked back through the door, smug and confident. I was sure if they arrested him enough, they would see he couldn't follow the law and stop letting him go.

And then, one day, Seyvn told me something that stopped me cold. "The officers said they think you're the one calling," he said casually, his tone laced with disbelief. "But I told them, nah, she wouldn't do that to me."

My stomach dropped, and for a moment, I couldn't even breathe. Why would they tell him that?

Didn't they realize what they were doing? They weren't just planting a seed of doubt. They were serving me to him on a silver platter, handing him every excuse he'd need to turn his wrath on me again.

I felt a sharp pang of disbelief. They were supposed to protect me. That was their job: to serve and protect, to enforce the restraining order, to make sure people like Seyvn couldn't keep hurting people like me.

But instead, they'd done the unthinkable.

They hadn't just failed me; they'd actively endangered me. Their words were a reckless betrayal, undoing what little faith I had left in the system that was supposed to keep me and my children safe.

I forced a laugh, shaking my head as if it were the most ridiculous thing I'd ever heard. "That's crazy," I said, my voice steady despite the tremor in my hands. "Why would I do something like that?"

He chuckled, shaking his head as though the officers' accusation was too absurd to entertain. I studied his face, my heart pounding, desperate for some sign that he wasn't questioning me.

To my relief, his smile didn't falter. He believed me.

But the disbelief and anger inside me churned like a storm.

How could they be so careless?

Every call I'd made, I'd done in desperation. My hands shook with fear every time I dialed, praying that this time they'd help, that this time they'd keep him away just long enough for me to escape.

But now, that hope was gone.

How could I call again, knowing they'd planted the seed of doubt? Small now, but capable of growing into something dangerous. I couldn't. I absolutely wouldn't.

It wasn't worth the risk.

The disbelief burned in my chest, a bitter reminder that the people I thought might save me had become another source of danger.

Seyvn's smile lingered, his obliviousness both a blessing and a curse. I bit back the words I wanted to scream, my anger boiling under the surface.

They were supposed to protect me.

CHAPTER 69

He's Back

"When someone shows you who they are, believe them the first time."

— Maya Angelou

Months passed, and the house settled into a strange rhythm. Seyvn's upbeat demeanor never faltered, and for a while, the kids seemed genuinely happy again, finding joy in the quiet even if I couldn't.

I couldn't relax. That man had tried to kill me. He had stood over me with fists and rage and no sign of stopping. I knew what he was capable of, and no amount of calm or kindness could erase that. And the officers only made it worse. Their betrayal still haunted me. I couldn't call them, even if I wanted to. I was truly on my own.

So, I stayed ready. I didn't trust the quiet. I didn't trust the smiles. I focused on what I could control.

The boxes by the door still packed. I rearranged them now and then to make them look like they were just out of place, not part of an escape. I kept the house functional but sparse, leaving out only what we could afford to lose.

Seyvn didn't seem to notice. He was content, happy even, acting as though everything was back to normal. He joked with the kids, brought in new furniture, and talked about a future I knew would never exist.

Eventually, the night settled in.

The kids had finally gone to bed, their soft murmurs fading into silence as the house settled for the night. I lingered in the living room for a moment, relishing the rare stillness, before heading into the dining area where Seyvn was sitting at the table.

He was unusually relaxed, leaning back in his chair with an easy grin, recounting a story from earlier in the day. His hands moved animatedly as he spoke, and his laugh echoed through the room as though nothing in the world could dampen his mood.

I sat down across from him, nodding at the right moments, offering small smiles, but my mind was elsewhere. My thoughts circled around the packed boxes by the door, the money I'd tucked away, and the unfinished plan I needed to make work.

"You're quiet," he said suddenly, his tone curious but casual.

I blinked, forcing myself to meet his gaze. "Just tired," I said, managing a soft smile. "It's been a long day."

He studied me for a moment, then nodded. "Yeah, I guess it has."

Encouraged by his relaxed demeanor, I decided to bring it up.

"I've been thinking," I began cautiously, keeping my tone light. "It's been a long time since we've seen my family. Maybe we could take a trip back to Wisconsin? The kids haven't seen their aunt and granny in ages, and I'm sure they'd love to reconnect."

For a split second, his face remained neutral, and I let myself hope he'd agree.

His body stiffened, and without warning, his hand shot out, slapping me across the face with such force that I fell out of the chair.

The impact was dizzying, my vision blurring as pain exploded across my cheek. I hit the floor hard, my heart racing, my mind struggling to catch up with what had just happened.
"I'm your family," he hissed, standing over me, his voice low and menacing. "What the hell do you need to see them for?"

I stared up at him, stunned, my hand instinctively covering my cheek as the sting spread.

He crouched down then, his face softening, his voice trembling with fake remorse. "I'm sorry," he whispered. "I didn't mean to do that. It's just... it felt like you were rejecting me. Like I'm not enough for you. Do you know how that feels?"

His words hit my ears, but they didn't register. My mind was still replaying the swing. The mask had slipped, and the real Seyvn was right in front of me. His apology meant nothing. That slap was a declaration.

I wasn't staying.

I was getting me and my kids out of there, no matter what it took. I picked myself up off the floor slowly, every movement deliberate as I fought to keep my emotions in check. Seyvn stood there, his eyes watching me closely, as though he expected me to lash out or break down.

But I wouldn't give him that.

Instead, I muttered, "I need some air," and walked toward the back door, keeping my steps steady, refusing to let him see the way my legs were shaking.

The cool night air hit me as I stepped outside. I closed the door behind me, leaning against it for support.

I had already decided to leave. It had always been a matter of when.

But now, I knew the answer. It had to be soon. As soon as possible.

There was no room for doubt anymore. The slap, the words, the empty apology. Every part of it proved Seyvn would never change.

When I went back inside, he was sitting at the dining table, his head resting in his hands. He looked up as I walked in, his expression unreadable.

"Look," he started, his voice soft, almost pleading. "I didn't mean to hurt you. You just caught me off guard. I thought we were okay, you know? Like... really okay."

"I just want us to be a family," he continued, his tone almost desperate. "Is that too much to ask?"

I turned to him with a forced calm. "No, it's not," I said quietly, my voice devoid of emotion. "I never should have asked. You have been doing better. I'm sorry."

He nodded, relief flooding his face as though my words had erased the slap, the rage, the fear.

But they hadn't.

CHAPTER 70

Til Death Do us Part

"Death is sometimes kinder than love."

— Rick Riordan, The House of Hades

The slap didn't just mark my face. It marked my heart. It marked my mind. It took over my thoughts, reminding me that nothing had really changed.

The fear, the pain, the feeling of being trapped were all closing in. And in my darkest moment, I made a chilling decision. I was getting out, one way or another.

The next night, everything looked normal. The kids were gathered around the table, laughing over bowls of ice cream like they had no idea our world was on the edge of collapse. I smiled with them, laughed when they laughed, then quietly slipped into the kitchen. Their joy faded behind me, soft and distant.

My hands shook as I reached for the sleeping medication, my breath coming in shallow gasps. I poured the pills into a small bowl and began crushing them into a fine powder. The repetitive motion felt surreal, like I was watching someone else do it. The white dust gathering at the bottom wasn't just medicine anymore. It was a symbol of my desperation, a measure of how far I'd been pushed to escape.

Then I grabbed his bowl and started scooping ice cream, careful and deliberate, as though I were preparing the most important dish of my life. I stirred the powder into the creamy swirls, mixing it thoroughly until no trace of it remained.

But I didn't stop there.

On the counter sat Seyvn's big black steel mug, the one he used for everything. I filled it with juice and ice, and then poured in a splash of antifreeze, watching the liquid blend seamlessly. My heart pounded in my chest as I placed the mug and the bowl on the dining room table.

This wasn't just a sweet treat and a drink. It was my escape plan.

Seyvn walked in from the living room, glancing at the table that boyish grin plastered across his face. "Ice cream for me, too?" he asked, glancing at the bowls on the table.

"Of course," I said lightly, forcing a smile that I prayed looked natural. "And I even got your favorite mug ready."

He kissed my cheek, then walked over to the table and picked up the bowl of ice cream.

The kids were giggling and eating happily, oblivious to the tension humming in my veins. My hands fidgeted with a napkin, my eyes glued to Seyvn as he took the first spoonful of ice cream.

But then he stopped, his face scrunching in confusion.

"This tastes funny," he said, his tone sharp, suspicious.

My breath caught in my throat, my mind racing for an explanation.

"Really?" I said, feigning surprise. I grabbed the bowl and took a small bite, forcing myself to appear calm even though my pulse was hammering in my ears. "Huh, it does taste a little weird. Maybe... dish detergent?"

Rayna, quick as ever, chimed in. "I washed the dishes earlier!" she said brightly, her voice cutting through the thick tension.

I turned to Seyvn, shrugging. "She's still learning," I said with a light laugh. "Maybe she didn't rinse them well enough. We'll work on it, won't we, Rayna?"

He seemed to relax, chuckling softly as he set the bowl aside. "Yeah, you gotta teach her better," he said, shaking his head.

But then he reached for the mug.

My heart skipped a beat.

"You know," I said quickly, grabbing the mug before he could take a sip, "if the dishes weren't rinsed well, the cup might taste weird, too. Let me clean it out again."

He shrugged, oblivious to the panic roiling beneath my calm facade.

I dumped the mug's contents down the sink, the bright liquid swirling away, and immediately grabbed the sponge. My hands moved automatically, scrubbing the mug and bowl with precision, rinsing away any trace of my desperation.

When I was done, I refilled the mug with fresh juice and ice and scooped a new bowl of ice cream, this time without any "extras." My movements were methodical, deliberate, as if this small act of normalcy could erase what I had just attempted.

I carried them back to the table, placing them in front of Seyvn with a forced smile. "Here," I said softly. "Let's try this again."

He grinned, none the wiser, and dug into the fresh bowl.

The kids laughed and chatted around the table, the innocence of their joy a reminder of why I couldn't afford to lose control like that again. Seyvn joined in their conversation, cracking jokes and acting like the doting father he always pretended to be.
I stood quietly, watching the scene unfold, my hands resting on the edge of the table, clenched just enough to keep them from trembling.

The room was filled with laughter, the kids' joy filling every corner, but inside, I was unraveling.

Later that night, as I lay awake staring at the dark ceiling, the weight of what I had done or nearly done left me disappointed.

What was I thinking?

What if he had eaten the ice cream or drunk from the mug? What if he had died right there in front of the kids?

I couldn't bear the thought.

And yet, the reality I was living was no better.

I pressed my hands to my face, tears slipping through my fingers as I grappled with the choices that had led me here.

I hadn't killed him, but I needed to find a way out before he killed me.

CHAPTER 71

Caught

"In a closed society where everybody's guilty, the only crime is getting caught."
— Hunter S. Thompson

After what I had almost done the night before, after how close I had come to crossing a line I couldn't uncross, I knew I had to leave. For my life. For my children. For my freedom. For my sanity. For everything.

Seyvn's grip on me had taken more than just my happiness. He had stripped away my sense of safety, my dignity, my very autonomy, and I couldn't let him take anything else.

I couldn't keep living like this.

I had said that to myself a hundred times before. Thought it, cried it, and even prayed it. But this time felt different. The fear was still there, but I wasn't letting it stop me. I didn't know if I was brave, numb, or just plain stupid, but I knew I was leaving.

He hadn't disabled the truck. He hadn't bothered in weeks. Things had been calm enough that he let his guard down. He didn't think I'd go. I'd taken him back after every bruise, every insult, even after he nearly killed me. Why would he believe I'd actually leave?

But when he got in the shower that evening, whistling to himself like everything was fine, I knew that was my moment.

I hurried to gather the kids, my hands trembling as I whispered for them to grab their coats and put on their shoes. In the rush, I didn't even notice Abigail was barefoot. She always needed a little extra help, but I hadn't given it. I couldn't. There was no time.

We climbed into the truck, the cool night air wrapping around us. My heart was pounding as I started the engine, half-expecting Seyvn to come storming out of the house. But he didn't.

I didn't have a plan. I just drove, needing somewhere that felt safe, somewhere I could think.

I went to the emergency room.

It wasn't just a hospital. It was a place where I could disappear into the crowd. No one would question a woman sitting in the waiting room with five kids. People waited there all the time, whether to be seen, to get test results, or for someone to come out from the back. No one needed to know what I was really there for.

I just needed to think.

The hospital had a kids' room just off the main waiting area, a small, brightly lit space filled with games, books, and toys scattered across colorful rugs. The kids walked in quietly, their eyes lighting up at the sight. For a moment, their excitement allowed me to exhale. We had finally gotten away.

Rayna carried Abigail to a corner with a plush chair, gently setting her down before joining the others at the game console. Lilly, ever curious, toddled over to a stack of books, her tiny hands patting the pages, flipping through them like their textures and colors held secrets only she could understand.

I went into the kids' waiting room and sank into an empty chair, exhaustion settling into every muscle.

In my rush to leave, I hadn't brought any money. Not a single dollar. My only thought had been to get out and get safe. And we were safe now, or at least safer than we had been, but I couldn't stop thinking about what came next.

How was I going to get to Wisconsin?

I stared at the cracked tile floor, my mind racing through possibilities. The plan that had seemed so clear a few days ago now felt like a tangled mess, but I had no choice but to untangle it.
For now, I decided to just sit in that waiting room and figure it out.

The hum of the hospital, the steady beep of monitors, and the faint sound of my kids laughing formed a strange kind of cocoon around me. It wasn't ideal, but it was a pause. A moment to breathe. A chance to figure out the next step without fear hanging over me.

I was so deep in thought that I didn't register the sound at first. A faint, high-pitched voice pierced through my haze.

"Daddy?"

My heart stopped.

I looked up sharply, my eyes darting toward the sound. For a split second, I told myself it couldn't be. Seyvn was in the shower when we left. There was no way he could have known where we were.

The sound jolted me out of my trance. My head snapped up, my heart pounding in my chest. I looked toward the hallway, praying I had misheard. There was no way. He couldn't be here.

But when I looked past the colorful doorway, my worst fear became reality.

Seyvn.

He stood just inside the main waiting room, his eyes scanning the area with the sharp focus of a predator. The cold stare he gave me when our eyes met sent a chill through my body.

How did he find us? How was this even possible?

I froze, panic taking hold of me as he walked toward the kids' room, his heavy boots echoing in the sterile hospital air.

"Let's go," he said quietly, his tone calm but laced with the kind of authority that left no room for argument.

I couldn't move.

I looked around the waiting room, desperate to find someone, anyone who could help us. A nurse passing by, a security guard, anyone.

But Seyvn leaned closer, his voice dropping to a dangerous whisper.

"If you say one word, I'll kill you. Right here."

His words weren't a threat.

The fear in my chest was suffocating, but I forced myself to keep going.

My legs felt like they were moving on their own as I walked toward him, my body betraying me yet again.

The main waiting room was packed with people. Families clutched each other in worry, lone figures sat hunched over in exhaustion, children fussed, and phones buzzed quietly in laps. It was a sea of urgency, each person lost in their own struggles, their own emergencies.

No one noticed us as Seyvn ushered me and the kids out of the hospital.

As we stepped through the automatic doors, the cool night air hit my face. That's when I saw them, two police officers sitting in their patrol cars just beyond the curb.
Hope flared in me, brief and bright, like a match struck in the dark.

Maybe I could go to them. Maybe I could break away, scream for help, and they'd step in before Seyvn could do anything.

But as if he'd read my mind, Seyvn leaned in close, his voice low and icy.

"Don't even think about it," he warned, in a way that sent a shiver down my spine.

I froze.

There was no guessing what he meant. He could take me out right there, and the officers would be too late to do anything about it. And even if I made it, what then?

The memory of every time I'd called the police before came rushing back. The restraining order, the violations, the endless cycle of arrest and release. Seyvn was a master manipulator. He could charm, lie, and twist reality until even the most seasoned officers doubted what they'd seen.

What if they didn't believe me? What if he convinced them I was the problem, just like before, when I was the one arrested and charged with assault, even though my nose was the one that had been broken?

The hope that had sparked so brightly just moments before extinguished with a cruel finality.

Defeated, I kept walking, my heart screaming for the officers to notice something, anything. But they didn't even glance our way.

We slipped past them, Seyvn's presence looming behind me like a shadow I couldn't escape.

When we reached the truck, I saw Seyvn lift the hood. My stomach churned as realization set in. He had disconnected it after he arrived, ensuring that if I tried to leave before he found me, I wouldn't be able to go anywhere.

He must have had a tracker on the truck. Seyvn was a mechanic, skilled with electronics, and it would've been nothing for him to put in a tracking device. I had been none the wiser, blindly thinking I could escape. How else would he have found me? How would he have known exactly where I parked?

I was so careful.

But it hadn't mattered.

CHAPTER 72

Defeated

"There are defeats more triumphant than victories."

— Michel de Montaigne

The drive home felt like a crawl through molasses. Seyvn was behind the wheel, his grip tight on the steering wheel, his eyes locked on the road. I sat in the passenger seat, pressed as far against the door as I could manage without making it obvious.

The tension was unbearable, thick and suffocating, filling the small space of the truck. Not a word was spoken. Not a glance exchanged. The kids sat quietly in the back, their usual laughter and chatter replaced by a strained silence that felt unnatural. Even Lilly, who always seemed to have something to say, was unusually subdued, her little hands clutching the straps of her car seat like she was holding on for dear life.

I wanted the drive to last forever, to stretch the minutes into hours, anything to delay stepping back into the house. But at the same time, I wanted it over, the unbearable silence to break, the weight of his presence to dissipate.

When we finally pulled into the driveway, the headlights illuminated the house like a spotlight on the stage of my worst nightmares. Seyvn killed the engine, and the sudden silence was deafening.

"Let's go," he said, his voice calm but carrying that undercurrent of authority I didn't dare question.

The kids began climbing out of the truck, moving slowly, their steps hesitant. I stayed in my seat for a moment, taking a deep breath to steady myself before opening the door.

I helped Lilly out of her car seat, taking my time adjusting her coat, kissing her face, anything to delay going inside.

"Come on," Seyvn said again, this time sharper, his tone making it clear there was no room for stalling.

I nodded and followed him toward the house, my legs heavy, each step feeling like I was walking to my own execution.

The kids went in ahead of us, their small forms disappearing into the shadows of the hallway. I lingered at the doorway, the night air cool against my face, wishing I could just turn around and run.

But I couldn't.

Seyvn stood there, waiting for me, his expression unreadable but his presence suffocating. I stepped inside, the door closing behind me with a finality that echoed through the silent house.

When we got inside, Seyvn's voice was unnervingly calm, as if we'd just returned from a pleasant family outing.

"Kids, go to your rooms. Straight to bed," he instructed, his tone leaving no room for argument.

The kids froze, their eyes darting between him and me. I could see the unspoken question in their faces: Was it safe to leave Mommy alone with him?

I adjusted Lilly in my arms, pressing her small body closer as if that alone could keep us in this moment a little longer.

"I'll tuck them in," I said quickly, the words tumbling out before I could think better of it. I needed more time, just a few more minutes away from him. "I just want to make sure they're okay."

Seyvn's eyes locked onto mine, his expression unreadable. "Upstairs," he said, his voice low but firm.

I hesitated, my arms tightening around Lilly.

"Now," He repeated, the shift in his tone so subtle, so sinister, my spine stiffened.

Reluctantly, I knelt down and set Lilly on her feet, brushing a kiss against her soft cheek before gently nudging her toward Alyra. Without a word, Alyra took her hand, gripping it tightly as she led her toward the hallway.

The finality in his tone made it clear there was no room for negotiation.

I nodded, swallowing the lump in my throat as I turned toward the stairs. My legs felt like lead as I climbed, each step heavier than the last. Seyvn followed closely behind, his presence suffocating, his silence deafening. At the top of the stairs, I hesitated, gripping the banister like it was the only thing keeping me upright. Seyvn's shadow loomed behind me, his presence oppressive, filling every corner of the narrow hallway.

"Inside," he said, nodding toward the bedroom door.

My feet moved before my mind caught up, carrying me into the room. I stopped just inside, standing stiffly by the wall, my back pressed against the cold plaster.

Seyvn closed the door softly behind him, the quiet *click* of the latch sealing my fate. He didn't yell. He didn't rage. Instead, he stood in front of me, watching me.

The silence stretched between us, heavy and unbearable.

With brutal force, Seyvn grabbed the sides of my head. Before I could react, he slammed my head back against the wall.

A shockwave tore through my skull. The crack of drywall splitting filled the air, but the pain drowned out everything else. My vision blurred, a sharp ringing in my ears as my head went through the wall. I gasped, dizzy, my body struggling to process the sheer force of it. The world tilted, unsteady beneath me. There was no time to catch up. Only pain. Only his looming presence.

"You're not leaving me," he snarled, his face inches from mine. 'Not with my kids. Not ever.

Then, with a sudden force, he shoved me backward. The hits were just as vicious as the night he tried to kill me, one after another, hard and unrelenting. I curled into a ball, trying to protect my head and ribs, but it didn't matter. Seyvn was bigger, stronger, and in that moment, unstoppable.

"You think you can leave me?" he shouted, each word punctuated by another blow. "You think you can take *my* family?"

I tried to hold it in. I didn't want the kids to hear. But the pain forced its way out in broken, uneven cries. Not loud enough to be a scream, but not quiet enough to keep hidden. Then I heard Alyra's voice carry up the stairs, trembling and scared.

"Mommy? Mommy, are you okay?"

Her voice broke through at the exact moment I needed it most. It might have been the only thing that stopped him. For a split second, he froze, his head turning toward the door, his body still hovering over mine. If she hadn't spoken, I don't know if he would have stopped at all.

Without missing a beat, his voice cut through the silence, calm and controlled, like he hadn't just been kicking my ass a second earlier.

"Mommy's fine," he called back. "Go to bed."

Her small footsteps retreated, and I prayed she wouldn't come up, wouldn't see me like this.

410

Her voice had stopped him this time, but I knew it was only temporary.

He turned back to me, his eyes cold and lifeless. "If you leave, it won't be with your life," he said, his voice barely a whisper.

I nodded weakly, my body trembling, my spirit crushed.

As he left the room, I heard him lock the door from the outside, trapping me in my own personal hell.

At that moment, I knew.

I couldn't fight him anymore.

I was defeated. Every time I tried to leave, he found me and made me regret it. He would have killed me without hesitation. At that point, staying wasn't about hope. It was the only way to make sure my children didn't lose their mother and I didn't lose my life.

CHAPTER 73

Just Two More Days

"Of all the hardships a person had to face, none was more punishing than the simple act of waiting."

— Khaled Hosseini, A Thousand Splendid Suns.

The knock at the door was heavy and deliberate, the kind that signaled authority and confrontation. My heart leapt to my throat as I opened it to see police officers and a pair of CPS workers standing on my porch.

"Ms. Matrice, we need to speak with you," one of the CPS workers said, clipboard in hand.

"Is everything okay?" I asked, trying to steady my voice.

She glanced down at her notes. "We received a report from the school. Your daughter Abigail shared some... concerning information. She told her teacher that Seyvn put your son in the freezer a few days ago."

I blinked, completely caught off guard. "Seyvn put... what? No, that doesn't make sense."

But the CPS worker's expression remained stern.

"She was very specific," the worker continued. "Abigail said that she and Alyra were scared to let him out."

My head spun. I had no idea where Abigail could have gotten this story. Seyvn had done a lot of terrible things, but this? This couldn't be true... could it?

413

"I don't understand," I said, shaking my head. "There's no way that happened."

And then it hit me.

Abigail, my sweet, developmentally delayed daughter, must have gotten confused. She had to be talking about the *I Love You More* game.

"No," I said quickly, the words rushing out. "No, that's not true. She must've misunderstood. She's delayed, and sometimes she mixes things up. It wasn't Seyvn. It was me. I put Enrique in the freezer. We were playing a game."

The workers exchanged glances, and one of them frowned. "Can you explain the game?"

I took a deep breath, steadying my voice. "It's the *I Love You More* game. Enrique and I go back and forth saying, 'I love you more,' and we do stuff to make the other take it back. We were laughing. I lifted him up, but I'd never hurt him. They weren't scared."

"Abigail said it was Seyvn," one of them pressed. "It sounded like a separate incident from the game."

"That's not possible," I insisted, my voice rising in desperation. "Seyvn didn't do anything like that."

One of the officers cleared his throat. "Is Seyvn here now?"

"No," I said quickly, probably too quickly.

The CPS worker frowned. "Are you aware that the PFA is still in place?"

"Yes, I'm aware," I said, my heart pounding. Of course I was. I'm the one who put the worthless order in place. "But the issue isn't just the order. It's what Abigail said in that report, and I'm telling

414

you, it's not true." Seyvn hasn't even been here." I added not even remotely true.

The workers exchanged looks before nodding.

One by one, they interviewed the children.

Rayna, ever calm and protective, explained that Mommy loves Enrique. Enrique is her favorite and that it was just a game. She described the laughter and how we were all playing, her voice steady and unwavering.

But when they spoke to Abigail, her story didn't change. She repeated what she'd told her teacher, adding chilling details about how she and Alyra had been scared to let Enrique out of the freezer. She also mentioned the game but insisted it was different from the time with Seyvn.

Listening to her recount these moments, even I started to wonder. She spoke with such certainty and detail, it almost made me question what I knew to be true.

When the interviews were over, the CPS workers regrouped, their faces grim.

"This is a serious allegation, Ms. Matrice," one of them said. "We'll need to follow up on this."

I nodded, not sure how to feel. I wasn't worried, exactly, but I knew better than to trust how any of this might turn out. These CPS people could be unpredictable.

After they left, I slumped onto the couch, my head in my hands. The house felt heavier, quieter. The kids hovered nearby, their eyes wide with fear and confusion, waiting for me to say something. Anything that might make sense of what had just happened.

But I didn't have the words to reassure them. Not yet.

For a long moment, I just sat there, replaying Abigail's story in my mind, trying to make sense of it, trying to understand why she would say something like that.

Finally, I took a breath and sat the kids down, my voice trembling as I forced myself to explain the gravity of the situation. "Listen to me," I said, my heart still pounding "They're going to come back to your school," I said, my heart pounding. "They're going to ask you questions, but you have to say you don't know. Tell them to ask your mother."

The kids' eyes widened, fear creeping into their innocent faces. I pleaded with them, my voice breaking. "If you answer their questions, they'll take you away from me. They'll put you in foster care. That's what they came to do tonight, but they couldn't find a reason. Please, don't give them one."

Tears threatened to spill over as I looked at them, their small faces etched with confusion and worry. I had to make them understand.

That night, I also sat down with Seyvn, desperation in my voice as I tried to reason with him. "You need to leave," I said. "CPS is investigating now. They're not going to stop until they find a reason to take the kids, and if they find out we're violating the no-contact order, it's over."

Seyvn shrugged, his indifference cutting me to the core. "They're not going to do anything," he said, brushing off my concerns. But I didn't want to take that risk.

The encounter with CPS had lit a fire under me. I couldn't wait any longer. I had to get us out. I still had the money I'd saved from selling Seyvn's electronics, hidden in the pocket of a jean jacket at the back of my closet.

But Abigail's upcoming field trip was all she could talk about. Her excitement was deep, filling every conversation, every meal, every moment of the day. She had counted down to this for weeks, bubbling over with details about the itinerary, the bus ride, the friends she'd sit with. Her joy was a fragile thing, something I couldn't bear to shatter. So, I told myself just two more days. I would leave the moment she got home on Wednesday.

That promise should have felt reassuring, but it didn't. Because before I could get to Wednesday, I had to get through Tuesday.

Tuesday was Seyvn's court date from the night he tried to kill me, and the closer it got, the sicker I felt. I already knew how it would go. I had seen it too many times. He'd walk in looking calm and clean, like somebody who had it all under control. Button-down shirt. Hair laid in waves he spent way too much time perfecting.

Then he'd start talking. Voice low, steady, almost gentle. He'd tell his version of events, his carefully crafted story, and somehow make it all sound believable.

And the courtroom would sit there nodding, like they had never seen a man lie with a straight face. Like what he was saying made sense. Like it was possible he was the one who needed protection.

I could already hear the prosecutor's dispassionate tone, see the judge flipping through his file as though it held mere paperwork, not the sum of all the terror he had inflicted. The charges were just words on a page to them. To me, they were bruises, threats whispered in the dark, the way he would tighten his grip just enough to remind me how easily he could take everything away.

And yet, they wanted me to risk my life to come to court and testify?

This wasn't a man who got angry and walked away. This was a man who had beaten me to the brink of death. A man who had slammed my head into a wall so hard that the drywall crumbled. A man I once had to jump from a moving car to get away from. A man who had attacked a police officer just to get back to me. There were no limits to what Seyvn would do, and they expected me to risk my life by showing up?

Their own officers had put me in danger by telling Seyvn I was the one reporting his violations of the no-contact order. How could I trust a system that had practically served me up on a platter? Did they really believe a piece of paper was going to stop him if he decided to come after me again?

I wasn't about to find out.

Seyvn knew exactly how the game was played. If I didn't show up, he wouldn't be penalized. And if he wasn't penalized, he wouldn't penalize me. Their penalties were too soft anyway, their consequences temporary, like a warning or a court date could ever make a man like Seyvn stop being a tyrant.

I should have left while he was in court. Grabbed what I could and drove. But I promised Abigail Wednesday.

So, I stayed.

Just two more days.

CHAPTER 74

Their View

"Perception is real even when it is not reality."

— Edward De Bono

I stayed home, hoping my absence would go unnoticed, that I could quietly focus on getting out of Delaware with my kids. I wasn't running from the legal process. I was making the only choice that made sense.

Showing up wasn't going to protect my children. It definitely wasn't going to protect me.

The system had already shown me, time and time again, that its version of justice didn't extend to people like us.

Seyvn would walk free, and I would be left dealing with the consequences. Again.

What I didn't know was that I wasn't the only one making a decision that day.

CPS was at the courthouse that day, watching to see if I'd show up. To them, my absence wasn't about survival. It was a red flag. A warning sign. Proof, in their eyes, that I wasn't willing to protect myself or my children from violence.

What they didn't realize was that by not showing up, I was doing exactly that. I was protecting us the only way I knew how.

But while I was focused on keeping my children safe, they were drawing their own conclusions. Decisions were already being made, judgments already forming and I didn't even know it.

Later that day, CPS came to my house. Not to understand why I was afraid. They came to figure out why I hadn't been in court. Why, in their eyes, I was letting him get away with nearly taking my life.

Their timing couldn't have been worse. Just as they arrived, Seyvn was driving my truck down the street. Everything I had tried to do to keep us safe, every precaution, every careful step, fell apart in that one moment. To them, it didn't matter why he had the truck or how he got it.

What they saw was a man I should have been protecting my children from, behind the wheel of my vehicle. And that was all they needed. My life was under review again, rewritten through their eyes without a single word from me.

I, on the other hand, wasn't worried about CPS, they could think what they wanted.

Tomorrow, I was getting them out of Delaware for good.

The plan was set, but I still wanted them to have one final memory before everything changed.

That evening, I took the kids and their best friend to family skate night. It was our last night there, and I wanted them to have one final memory before everything changed.

When we pulled into the driveway, the energy from the rink was still with us. Abigail was in the back seat, talking a mile a minute about her upcoming field trip. Rayna was humming one of the songs from the skate floor, her fingers tapping out the rhythm on the window.

For that little while, we were just a family coming home.

Then I saw it.

CHAPTER 75

Please Don't Do This

"And if thy sons were ever dear to thee, O, think my son to be as dear to me."

— William Shakespeare, Titus Andronicus

A large black Suburban sat parked across the street.

At first, I didn't think much of it. It could have been a neighbor's visitor or someone passing through. But something about it felt off. It wasn't a car I recognized, and it didn't seem to belong there. I glanced at it a second longer before shaking off the unease. Maybe I was just on edge from everything that had happened recently.

We got out of the car, the kids chattering away, still riding the high from the night. I lingered, helping Lilly out of her car seat and taking my time with the diaper bag, stalling for reasons I couldn't quite explain. The suburban sat there, silent and unmoving, but its presence felt heavy, almost ominous.

Inside the house, the kids ran off to their rooms to put their stuff down, their laughter echoing down the hallway. They knew the routine. Skating nights didn't mean skipping chores. Rayna grabbed the broom to sweep the kitchen, Alyra got mop water, and Enrique went to pick up toys that had been left out earlier while Lilly followed him around, mimicking his every move.

I started tidying up the living room, my mind racing with plans, making sure everything was ready for tomorrow. With every move, the plan solidified in my mind. Tomorrow, I thought. By this time tomorrow, we'd be on the road. Leaving Delaware and Seyvn behind us.

The sounds of chores moved through the house. Sweeping. Drawers opening. Toys being picked up. Nothing special. Just a regular night.

It felt normal. Comfortable, even.

Then came the knock.

Hard. Intentional.

It stopped everything.

I froze mid-step, my heart leaping into my throat. The kids paused, their eyes darting to me, and the unspoken question hung heavy in the air: Who could it be?

I swallowed hard and took a steadying breath. "Keep going with your chores," I said, trying to keep my voice calm, but the tremor betrayed me.

Approaching the door, I wiped my hands on my jeans, the weight of the moment pressing down on me.

Through the peephole, I saw them. A group of people standing in a semi-circle on the porch. Their faces were serious. Posture stiff.

Police officers.

And the person who made my stomach drop. The CPS worker.

The black suburban suddenly made sense.

I rushed to grab my phone and call my mother.

We hadn't been close in years, but she was still my mother, she loved those kids, she had been willing to let us stay with her. and she had worked for CPS. She'd know what to do.

My hands shook as I held the phone. Her voice came through, steady, trying to calm me, but the panic was deafening. My mind raced with thoughts of my kids, myself, of everything about to collapse.

"Marla, you *have* to let them in," my mother's voice cut through the panic, each word striking with urgency. Her tone was steady, but I could hear the tremor beneath it, the cracks betraying her own fear.

"They're going to take them!" I whispered harshly, my voice breaking under the weight of the inevitable. "Do you understand what that means? My babies. *Gone.* How do I just let that happen?"

"They'll come back," she insisted, though her voice faltered, laced with hesitation. "You'll get them back, Marla. You just have to trust the process. Don't make it worse by refusing."

Trust? How could I trust anyone who sent strangers to my door to steal my children? I gripped the phone tighter, as if holding it could keep the ground beneath me from crumbling. I wasn't sure what was more infuriating, her helpless logic or the fact that she was probably right.

The knocking at the door grew louder, more insistent. Each pound sent vibrations through the frame, and through me. The kids had stopped moving, paralyzed with fear.

Abigail stood frozen, her eyes locked on the door. Enrique pressed himself against Alyra's side, his small hands clutching her shirt. Lilly, too young to fully grasp what was happening, her face confused and fearful, silently asking me to fix it.

I looked at them, all of them. I had no answers. I couldn't promise anything. My chest tightened with panic as I realized how utterly helpless I was in that moment.

"Ms. Matrice, this is the Department of Family Services. Open the door, or we'll be forced to enter," a voice boomed from the other side.

The reality crashed over me like a tidal wave. Seyvn was upstairs. I hadn't even thought of him. He was hiding, protecting himself while I stood here on the front lines, trying to shield *our* children from the fallout of *his* actions. He wasn't going to help. He never helped. He'd left me to face this alone.

"Marla, let them in," my mother's voice broke through my spiraling thoughts. "If you don't, they'll force their way in, and it'll only be worse for the kids."

My throat tightened as I looked at my children, their faces etched with fear. My mind screamed at me to protect them, to find a way out. But the options were slipping through my fingers, like trying to hold water in a fist.

The knocking turned into pounding.

I had no choice. My fingers, trembling uncontrollably, reached for the door. My hand hovered over the lock for a second, the weight of the moment crashing over me.

"Please, God," I whispered under my breath. "Please don't let them take my babies."

With a shaky breath, I turned the lock and opened the door.

The sight of the CPS worker standing at my door, flanked by two police officers, felt like the world had been ripped out from under me. I clutched the doorframe, my breath caught in my throat as I stared at them. They weren't here for a conversation. They were here for my children.

"Ms. Matrice," the worker began, her tone clipped and emotionless, "we have an emergency order to take custody of your children."

Her words hit like a sledgehammer. My knees buckled, and I stumbled back, gripping the doorframe to keep myself upright.

"What?" I croaked, the word barely escaping my lips. "Why? My children are fine! They're fine!"

Behind me, the kids froze, the weight of the moment crashing down on them. Rayna was the first to react. Her face twisted with fury, her voice shaking as she screamed, "You can't take us! We're not going anywhere with you! You're not our family!"

Her anger erupted like a storm, fierce and unrelenting. She cursed at the workers, her words sharp and venomous, a side of her I had never seen before. This wasn't just rage, it was desperation. Her voice trembled with fear, but she stood her ground, refusing to back down.

Abigail clung to my leg, her tiny fingers digging into my skin, her body trembling with each ragged sob. 'Mommy!' she cried, her voice breaking as she buried her face against me, as if she could disappear into my shadow and escape what was coming.

Enrique stood beside me, his small hands gripping the fabric of my pants. My Momma's Boy, so full of energy and confidence on any other day was now frozen, his wide eyes darting between me and the strangers who had come to take him. He didn't speak, didn't cry. He just held on, his silent plea heavier than any words.

Alyra stood motionless, her favorite toy clutched against her chest, her expression unreadable. She wasn't crying. She wasn't moving. She just watched, her stillness eerie against the chaos unraveling around us.

In my arms, Lilly wailed, her small hands tangled in my shirt, fists curling tight, as if she could anchor herself to me and make it impossible for them to pull us apart. Her face was damp with tears, her cries raw and piercing, the only words she knew lost in the

425

choked sobs that rattled her tiny body. She was too young to understand the details, but she understood enough. She knew something was terribly wrong.

And I knew, no matter how tightly they held onto me, I couldn't stop what was coming.

I turned to the worker, my voice breaking as I begged, "Please, don't do this. They need me. *Please!*"

The officers exchanged glances, their faces devoid of any emotion. The worker handed me a piece of paper, her expression cold and detached, as though she were handing me a utility bill instead of an order to destroy my family.

"This is temporary," she said flatly, as if those words could somehow soften the blow. "They'll be placed in foster care until the investigation is complete."

Temporary? Investigation? The words swirled in my head, but they didn't mean anything. What investigation? What could possibly justify this?

I looked down at the paper, my eyes scanning the accusations as my heart shattered: "Failure to follow a no contact order. Chronic domestic violence. Bizarre punishment of Enrique."

Bizarre punishment. Chronic domestic violence. I couldn't even process it. Every moment of my life had been spent shielding my children from Seyvn's rage, enduring his abuse so they wouldn't have to. And now, because of him, I was losing them.

My voice rose, shaking with fury and desperation. "Are you kidding me? *This is absurd!* My children are not abused! They're not hurt! They're healthy, they're loved, they're everything they're supposed to be because I make sure of it!"

The worker's face didn't change. She simply stood there, unmoved. "If you want to get beaten every day, that's your choice," she said, her voice cutting through me like a knife. "But your kids shouldn't have to see or hear it."

My jaw dropped. I stared at her, my anger boiling over. "*Choice?*" I hissed. "Do you think I *choose* this? I called the police. I begged for help. And what did they do? They told *him* I was calling! They let him walk free every time! How is that my fault? What exactly was I supposed to do?"

The officers behind her shifted uncomfortably, their gazes averted. Of course, they didn't answer. They didn't care. None of them did.

Rayna's rage erupted again, her voice breaking through my thoughts. "You're monsters!" she screamed, tears streaming down her face.

I looked at her, at all of them, my heart shattering into a million pieces. They didn't deserve this. None of us did.

I turned back to the worker, my voice a desperate whisper. "Please," I said again, the word barely audible. "Please don't take them. Don't do this."

But it was too late. The decision had already been made.

CHAPTER 76

The Silence That Followed

"In the silence of the heart God speaks."

— Mother Teresa

The worker stepped forward, her expression unyielding. "Ms. Matrice, I need you to gather the children's belongings. Just the essentials."

Her words were like a bolt of lightning. Essentials? How could she expect me to distill my children's lives into "essentials"?

Everything in this house was theirs. The toys they played with, the clothes they wore, the drawings on the fridge that marked every milestone, every memory. How was I supposed to reduce their existence to a single bag?

Rayna didn't move. Her feet were planted firmly on the ground, her arms crossed over her chest like a shield. "We're not going anywhere," she spat, her voice trembling with anger and defiance. "You can't make us."

The worker knelt slightly, her voice softening as if she thought she could reason with her. "Rayna, this isn't forever. We're going to make sure you're safe, and then you'll go home."

Rayna's laugh was cold and bitter, a sound far too mature for a girl her age. "Safe?" she repeated. "You're not keeping us safe. You're tearing us apart!"

She was right. They weren't protecting them. They were destroying them. But no amount of logic or pleading would change what was about to happen. The system seemed built to dismantle families like mine.

Behind me, Abigail clung to my leg, her sobs shaking her small body. "Mommy, please," she begged, her voice barely audible. "I don't want to go. Don't let them take us."

I wanted to promise her that I wouldn't let them. That I'd fight until my dying breath to keep them here, with me, where they belonged. But I couldn't stop it.

Tears blurred my vision as I kissed her forehead, whispering, "It's going to be okay." But even as the words left my mouth, I knew they were a lie. Nothing about this was okay.

"Ms. Matrice, we don't want this to escalate," the worker said, her tone firmer now. "Please, for the children's sake, cooperate."

I nodded numbly, my body moving on autopilot as I went to gather bags and clothes. My hands shook as I held Lilly, balancing her against my hip while folding their favorite pajamas, their tiny socks, their beloved stuffed animals. Each item felt like a betrayal, a confirmation that I was letting them go.

Rayna hovered beside me, her hands gripping the edge of a bag. She didn't say anything at first, just watched, her chest rising and falling in shallow, angry breaths. Then, without warning, she grabbed a handful of clothes and shoved them inside.

She was helping me pack.

Not because she had accepted it, but because it was the only thing she could control.

Her movements grew more frantic, her hands trembling as she stuffed her things into the bag with sharp, jerky motions. Then, all at once, the anger exploded out of her.

"This is your fault!" she screamed at the workers. "You're ruining everything! I hate you!"

430

I turned to her, my heart breaking all over again. "Rayna, stop," I said gently, trying to soothe her, even though I wanted to scream just as loudly. "I know it's not fair. I know this shouldn't be happening. But right now, we don't have a choice."

She spun on me, her eyes burning with pain. "Why are you letting them take us?" she demanded, her voice cracking.

My chest tightened, guilt crashing over me like a wave. She didn't understand. How could she? How could any of them? I was fighting, but I was fighting a battle that had already been lost.

When the bags were packed, I forced myself to hand them over. My fingers trembled as I passed them to the worker, but she took them without hesitation, without emotion. Her face remained blank, her demeanor professional. This was just another case for her. Just another child screaming. Just another mother breaking.

But for us, it was obliteration.

"It's time to go," one of the workers said.

Rayna stood frozen, her fists clenched at her sides, her whole body rigid with defiance. When they reached for her, she jerked away.

"No!" she screamed. "Let me go! You can't take us!"

Two officers stepped in, their movements careful but firm. They took her by the arms, and she thrashed against them, kicking, twisting, fighting with everything she had.

"Mommy! Please! Don't let them take us!"

The sound of her cries shattered me. I rushed to her, pulling her into my arms, holding her as tightly as I could.

"Rayna, listen to me," I whispered, my voice thick with the weight of a promise I had no choice but to keep. "I swear to you, this is temporary. I am going to get you back. But right now, I need you to go. I need you to be strong, okay?"

Her body trembled against mine, her breath coming in ragged sobs. For a moment, she didn't respond, just clung to me, unwilling to let go.

"You hear me?" I pressed, gently pulling back just enough to look into her tear-filled eyes.

She sniffled, nodding weakly.

I swallowed hard and cupped her face, pressing a kiss to her forehead. "I love you," I said quietly. "I love you so much."

Her grip on me loosened. Slowly, reluctantly, she stepped back.

The workers waited, impatience etched across their faces, their irritation barely concealed. Rayna wiped her face with the back of her sleeve and, with one last glance at me, turned and walked toward them on her own.

It didn't make it right. It didn't make it hurt any less.

But at least she wasn't being dragged away.

Alyra stood frozen. She didn't cry, but the way her lips trembled betrayed the storm of emotions swirling inside her.

Abigail sobbed as she walked out, her small hands reaching for me. Lilly screamed until her voice cracked, her arms outstretched. "Mommy! Mommy!"

And Enrique... my sweet boy didn't say a word. He just looked at me, his eyes filled with betrayal and heartbreak.

I crouched down, reaching for his hand before he could go. He let me wrap my arms around him, his small body pressing into mine.

432

I held him close, pressing my cheek against his, breathing him in like I could somehow make this moment last.

"I love you, Momma's Boy," I whispered, my voice thick with everything I couldn't say.

He clung to me for just a second longer before slowly pulling back. His voice was barely above a breath.

"I love you, Mommy."

His little shoulders trembled. Small and firm.

And then, they took him.

The door shut, and they were gone.

I stood there, fists clenched, my whole body shaking. Not with sorrow, but with rage. My babies were gone. Ripped away. And for what?

Upstairs, I heard Seyvn's footsteps, the floor creaking under his weight. He never came down. Never offered a word.

He stayed hidden, too much of a coward to face what he had done. Too spineless to show his face while his own children were taken. Not even enough of a father to offer them even the illusion of protection.

And me? I was still standing there. Helpless. Furious. Empty.

I'd failed them. I'd failed all of them.

And the silence that followed was the loudest sound I'd ever heard.

Chapter 77

What Good is Too Late?

"Better three hours too soon than a minute too late."

— William Shakespeare

The moment Seyvn came downstairs after the kids were gone, every ounce of rage and hatred I felt boiled to the surface. He had the audacity to look confused, even shocked, like he had no idea how it came to this. My hands shook, my jaw clenched so tight I thought my teeth might shatter. He was the reason my babies were gone, and yet here he stood, playing dumb.

This man had beaten me near death, had violated the no-contact order, stayed even when I begged him to leave. I hated him more than I thought it was possible to hate another person. I wished I had killed him when I had the chance. Maybe if I had, my children would still be here.

Instead, he stood there with that empty stare asking, "What happened?" his tone flat, almost indifferent. "Why did they take them?"

"Why?" I spat, the word coming out like venom. "Because of you, Seyvn. I told you this would happen. I begged you to leave. But you didn't listen! And now they're gone."

He looked at me, his face blank, as if he couldn't comprehend what I was saying. It made me hate him even more.

Finally, some version of reality had managed to reach him, he mumbled something about needing to leave. Now he wanted to go. Not because he felt guilty or regretted anything. He didn't. He was just trying to protect himself. My children were already gone.

435

The damage was done.

He grabbed a few things and said he'd get an apartment to prove to CPS that he didn't live there. I wanted him gone. But more than that, I wanted him to pay.

And pay he did. Two days after the kids were taken, his probation officer told him to come in. Seyvn walked into that office with a lease in his hand, convinced he had it all figured out. He thought securing an apartment would be enough to make it look like he was following the rules, enough to get the system off his back. But instead of a routine check-in, they put him in handcuffs. Arrested him for violating the no-contact order.

And the irony was, when they finally arrested him, he wasn't even violating it. He hadn't been caught in the act. I hadn't called or reported anything. He had already left. But that's when they chose to do something. Not when he was in my house. Not when I was afraid for my life. Not when my children were home.

They could have acted sooner. They could have stopped him a hundred different times. But they didn't.

They moved when it suited them.

I should have felt relief. Maybe even vindication.

Instead, all I felt was anger. Why now? They could have done it when it mattered most, before my children were ripped from my arms and my life was left in shambles.

For months I had begged for help. I called the police. I pleaded for enforcement of the order. I risked everything trying to keep Seyvn away, and every time the system turned a blind eye.

The bitterness was overwhelming. Their actions felt like a cruel joke. They'd let the damage happen, then swooped in, pretending they were solving the problem.

My children placed in state custody, kept with strangers, forced to adjust to new homes, new rules, new people, while I jumped through endless hoops to prove I was worthy to parent my own children.

It made no sense. These were people with degrees, training, years of experience. Yet somehow, they couldn't see the harm they were causing. Or maybe they didn't care.

Seyvn was gone. The danger was removed. Yet they still refused to return my kids. Common sense would say this was the moment to reunite us. To let me rebuild. To finally get out of Delaware and take my children somewhere safe. But common sense had no place here.

They said it was about protecting children. But all I saw was destruction. I didn't know how I'd do it, or what it would take, but I would get them back.

CHAPTER 78

Nobody Else to Call

"Healing takes time, and asking for help is a courageous step."

— Mariska Hargitay

There was no handbook for this. No guide on who to call when the state takes your children and tells you there's no family close enough to take them.

My mom was too sick to travel. I didn't have any other family nearby. And that's what they clung to, that technicality. Like love only counted if it came with a local address. I didn't have time to sit around hoping someone would magically show up. I needed help. I needed somebody, anybody, who could step in and help get my babies home.

The only person I could think of was Wilma. Noah's mother. Their paternal grandmother. We hadn't spoken in years, but I never doubted that she loved those kids. And perhaps even more than that, she loved playing the hero. I knew if anybody was gonna lace up and wade into some bullshit, it was her.

My hand shook as I dialed. I didn't even have a speech ready. The phone rang a few times before she picked up. Her voice came through calm, curious, like she already knew something was wrong.

"Hello?"

"It's me," I said, my voice cracking. "I need your help."

Her tone softened, curiosity laced with something that almost sounded like satisfaction. "What's going on?"

I barely got the words out before they started tumbling over each other. "CPS took the kids. They're in foster care. They're saying I don't have any family nearby, that there's no one for them to go to. Can you come to Delaware for a little bit?"

A pause. I could almost hear the wheels turning in her head. Then, finally, she spoke. "I'll come."

True to her word, Wilma arrived. She didn't hesitate. She came ready to help, ready to step in. But her arrival came too late. She didn't make it in time for the first court hearing.

That hearing was supposed to determine whether the state had enough evidence to justify keeping my children in custody. And going into it, I already knew exactly what the state was going to say. But I truly believed deep in my soul that the judge wasn't going to let the state take children from their mother over domestic violence. Especially not when they weren't hurt.

So, when she started talking and said that domestic violence alone wasn't a reason to take children away, I finally let myself breathe. She said it was something I should educate myself on. I could've cried right there. Finally, someone with sense. She was a woman.

She had to understand what it meant to fight for your family.

She even acknowledged the evidence didn't support the reasons for removal CPS had initially cited.

I just knew she was going to send my babies home.

But then she kept talking.

"While I understand this was intended as a game and the kids were all giggling," she said, her voice flat and cold, "the court cannot overlook the potential for harm. It's reckless to place a child in the freezer. The children will remain in CPS custody."

Potential for harm. Not actual harm. Not injury. Just the idea that something could have happened. And that was enough to justify tearing my children from me.

Enrique hadn't been scared. He had been laughing, writhing in my arms, kicking and giggling as I teased him. There was no malice. No fear. No harm. Only joy.

But here? In this courtroom? They twisted it into something monstrous.

How was this possible? Even CPS, as much as they scrutinized every aspect of my life, informed the judge that it was a game.

That they had spoken to me about it, expressed their concerns, and I had listened.

And yet, here I was.

My children in state custody. My family shattered. My life under review because of a game I played with my son. My son who is the living, breathing heart outside my body.

And just when I thought it couldn't get any more absurd, the judge looked me in the eye and said words that made my blood boil:
"I want to hear remorse at the next hearing…"

Remorse? As if I had hurt him. As if I had done something cruel, something unforgivable.

If she wanted remorse, I could give her remorse right now!!!

How was keeping my children in foster care separated from their mother, from everything they had ever known a reasonable response to a mother playing with her child.

How was this *in their best interest?*

I wanted to scream. I wanted to shake the whole damn courthouse until someone, anyone, made it make sense.

CPS didn't care. They didn't care that their original reasons for removal had been thrown out. They didn't care that their own argument had crumbled in court. They were satisfied with the ruling. To them, it was a win. The judge had rubber-stamped their decision, and that was all that mattered.

I turned to my court-appointed attorney, desperate for him to fight back, to argue this insanity. But he barely raised his head. "Do you want to be the lawyer?" he said, his tone laced with disdain. "Because if you think you can do better, you're welcome to represent yourself."

I couldn't believe it. This was supposed to be my advocate, the person standing between me and the loss of my children. Instead, he was dismissive, indifferent, treating me like an inconvenience instead of a mother fighting for her children.

When Wilma finally arrived, it was too late to change anything. She hadn't been there for the hearing, but she still tried to step in by filing an emergency petition for custody. If the children couldn't be with me, at least they could be with someone they knew. At least they wouldn't be trapped in a stranger's home, scared and confused.

She told them she would stay at my house if that's what it took to satisfy their so-called concerns. She told them she had the resources, the ability, everything needed to take them in.

But then came the ruling that shattered what little hope I had left: *"It's not in the children's best interest."*

Not in their best interest.

Keeping them in foster care? Not letting them stay with their grandmother who came all the way from Kentucky? Tearing them away from their home, their family, and each other? That was supposed to be in their best interest?

It was asinine.

Thirty days.

That's how long the judge set the next court date for. Thirty long, agonizing days where my children would remain in the custody of strangers.

As if to placate me, or maybe just to check a box, CPS told the judge the children missed me. They wanted to go home. As if that was some kind of revelation. As if a mother's love and a child's need for their parent were groundbreaking discoveries.

And in her infinite "grace," the judge granted weekly visits and phone calls.

Weekly visits. One day a week.

It was framed as a gift, a kind gesture from the court. But it was not a gift. It was a slap in the face. A cruel substitute for the family they had torn apart. Just a reminder of everything we had lost and proof that the system never cared about what my children truly needed. They needed their home. Their family.

Their mother.

But that somehow wasn't in their best interest.

CHAPTER 79

Divine Intervention

"Sometimes the answers we seek come from the most unexpected places, and in the most unexpected ways."

— Haruki Murakami

After that first CPS hearing, I stumbled out of the courthouse feeling like a hollowed-out shell. The judge had ruled against me, and my children, my babies, were staying in foster care. My world had just ended, and I was expected to just keep moving. I headed to my truck, the only plan in my head being to get home and somehow hold myself together before I ended up on an episode of snapped.

But nooooooo. That would've been too easy for the universe, wouldn't it?

Because there it was. A bright yellow boot clamped onto my truck's tire. At first, I thought maybe I was so out of it I'd walked to the wrong truck. But then I saw the note. A citation from the parking authority. Three hundred dollars in unpaid tickets. And a warning that tampering could result in criminal charges.

Charges. I didn't even know what a boot was, how was I going to tamper with it.

Was this real? Had I run over a leprechaun in another life? What kind of karma was I carrying to deserve this?

I just stood there, staring at the note, waiting for a hidden camera crew to pop out and tell me I was being pranked. But no one came. So, there I was, stranded downtown with no idea how to get home. I hadn't taken a bus since before I'd moved to Delaware, and I barely knew my way around.

445

I started walking, hoping maybe I could find someone to help me figure it out. That's when I saw him.

Standing on the corner was a man. Older, disheveled, layered in mismatched clothes, like he was preparing for a winter apocalypse in the middle of spring. Wool hat, multiple jackets, and sandals. *Sandals!* I couldn't make sense of it, but honestly, I didn't care.

He looked approachable enough, and I figured a homeless man who stood on the corner all day probably knew how the buses worked better than most.

"Excuse me, sir," I said, trying to keep the shakiness out of my voice. "Do you know which bus I can take to get to Prices Corner?"

He turned toward me, his weathered face kind but cautious. "Well," he said slowly, "You've got a couple of options," he said, his voice raspy but patient. "You can walk four blocks to Rodney Square and catch the 52, or you can go two blocks the other way and take the 8. Either one will drop you off at Prices Corner."

I nodded, trying to process his directions, but my mind was a jumbled mess. Four blocks? Two blocks? I barely had the energy to stand, let alone walk blocks in either direction. He must've seen the confusion or maybe the pure defeat on my face, because he tilted his head and asked, "Would you like a ride?"

I blinked at him, sure I'd misheard. A *ride?* From him? This man, dressed like he'd just time-traveled from two climates at once, wanted me to get in his car. All the true crime shows I'd ever watched flashed in my mind. This was the kind of guy who offered you help only to drive you into the woods and... well, you know the rest.

But the truth was, the worst had already happened. My children were gone. My life was crumbling. What was he going to do? Kill me? At that moment, that didn't even sound so bad.

"Sure," I heard myself say, like a fool in one of those movies where you yell at the screen, *"Don't do it!"*

We walked to his pickup truck, and it was *exactly* what I pictured a kidnapper would drive. Dingy, nondescript, and, of course, white.

As I climbed in, my brain screamed, *this is how it ends. He's going to drive me to some abandoned field, and that's it.* But I climbed in anyway, my movements stiff with fear. As soon as I shut the door, he said, "Put your seatbelt on."

Now, in my already-paranoid mind, that wasn't for safety. That was so I couldn't escape. Still, I clicked the seatbelt into place because, what else did I have to lose?

As we pulled off, he started talking. And let me tell you, it was *a lot.* "This isn't an accident," he said. "God put me on that corner for you."

I stared at him, deadpan. *God?* Was this man serious? I was trapped in a white pickup truck with someone who thought he had a hotline to God himself. He didn't stop. He went on about how this was divine intervention, how everything I was going through would work out because God had a plan for me.

I wanted to scream, *Are you out of your mind?* My kids were in foster care. My husband was a lunatic. My truck was booted. God wasn't planning anything but my misery. But I didn't scream. I just sat there, clinging to the door handle, nodding along while he rambled about faith and hope and divine timing.

At some point, I realized we weren't going in the direction of Prices Corner. "This doesn't look right," I said, trying to keep the panic out of my voice.

He looked at me, completely calm. "Which way would you like me to go?"

I had no answer. I didn't know my way around well enough to say, so I just slumped back into the seat, defeated. If he was taking me somewhere to kill me, I'd already resigned myself to it.

By the time we got close to Prices Corner, I made a split-second decision. "Actually, can you take me to my house?" I said, giving him my address.

He nodded without question, driving me all the way home. When we pulled into my driveway, he asked for my phone number so he could "check in on me." Against all logic, I gave it to him. Why? I don't know. Maybe I was grateful. Maybe I was too drained to say no. Either way, I made it home alive.

When I got inside, I locked the door and collapsed onto the couch, still wondering if God had actually sent me a guardian angel or if I'd just narrowly escaped being the lead story on the evening news.

Whatever it was I hope God didn't tell him to come back and kill me.

CHAPTER 80

Fractured Justice

"Be more concerned with your character than your reputation, because your character is what you really are, while your reputation is merely what others think you are."

—John Wooden

That first family court hearing set the tone for a nightmare of contradictions. The judge claimed domestic violence was not the reason my children were found dependent. But that was nothing more than a lie dressed up in legal technicalities. Everything that happened after proved it. Domestic violence dictated every decision, all of them centered on Seyvn.

Every hearing was a performance. A courtroom ritual with a predetermined ending. They kept asking the same questions, like a script they couldn't let go of.

What if he comes back?

What if she lets him in?

What if the cycle starts again?

It didn't matter that Seyvn was still incarcerated or that I had fought with everything I had to protect my children.

There were no bruises on them. No threats. No emergency. None of that mattered. CPS didn't need a crisis. They needed a justification. And when they wanted to keep your children, they would create one.

A glance. A sentence. A gesture. Not because it made sense. But because they could.

449

They didn't stop at twisting small moments. They reached back, digging through every part of my life for anything they could use. They picked apart every decision I had ever made.

They asked why I hadn't called the police more, ignoring that calling had only put my life in more danger. As if surviving wasn't already a full-time job.

They even brought up the "I Love You More" game Enrique and I used to play and warped it into something dangerous. They twisted a moment of love into evidence, bending reality to fit the narrative they needed.

They kept making it up as they went. It didn't matter that the judge had said it wasn't about domestic violence. DFS never followed her lead. And the longer it went on, the more it felt like even the judge forgot what she had said.

Nothing made sense. So, I started asking questions, hoping for anything that resembled honesty. But every response was vague. Contradictory. It was like chasing smoke through the air.

CPS couldn't keep their story straight. Even the foster mother would ask me when the children were coming home, like I had some magical insight into the state's incoherent, baseless decisions.

But yet, these same people who couldn't even keep their own story straight were given complete control over my children's lives. They decided when I could see them, how I could see them, and for how long. Even the smallest connection had to be on their terms.

Once a week, for one hour, I was allowed to be their mother. Always under the watchful eye of someone from CPS, monitoring every word, every interaction, as if I might suddenly reveal myself to be the monster they were trying to make me out to be.

The first visit was almost too much to bear. The moment they saw me, my babies ran. Enrique gripped my waist like he could hold the world together with his arms. Abigail buried herself in my chest, her whole body trembling. Lilly clung to my leg, her fingers digging into my clothes. Rayna and Alyra pressed against my sides, eyes wide and full of fear.

I held all five of them as tightly as I could. None of this was fair.

On the other side of the mirrored glass, the CPS worker sat watching. Noticing. Judging. Writing. Their pen scratched against paper, turning our love into documentation.

The moment should have been about my children, but they made it clinical. Mechanical. Something to be studied.

Wilma sat beside me. She had been fighting too. Petitioning for custody, pleading for the children to be placed with her, but CPS had denied her again and again. Still, she kept showing up.

"Mommy, why can't we come home?" Alyra asked, her big eyes searching mine for the truth.

They didn't understand. They begged for answers I couldn't give, their voices trembling with confusion and fear.

I wanted to tell them everything. I wanted to scream about the injustice, the lies, the bureaucratic nonsense that had stolen them from me. But I couldn't. I had to smile, to reassure them, to pretend like everything would be okay, even as I felt my own heart breaking.

"I'm trying, Alyra," I said, my voice shaking. "I'm doing everything I can to bring you guys home."

Alyra's little hands curled into fists. "That's not an answer," she said, her voice cracking. "Why can't we come home?"

She was right. It wasn't.

Because they won't let you.

Because they don't care about what's right.

 Because I don't know how to fight them.

I blinked hard, steadying my breath. "I don't know, baby," I admitted. "But I promise, I will not stop trying."

And just like that, the visit was over. I watched them being led away, their tear-streaked faces turned back toward me, little hands reaching for one more second, one more hug, one more moment.

Reaching until they were gone.

CHAPTER 81

The Best Interest of the Child

"There can be no keener revelation of a society's soul than the way in which it treats its children."

— Nelson Mandela

First, they took them from me. Then they took them from each other.

At the start, at least there was that. They were placed in the same home. They could sleep under the same roof. Eat at the same table. Hold onto a little piece of what we had. But even that didn't last.

The foster mother complained that Rayna was "parenting" her siblings. As if that was a crime. As if loving too deeply, caring too much, made her a threat. Rayna had always been their shield. Their voice. Their comfort. Not because she had to be, but because it was who she was.

But CPS didn't see her instincts as a strength. They saw interference. A problem to be solved.

Their solution? Separate her.

She was sent to live in a different foster home.

Ripped from the only family she had left. Alone. Thirteen years old, carrying more than any child should ever have to carry, and now expected to figure it out by herself. Her only crime was loving her siblings too much.

The world she was thrown into was nothing like the one she had known. Her days were spent at the Boys and Girls Club, surrounded by children hardened by survival. The language was rougher. The habits sharper. The faces less forgiving. She was exposed to behaviors born from survival, not innocence.

And so, she adapted.

Unfortunately, her nights were no better. She would get in an unfamiliar bed, her small body tensing at every distant pop of gunfire, every unfamiliar sound from the streets below. She had never known that kind of fear before. The kind where someone might hurt you just because they can.

The absence of her siblings, her built-in safety net, made every day more unbearable. She was no longer the big sister, the protector, the confident, bubbly girl I had raised. Now she was just another scared child trying to navigate a world that was foreign and unkind. She was terrified, alone, and adrift in an environment that felt less like a temporary home and more like a punishment.

The younger children fared no better.

When their foster mother left the state, Enrique and his sisters were placed in the same home where Rayna stayed. It was around Enrique's birthday, and for the first time in a long while, my heart felt warm. I was truly excited knowing my babies would be together to celebrate even if I couldn't be there with them.

But instead of birthday cake and laughter there was silence. No party. No joy. Just an empty space where happiness should have been.

My sweet boy, the one who loved wrestling and our "I Love You More" game, was thinking about ending his life.

Seven years old.

He wasn't thinking about cake. Or presents. Or making a wish.
He was thinking about how to make it stop.
Because the pain was too much.
Because he had been taken from everything he knew.

Because he was in an unfamiliar place, forced to share a bed with boys he didn't know, while his sisters were just a room away. Because no one cared.

He cried. And cried.

Instead of holding him, instead of telling him it was going to be okay, instead of showing him even an ounce of compassion, the foster mother threatened him.

"If you don't stop crying, I'm taking you to juvenile detention."

As if fear was something he could just turn off.

As if he hadn't already lost everything.

As if a seven-year-old's tears were some kind of crime.

And when the crying didn't stop, she followed through.

She put my baby in the car and drove him to a place meant for criminals.

Because he was grieving.

Because he missed his family.

Because he was breaking under the weight of a nightmare no child should experience.

Because she didn't even have the common decency to buy the boy, at the very least, a cupcake on his birthday!

Thankfully, the detention center, a place meant to house kids who had committed real crimes, showed more decency than anyone else and refused to take him

They knew the truth.

Enrique wasn't a delinquent.

He was a seven-year-old child who wanted to die.

But, instead of helping him, instead of calling someone, anyone, who might actually care, they handed him right back.

Back to the woman who thought jail was the right answer for a scared, grieving little boy.

Back to someone who saw his pain as an inconvenience, not a cry for help.

Back to a house where his birthday didn't exist.

No cake. No candles. No kindness.

Just another day in a world that had already failed him.

And it was not only Enrique.

Lilly was the hardest to watch. My perfect princess, barely two years old. Too young to understand why she couldn't stay with her mother.

Every visit ended the same way, her tiny hands clutching my shirt, her face buried in my chest, screaming as the CPS worker pried her away. Her voice, shrill and piercing.

"Mommy! Mommy! Noooooooooo!" she cried, her little fingers gripping tighter as tears streamed down her cheeks.

I tried to comfort her, whispering, "It's okay, baby. It's okay. I'll see you soon."

But how could she understand "soon" when every moment apart must have felt like forever?

Within those moments apart, there were supposed to be phone calls. They were meant to be a lifeline, a way to keep me connected to my children. Instead, they became another source of pain for all of us.

The foster mother of the youngest children eventually asked for the calls be stopped altogether. She said they were too upsetting, that the kids would cry for hours after hanging up, inconsolable and desperate.

As much as it angered me, I couldn't blame her. The children were suffering, and as much as I longed to hear their voices, I knew these calls were only adding to their pain.

This system, this process, was ripping us apart piece by piece.

They called it "temporary," but every day felt like an eternity.

How could they not see the damage they were doing?

How could they not understand that ripping a child away from their mother causes scars that may never heal?

They claimed my children were taken because I had not done enough to protect them. Why? Because I refused to be hunted down and killed.

I fought every second to stay alive so my children would not have to attend my funeral far too early. And while I was fighting for them, the system turned its back on me and told the man who was trying to kill me that I was the one calling the police on him. But I was the one accused of failing to protect them.

Now THEY claimed to be protecting my children and keeping them safe, but the emotional wounds my children were now suffering from were just as real as the physical scars I had spent years trying to shield them from.

Instead of helping us escape the violence, the system punished me for it. Instead of offering resources to heal my family, they only made things worse.

This same system exposed my children to dangers far worse than anything they had faced at home and showed no concern for the psychological damage they caused.

My children were assigned three different guardian ad litems during this time. Three.

After the judge gave custody to the state, not one of them ever spoke to me, and not one spent meaningful time with my children. They never even tried to understand the trauma we had been through.

Yet they stood in court making bold recommendations, pretending to know what was in the best interest of my children.

They were nothing more than proxies for CPS.

They didn't question. They didn't challenge. They didn't even acknowledge the contradictions staring them in the face.

They weren't advocates. They were accomplices.

And in every decision that tore my family apart, deepened my children's suffering, and turned our love into evidence, they hid behind the same lie: it was in the best interest of the child.

CHAPTER 82

Twisted Perceptions

"All things are subject to interpretation. Whichever interpretation prevails at a given time is a function of power and not truth."

— Friedrich Nietzsche

The envelope sat in my hands, thick and official, the New Castle County Police Department's name printed across the top.

My first instinct was that it had something to do with Seyvn. Maybe an update on his incarceration, maybe a request for me to testify.

One of CPS's latest demands was that I petition the state to reopen the charges against him for nearly killing me.

It was almost laughable.

Where was this energy before?

Where was their urgency when I was calling the police, reporting his violations, fighting for my life, and trying to survive?

They didn't care when it mattered. But now, when it served them, they suddenly wanted justice?

I shook my head and tore open the letter, ready to skim through whatever nonsense they were throwing at me this time.

Then I saw it.

NOTICE OF ARREST WARRANT.

I stopped breathing.
The words didn't make sense. I read them again. And again.

My vision blurred.

I blinked hard, forcing my vision to focus, certain I had read it wrong.

But the words didn't change.

They sat there, bold and unmistakable.

My name.

My address.

My charges.

My hands started to shake, the paper crumpling slightly beneath my fingers.

What the hell?

I wasn't being called as a witness. I was being called the criminal.

Charge: Endangering the Welfare of a Child – Knowingly Act in a Manner Likely to Injure In Violation of 11 Del. C. subsection 1102 0a1a M A

TO WIT: Marla, on or about the 2nd day of MARCH 2012, in the County of NEW CASTLE, State of Delaware, did being a parent legally charged with the custody or care of a child less than 18 years old, MARLA KNOWINGLY PLACED HER SON, ENRIQUE, IN AN OPERABLE FLOOR-TYPE FREEZER. THIS ACTION WAS LIKELY TO BE INJURIOUS TO THE PHYSICAL, MENTAL, AND MORAL WELFARE OF ENRIQUE.

That's what it said.

As if putting it in bold capital letters could make it true.

460

Yes, I played the game. Maybe using the freezer wasn't the smartest choice. But the judge already kept my children for it.

She dismissed domestic violence as a reason to keep my kids, then turned around and gave CPS a reason they could use.

One I now had a warrant for.

They could arrest me anywhere. Pull me over. Drag me out of my home. Humiliate me all over again.

If they wanted me, fine.

But they weren't going to get the satisfaction.

I was going to them. I would turn myself in.

Walking into that police station felt like placing myself in the hands of those who had no intention of letting me go. My stomach twisted into knots. My pulse hammered in my ears as I pushed through the doors.

As I stepped up to the thick glass, the officer sitting behind it barely looked up.

"Can I help you?"

I took a breath, steadying my voice. "I'm here to turn myself in.

There's a warrant for my arrest."
That got his attention.

His fingers paused over the keyboard, his expression shifting from indifferent to something more alert. He looked at me properly now, scanning my face like he was trying to place me in in whatever cell they already had waiting for me.

"What's your name?"

I told him.

He typed, his eyes flicking back and forth between the screen and me. A few seconds passed before he nodded.

"Give me a moment."

Then he disappeared.

I stood there, my stomach twisting tighter, waiting.

I heard the heavy door unlatch before he stepped out, now on my side of the glass.

"Alright," he said, his tone neutral. Not cruel. Not kind. Just procedural.

I swallowed hard.

"Come with me."

I followed him down a short hallway, my heart pounding.

He stopped and gestured for me to face the wall. "I have to cuff you."

Cold steel closed around my wrists. Not tight. Not loose. Just there. Another reminder that I had no control over anything in this moment.

They fingerprinted me like I was some violent offender, took my mugshot, and then, they led me to the cell.

It was freezing. I sat stiffly on the wooden bench, my body tense from more than just the chill in the air. The walls were streaked with grime, as if they hadn't been scrubbed in years.

And the toilet?

There wasn't one.

Just a hole in the floor.

No seat. No stall. No privacy.

No toilet paper.

Nothing.

Not even the basic decency afforded to animals in shelters.

I exhaled slowly, pressing my hands against my knees to stop them from shaking. They wanted me to feel broken. To feel like nothing. I closed my eyes, forcing my breath to steady.

Time stretched in that freezing cell, each second dragging longer than the last.

At some point, an officer finally appeared, unlocking the door with a loud clank.

Hours crawled by until they finally came for me.

"Let's go. Bail hearing."

The bail hearing was just as absurd as the family court nightmare.

I was led into a small room, the walls just as lifeless as the cell I'd left behind. A monitor sat in front of me, and when it flickered to life, there he was. Another stranger with too much power. The Judge.

He didn't see a mother.

He didn't see a mistake.

He didn't see a moment taken out of context.

He saw a charge sheet and treated it like truth. Like I had no regard for my son's safety.

I wanted to scream.

I wanted to make him see it for what it was.

A game. A moment of laughter twisted into a crime.

But he didn't care.

And just when I thought this couldn't get more ridiculous, the judge set my bail conditions.

"No contact with your son. Pursuant to CPS approval."

I blinked, trying to process what I had just heard.
CPS?

How would the criminal court even know to put that condition in place if CPS wasn't involved?

Of course.

The same CPS the judge had just armed with her ruling.

They weren't just involved. They orchestrated it.

One moment I was a mother fighting to protect my children from a broken family court system.

Now I'm defending myself in a broken criminal one.

This wasn't two separate courts making separate decisions.

This was one system working together to destroy me.

Good luck with that.

CHAPTER 83

A Deal with Desperation

"Desperation can make a person do surprising things."

— Veronica Roth

The courtroom battles, the ceaseless scrutiny, and the relentless demands of the system had taken everything from me. My children. My dignity. And now, my sense of self.

By the time I met Levi, I was running on fumes.

Levi was my new caseworker, and nothing about him blended in with the cold, procedural world of social services. He had a presence that was hard to ignore.

He was massive, the kind of man who seemed to take up more space than the room could give. His clothes clung snugly to his frame but he carried himself with a confidence that was seemingly out of place. Out of place in the job, and out of place on him.

Still, for all that presence, he was just another worker. Professional. Direct. Another face in a system full of them.

That was all I needed him to be.

My focus was on getting my children back, doing everything I could to meet CPS's relentless demands. But the more we spoke, the more his tone changed. A softness crept in, too careful to be casual, too familiar to ignore. He asked about things that had nothing to do with the case. Remembered details I hadn't expected him to. Checked in more often than policy required.

Maybe he saw my desperation. Maybe it was my vulnerability, my raw determination to fight for my children. Maybe it was something more self-serving, a reflection of his own loneliness, his own need for connection.

Whatever his reasons, I didn't have the luxury of overanalyzing it. Levi's presence was a comfort in the airless rooms stacked with files and accusations. He walked the line between ally and opportunist. He listened. He was kind. And I was exhausted.

I had made a promise to my children. A promise that drove every decision I made, every compromise, every shred of dignity I was willing to sacrifice. I promised that I would bring them home, no matter what.

They were the reason I got out of bed in the morning. The reason I didn't let despair swallow me whole. They were everything.
That promise was what made me pick up the phone every time Levi called.

At first, the calls were professional. He'd check in about the case, give me updates on the court hearings, and discuss my compliance with the CPS plan. A lingering comment about how strong I was. A joke that danced just on the edge of inappropriate.

Then one evening, his tone changed.

"You know," he said, his voice low and conspiratorial, "I could make things easier for you. More visits. More time with your kids."

My stomach churned, a mix of dread and anger rising in my chest. His words hung in the air like bait, and I could see the hook beneath them. He didn't have to say it outright. I knew exactly what he meant. And I was past the point of caring.

If Levi wanted me, he could have me. I was ready to serve myself up on a silver platter if it meant getting my children back. Pride and dignity meant nothing compared to the gnawing ache of my children's absence.

So, I didn't ask what he meant. I let the silence stretch, My mind on my kids. Their faces, their laughter, the way they used to fill the house with life. If giving him what he wanted could bring even a fraction of that back, then I'd do it without question.

And Levi knew it.

The next time he called, the pretense of professionalism began to erode. It wasn't about court hearings or visitation schedules anymore. It was about me. His words became heavier, his tone slower, dripping with something different than before. He asked questions I didn't want to answer, but I did anyway, letting him guide the conversation where he wanted it to go.

"Do you ever think about me?" His voice soft, as if he were testing the waters.

"No," I said flatly. "I think about my kids."

"Of course," he said, his tone dripping with understanding. "But don't you think about what you need sometimes? About yourself?"

What I needed were my children, to hang up the phone.

But I didn't.

I stayed, letting his words settle in, even though they made my skin crawl. Each call stretched longer, drifted further from the case, and slid into territory I wanted no part of.

The promise I'd made to my children rang louder than my disgust. If this was the price to pay for getting them back, then so be it.

I had already done everything CPS demanded. The parenting classes. The domestic violence counseling. The drug tests. Every hurdle they placed in front of me, I cleared. Yet, it led nowhere. Progress was slow, restrictions remained, and my children felt further away than ever.

Now, he promised change. More visits, fewer restrictions, faster progress. The deal was unspoken but unmistakable: my children for me. And I agreed.

And Levi delivered. He arranged extra visits, more time than the court had ordered. Those visits were everything to me. Brief moments of joy in a life otherwise filled with despair. I convinced myself it was worth it, that I could live with the tradeoff if it meant being closer to my babies.

I hated myself for what I was doing, but I couldn't stop. Not while my children were still in the system.

CHAPTER 84

Debt Due

"A small debt produces a debtor; a large one, an enemy."

— Publilius Syrus

When Levi asked me to come in and sign releases, it carried the same false promise as everything else with CPS. Another pointless task, another line on the endless checklist they dangled in front of me, swearing it would bring my children home.

I was running on fumes, but fumes were enough to get me there. The office was quieter than usual, almost too quiet. He led me into a small conference room and gestured toward a chair.

But I didn't sit.

I stayed standing, arms crossed, waiting for him to tell me what needed signing. I had been through this routine too many times to pretend it mattered anymore.

He slid the papers across the table. I scanned them quickly, the legal jargon blending together like it always did.

Then I looked up.

His eyes were already on me. Not in the way someone checks to see if you understand. But carrying something personal that didn't belong in that room.

"You're really trying, aren't you?" he said, leaning back in his chair, his tone unusually soft.

I nodded. "Of course I am."

He smiled, slow and knowing. "I see that. You've been doing everything we ask."

His gaze dropped, then came back up to meet mine. "That's good."

Something about his voice unsettled me. It wasn't what he said.

It was how he said it.

The room felt smaller. The silence stretched longer than it should have.

Then he stood, walked around the table, and stopped behind me.

Close enough that I could feel his presence, the heat of his body radiating toward mine.

My breath caught. I stayed still.

His hands settled on my shoulders. "They don't make it easy for mothers like you," he murmured, fingers grazing my skin.

I nodded, my throat dry.

"They want you to fail." His grip tightened slightly. "But I don't."

I exhaled shakily, my pulse hammering in my ears.

I should have left.

I should have said something.

But I didn't.

Unlike the others, the caseworkers who barely looked at me, the attorneys who didn't fight, the judges who made up their minds before I even spoke, Levi had helped me.

He was getting me more visits.

I had to make sure I didn't lose the only person with the power to send my children home.

That was the logic in my head.

His hands slid from my shoulders, tracing lightly down my arms.

"You deserve this," he said, his thumbs grazing my neck. "After everything you've been through."

I tensed.

He was too close.

I wasn't moving.

Was I letting this happen?

I wasn't stopping it.

"I see how hard you're working," he murmured. "You deserve a break."

His hands slid lower.

Down my sides.

Fingertips grazing my waist before moving lower, slipping into the waistband of my joggers.

I froze. Felt my breath catch.

But I didn't move.

His fingers pressed against me.

Not roughly. Not urgently. Just enough to make it clear what he wanted.

I stayed still. barely reacting.

Not because I wanted this.

But because I was so damn tired.

Because fighting had never gotten me anywhere before.

Because I didn't have anything left to fight with.

Levi pulled his hand away, and I exhaled, only for him to bring his fingers to his lips, tasting me.

The groan that left his throat made my stomach turn.

Without a word, he gently turned me to face him.

"I can help even more," he said, his voice soft and careful.

I didn't move. I couldn't.

His hands went back to my waist.

I swallowed, my heart pounding so loudly it felt like it was inside my throat.

His hands curled under the waistband, tugging lightly.

I lifted my hips.
I don't know why.

Maybe because it was easier. Maybe because resisting wasn't an option. Maybe because CPS had already taken everything else.

What was one more thing?

The fabric slid down my thighs, pooling around my ankles.

He guided me up, pressing lightly on my hips until I was half-sitting, half-leaning against the conference table.
He gently guided me back until my spine met the cold wood under me.

The conference table. The same conference table where they had made decisions about my children's fate. Where they had called me unfit. Where they had written my life into a case file, stripped of context, of truth, of humanity.

And now, my caseworker was between my legs, his mouth on me, another piece of me taken, another shred of dignity gone.
His hands gripped my thighs, spreading me wider, his tongue inside me with a hunger that disgusted me.

I closed my eyes.

I tried to disappear inside myself. Tried to forget where I was. Tried not to think about how I had gotten here. How I had stopped fighting. How I had let myself be used. Again.

I had come here to sign releases. To comply.

To be the obedient mother they needed me to be.

And now, I was lying there, letting my caseworker devour me.

I told myself it was the price I had to pay for every extra moment with my children. That it was worth it.

I kept repeating that over and over, willing myself to believe it.

CHAPTER 85

Folded

"Under pressure, would I fold and disappear, or would I show everyone that when bad things happen, you fight?"

— Drew Brees

I broke the agreement.

I couldn't do it again. My moral compass wouldn't let me.
I cut it off. Stopped picking up when Levi called. Stopped letting him believe he still had access to me.

I thought if I backed away quietly, it would all go away.

But it didn't.

Levi didn't take the rejection lightly and made sure of it.

It started with the emails. On the surface they looked professional, but the questions had nothing to do with the case.

They were fishing lines, tugging for a response. When I gave him nothing, he moved closer to what would hurt.

The visits changed. He told the foster mom I was unavailable, even when I was waiting. Extra time with my children disappeared without warning, carved away as if it meant nothing. I could feel his hand in every cancellation, every excuse that cut me out of their lives.

Then the paper trail began to shift. Notes carried slanted details. Call logs showed what he wanted them to show. Sign-in sheets were recorded in ways that painted me as absent or unreliable. It was a slow bleed, piece by piece, until the story he wanted replaced the truth.

When the court pulled my file apart, all they saw was his version of me.

I confided in my court-appointed attorney about what was happening, but he warned me to stay quiet, said it would only make things worse. He gave me no guidance, no protection.

After the emails that went nowhere, after the visits he cut short, after the notes he slanted against me, I couldn't take it anymore. I filed a formal complaint with Levi's supervisor.

She shared it with the guardian ad litems, the state's attorney, and everyone tied to my case. They accused me of lying. I was no longer a mother fighting for her children. I was a manipulator, a woman inventing stories.

My very truth was under review. And in their hands, it became another excuse to silence, belittle, dehumanize, and discredit me.

But I had recordings. Pieces of our conversations they could not ignore. Faced with that proof, they had no choice but to acknowledge what had been done.

And still, their fury turned on me. They didn't care how it began or what he had promised. They didn't care that he used his position. They refused to see a caseworker abusing his power.

Instead, they saw me manipulating mine. In their eyes, I wasn't a victim. I was a woman who would do anything to get what she wanted.

My voice became a weapon. Another excuse. Another bullet point on the list of why I was unfit to be a mother.

Levi was pulled off my case, and after that CPS wanted nothing to do with me. Every door that had once cracked open slammed shut.

478

They hated me for what had happened, and they made sure I knew it.

I was furious at myself too. I should've kept going. That's what I told myself every night. Maybe Levi wasn't even trying to be cruel. Maybe he was more hurt than anything, convincing himself that what we had was real. With the way I failed to resist, maybe he even believed we were in a relationship. If I had endured a little longer, it was only a matter of time before he gave my children back to me.

But instead, I pulled away. And for what? To do the "right" thing?

After a lifetime of being used, discarded, and overlooked! I had taken whatever people dished out! And now I wanted something different?!

A little dignity?!

A little self-respect?!

And this was the moment I decided I just had to have it?! This was the moment I chose to draw the line?! When everything that mattered was hanging in the balance!

I was furious!

I played the game, and when it mattered most, I folded.

And now… I was paying for it.

CHAPTER 86

Not This Time

"As long as the world shall last, there will be wrongs; and if no man objected and if no man rebelled, those wrongs would last forever."

— Clarence Darrow

While the CPS case sat untouched, buried beneath silence and excuses, my criminal trial for child endangerment arrived. I had no reason to believe this trial would be any different from everything else they had already put me through. I knew exactly what I was up against. The same players. The same game. Every step of the way, the system had failed me. They created a story and worked backwards to make the facts fit.

Still, I clung to a sliver of hope. Maybe this would be the moment someone finally listened. Maybe the truth would finally matter. Maybe I would finally matter. But I knew better. I wasn't afraid of the truth. I was afraid of what they would turn it into. I had seen how easily the system twisted facts, how power trumped justice, and how a narrative built on lies could destroy lives.

That was the reality waiting for me in court. But before I could even step into the courtroom, I had to meet my public defender. The person who was supposed to fight for me, speak for me, and give the court no choice but to find me not guilty.

 I had hoped that he'd take one look at everything I'd been through and say, "Nah, we're not doing this." That he'd be the one to speak up, to tell the court this wasn't justice. This was wrong.

They walked me into a small conference room. That was where I saw him for the first time. And the moment he opened his mouth, I knew I was in this alone.

He didn't ask how I was doing. Didn't ask what happened. Didn't even ask if I understood the charges. He just glanced at the file in front of him and said, "The state's offering a deal." No introduction. No context. Just that.

A deal.

Like this was some kind of negotiation. Like this was a business transaction and not my life.

He told me, "Plead guilty to child endangerment and get a year of unsupervised probation." Said it like it was a favor. Like I was supposed to be thankful.

But accepting that deal meant saying I was guilty. It meant confirming everything they had said about me. Reckless. Dangerous. Unfit. It meant putting a permanent stain on my name, on my record, and on my motherhood. And he expected me to accept it without hesitation, without resistance, without a voice.

I stared at him, waiting for the punchline. Because surely, this was a joke.

"Plead guilty?" I repeated. "To child endangerment?"

"You want me to plead guilty to harming my child?" My voice trembled, not with fear, but with a rising fury. I wasn't sure if I was going to cry or scream.

His eyes narrowed, his irritation bubbling just beneath the surface. "You need to be realistic," he snapped, leaning forward like proximity might make me fold. "You're not going to win this. Take the deal, avoid a harsher sentence, and move on with your life."

Move on with my life?

After everything they had done to me, he really thought I could just move on with my life. Like this was just a bad day. Like I hadn't been dragged through courtrooms, labeled reckless, stripped of my children, humiliated, lied on, and torn apart from the inside out. Like pleading guilty wouldn't follow me everywhere I went. Like it wouldn't mark me in ways I could never undo.

The audacity of it made my chest burn.

How could I move on from admitting to something so unthinkable? Every part of me rejected the idea. Pleading guilty to harming my son wasn't just a lie. It was a betrayal. It was an insult to the bond we shared, to every moment I had spent fighting for him.

I folded before, I was not doing it again. Definitely not with this. "No," I said, my voice low and trembling with barely contained rage. "I'm not pleading guilty."

That was all it took for him to explode. His frustration, barely held back, erupted across the table. His face turned red. He slammed the file shut, stood up, and leaned over me.

"Just accept the fucking deal!" he shouted, the words hitting like a slap.

My anger bubbled up, hot and unrelenting, and I could feel it pushing past the lump in my throat. Who the hell did he think he was? This man who didn't know me, didn't know my son, didn't care about the truth. He was trying to force me to accept a lie that would haunt me forever.

"You must've lost your damn mind," I shot back, my voice shaking with rage.

I shoved my chair back and stood, the sound of it scraping against the floor loud and final. I wasn't shrinking. Not for him. Not for anyone. I squared my shoulders, staring him down with everything I had left.

"You go in there," I said, each word deliberate, "and you do your fucking job. Because I'm not accepting the fucking deal."

He blinked. For a moment, he didn't move. The tension between us was thick enough to choke on. He stared at me, stunned, like he didn't know what to do with the version of me that stood in front of him. And I stared right back, daring him to speak, daring him to push harder. Because if I was going to plead guilty to anything, it damn sure wasn't going to be endangering the welfare of my child.

I turned and walked out, slamming the door behind me, hard enough to make it clear I was done being silent. Let it echo. Let it remind them I was still standing.

As I walked down the hallway, my heart pounded with a storm of anger, fear, and resolve. I didn't know what would happen next. But I knew one thing for sure. I wasn't giving up. This was my fight. And I wasn't stopping until justice was mine.

I didn't know how, because only minutes later, we were called into the courtroom.

As the public defender and I sat at the defense table, it was obvious how little had gone into my defense. He was flipping through pages like he had just picked them up. He hadn't reviewed anything with me, hadn't gone over a strategy, hadn't asked a single question about what actually happened. It was like he had been planning for a plea, and now that I had said no, he was stuck figuring out what to do next.

CHAPTER 87

The Burden of Proof

"The burden of proof is always on the one making the claim, not on the one denying it."

— Carl Sagan

I was never even supposed to have this public defender they handed me. My case was supposed to stay with the same court-appointed attorney who had been handling my CPS case. But a few weeks before trial, that attorney was caught trading sex for services.

Suddenly, everything I hadn't understood before snapped into focus. He was the one who told me to stay quiet about Levi. Now I knew why. They weren't protecting me. They were protecting each other and themselves.

But I couldn't worry about that right now.

This wasn't family court. This wasn't CPS. This wasn't the same judge who had let CPS and the guardian ad litems control the narrative. This was criminal court. Here, they had to follow the rules. Here, the state had the burden of proof. They had to prove their case beyond a reasonable doubt.

The bailiff's voice cut through my thoughts. "All rise." My chest tightened as I pushed myself to my feet and took a steadying breath.

Whatever happened next would happen here, under oath, with evidence, in front of someone who was supposed to be neutral. When we were told to be seated, I folded my hands tightly in my lap and fixed my eyes on the bench.

The judge didn't smile. She didn't scowl. Her face gave nothing away. But she carried herself with the kind of quiet authority that told me she wasn't here for theatrics or games. She was here for the truth.

The state called its first witness.

When I saw her walk up to the stand, my whole body tensed. The CPS worker.

Not just any CPS worker. The woman who had filed for emergency custody of my children. The one who claimed they were at risk. The one who watched Seyvn drive my truck past the house and used that moment, to justify taking my kids.

I hated her. Not in a casual way. Not in a passing, temporary way. I hated her in a way I didn't even know I was capable of. I used to picture every horrible thing that could happen to her, and it still wasn't enough. She had taken my children, lied without flinching, and carried herself like it was a job well done. I wanted her to feel pain. Real pain. I didn't care how that made me sound. I didn't care if it wasn't right. When I looked at that wench, all I could think about was the nurse I once choked in a fit of rage. Wishing I could do the same to her.

When she walked up to the stand and raised her hand, I braced myself. I didn't know what was about to come out of her mouth. She had told the truth once before in family court, but that didn't mean she would do it again. Not here. Not with prosecutors watching. I had seen how people in this system could bend the truth, reshape it, or throw it out entirely. And she was one of them.

But when she started talking, she admitted the freezer incident was a game. She said it had been addressed, and I had responded appropriately. She didn't claim it was abuse. She didn't pretend I meant harm.

The prosecutor tried to push her, to cast doubt, but she remained firm.

Next, my children were called to testify.

One by one, they entered the courtroom, too small for the seats they were asked to fill, too young to be carrying the truth in a room full of adults trying to twist it. But they were calm. Clear. Unshaken.

Last was Enrique.

My Momma's Boy.

He climbed into the witness chair with the bailiff's help, his little legs swinging, eyes wide but focused. He found me and smiled. I smiled back.

The prosecutor softened her tone as if speaking to a toddler, but I knew exactly what she was doing.

"Enrique, do you remember living with your mom?"

"Yes," he answered.

"Did your mom ever do anything that made you feel scared at home?"

He squinted a little, thinking. "No."

"Not even when she put you in the freezer?"

"It was a game," he said, shaking his head. "We were playing I love you more."

The prosecutor's smile tightened. "Did your mom close the lid on you?"
He shook his head. "No. She never closed it. I was in her hands the whole time."

"Are you sure?"

"I'm sure," he said. "She was holding me. Until I took it back. She won that time, but I'm gonna win next time."

The judge leaned forward slightly, her expression softening as she addressed him directly. "And how did you feel when your mom played that game with you?"

Enrique looked right at her. "I felt love."

In that moment, I could feel the weight lifting. The truth was out there, undeniable and unshakable. My son, my beautiful, brave boy, had spoken from his heart. And the judge listened.

At the close of all evidence, it didn't take long for the judge to render her decision. She didn't mince words. "This court finds the defendant not guilty," she said firmly.

Her tone carried a hint of frustration, as though she, too, was angered by the waste of time and resources. The trial was over. I was free.

The public defender offered a half-hearted apology for his earlier behavior. But his words meant nothing to me. I didn't need his apology. I needed accountability.

But for now, I'd take the Not Guilty.

CHAPTER 88

Together Again

"Reunited and it feels so good."

— Peaches & Herb

After the situation with Levi, everything stalled. CPS stopped answering my calls, stopped moving the case forward, stopped pretending they cared. They let my file sit, collecting dust, while my kids sat in foster care with no timeline, no urgency, and no plan.

Every time I complied, they changed the rules. Every time I asked for help, they found a reason to ignore me. I had done everything they asked, more than they asked, and it still wasn't enough.

Not because I was unfit. Not because I was a danger. But because I didn't play by their rules. I challenged them. I argued back. I didn't accept the crumbs they tossed at me, and they hated me for it.

So, they decided to punish me. They twisted everything I did. One late visit turned into a claim that I was always late. One missed phone call became an excuse to say I wasn't trying hard enough. They didn't care about the truth. They cared about power. They wanted to show me who was in charge, no matter how much it hurt my children.

But the child endangerment charge that CPS had wielded like a weapon had been dismantled. The judge's not guilty ruling had stripped them of their flimsy excuse for keeping my children away and court was coming up. They couldn't keep stalling forever. They needed to save face. They needed someone who could clean up the mess they made and make it look like progress.

That's when they brought in Sheree.

She was different. From the moment she was assigned to my case, I could feel it. She listened. She didn't roll her eyes or talk over me or make excuses for the way I'd been treated. She paid attention. She saw the damage CPS had caused, not just to me but to my children. She saw how far I had come, how hard I had fought, and how little they had done to support any of it.

Where the others stalled, Sheree moved. Where they ignored me, she answered. Where they made excuses, she found solutions. She didn't try to defend what had happened before she came on. She called it out for what it was. She didn't let them twist the facts or hide behind vague policies. She held them accountable. She did the work.

Sheree wasn't there to play politics. She was there to reunite a family.

She reminded me what real advocacy looked like.

And because of her, everything changed.

"Your kids are coming home," she said.

For a second, I thought I had misheard her. Those four words hung in the air, almost too heavy to believe. My heart stopped, my body went still. I had played this moment over in my head a thousand times, whispering it to myself in the dark, clinging to it when I had nothing else to hold onto. But to hear it spoken out loud, here and now, was different.

I stared at her, not breathing. Not blinking. I had imagined this moment so many times that I wasn't sure if it was real.

But then she smiled, that small but certain smile that only Sheree could give, and I felt it. It was real.

I threw my arms around her, the tears coming before I could stop them. She held me without hesitation.

Sheree was the light in the darkest chapter of my life, and I owed her more than words could ever express.

"Thank you," I choked out. "Thank you for fighting for me. For them."

"They belong with you," she said quietly. "We can't let fools raise our children."

She meant it. The foster mom had a trip coming up, and instead of shuffling my children to another respite home like they usually did, Sheree made the only decision that made sense.

She brought them home.

For days, I replayed those words in my head, hardly daring to believe them. And then the moment came.

When my children walked through the door, it was as if the house came alive again. Their faces lit up with excitement, their voices filled the rooms with laughter and chatter, and their energy shifted the entire atmosphere. They were home, and they knew it.

But beneath their joy, I could see the toll those eight months had taken. Their trust in the world was fractured, their confidence shaken. My youngest clung to me tightly, her small arms wrapped around my neck as if she feared I might disappear again. My son's once-bright eyes held a flicker of uncertainty, a hesitance I hadn't seen before. My oldest, always the strong one, struggled to readjust to her role as a sister after months of being forced to grow up too quickly.

That night, as I tucked them into their beds, I made a silent vow to each of them. We would rebuild. We would heal. I would do whatever it took to restore the trust and stability that had been stolen from them. The system had caused so much damage, but it couldn't erase the love that bound us together.

491

I thought of Sheree as I sat holding my youngest, her tiny hand gripping mine as she drifted off to sleep. Sheree, who had fought for us when no one else would. Sheree, who had seen through the lies and bureaucracy and made it her mission to bring my children home.

Thanks to her my children were here, safe in their beds, and I would spend every day proving to them that nothing, not the system, not the past, not another person, would ever take them from me again.

CHAPTER 89

No

"No Today Doesn't Mean No Tomorrow."

— Yvonne Orji

For years, fear was my shadow. After my children were returned, it became my constant companion. I rarely left the house, barely breathed outside its walls. The walls stood as silent witnesses to my guilt, my anxiety, and my endless "what ifs." The same "what ifs" that CPS had weaponized against me. What if Seyvn came back? What if CPS knocked on my door again? What if the system failed me the way it always had?

Five years passed like that, years of waiting, hiding, and watching. I moved, but not far, convincing myself he would never think to look so close. I erased myself from the world. No social media. No trace to follow.

I hated it. The fear, the silence, the memories, the years of isolation. They ate at me. Isolation had always been my go-to, but something had to give.

I didn't know what the future would hold, but I knew I couldn't keep hiding. Not from Seyvn. Not from CPS. And not from myself.

What happened to my family was not just a personal tragedy. It was a travesty. A system riddled with indifference, incompetence, and injustice left scars far deeper than separation. When the court finally returned my children, I thought the nightmare was ending. I believed the fight was behind me. But the echoes of that fight followed me into every corner of my life.

I still saw the faces of attorneys who dismissed me as if my pain was an inconvenience. I still felt the sting of a judge who barely acknowledged I was human. I still heard the voice of a public defender screaming in my face, demanding I accept a deal for a crime I hadn't committed. Those moments didn't fade. They replayed in my mind like a broken record, a constant reminder of the contempt and cruelty I had endured.

Every one of those memories was unacceptable. Every one of them fed a fire inside me. The more I thought about it, the clearer it became. The system had not just failed me. It had betrayed me.

It had tried to break me and call it justice. It tore my world apart, piece by piece, and called it due process. They stole my children and dressed it up as protection. They charged me with crimes I did not commit and disguised it as accountability. They looked me in the eyes and told me to accept the unacceptable.

I was done hiding. They had taken everything they could, but I was still here and that was enough to start reclaiming my life.

The journey back to myself started with a decision. I realized that if I wanted to make sure no one else endured what I had, I had to understand the system that had failed me. So, I decided to fulfill my childhood dream and become an attorney.

With that decision came a new battle. The path to higher education was not just uphill. It was littered with roadblocks, and the first one came fast. My technical school withheld my transcripts because I owed six thousand dollars. No transcripts meant no enrollment. No enrollment meant no way forward.

I called the school again and again, desperate for someone to help. Every conversation ended the same. No release without full payment. It didn't matter how many times I explained my situation. It didn't matter that I had a plan to pay. To them I was nothing more than an account with a balance.

I was caught in a cruel loop. No job meant no money. No money meant no payment. No payment meant no transcripts. And without those transcripts, no future. The door stayed closed.

After exhausting every avenue, I decided to take a chance. I remembered a quote I had once heard from Kris Jenner: *If someone tells you no, you are talking to the wrong person.* And clearly, I had been talking to the wrong people.

So, I went higher. I wrote directly to the president of the school. I poured my heart into that email, explaining my dreams, my determination, and how much was riding on one simple step forward. Truthfully, I didn't expect much. I had been told no so many times that hope felt like a distant luxury.

To my shock, he answered. He acknowledged my email, and more than that, he agreed to release one copy of my transcripts. Just one copy. But that was all I needed.

I set up a payment plan right away. Every installment was more than money. It was a promise to myself that I would not let debt or bureaucracy decide who I was or who I could become.

With that single transcript, I enrolled at Wilmington University. I attacked school like my life depended on it. Eight classes each semester. Long nights. Early mornings. I poured everything into it. Most of my grades were As, with a few Bs scattered in, each one a step away from fear and a step toward the courtroom where I planned to stand for people who were overlooked, unheard, abused and accused.

I knew grades alone wouldn't get me to law school. So when a guest speaker from the Department of Justice came to one of my classes and offered internship opportunities, I saw it as a chance to step into the world I had been fighting for. It felt like the door I had been banging on for years was finally opening.

I submitted my application with confidence, believing my work ethic spoke for itself.

Then the background check came back.

I had a criminal record.

An arm- length criminal record.

I stared at it in disbelief. I knew I had charges in my past, but I had never expected to see them laid out like this. Dismissed charges. Acquittals. The ones that had stuck. All clumped together in black and white, painting a version of me that felt like a stranger.

The assault on the nurse. The worthless check. The disorderly conduct for trying to protect Noah. The assault charge when Seyvn claimed I hit him with a pipe. The child endangerment.

It was all there.

Every misstep. Every accusation. A record that told nothing about fear, trauma, or survival. Only labels. Labels that made me look like someone I didn't even recognize.

But I refused to let the system paint who I was. That record was not a reflection of me. It was a reminder. A warning. Proof that no matter how hard you fight forward, the past will try to pull you back.

I learned something that day that everyone should know.

Dismissed does not mean erased. Charges do not vanish on their own. Expungement is not automatic. If you want your name back, you have to fight for it.

So, I did.

I gathered records. I filled out petitions. I paid the fees, got fingerprinted, and waited for judges to review the files. Each time a petition was granted, a file sealed, or a charge wiped away, it was one more step forward.

And through it all, I kept going. Studying. Writing papers. Raising my children. Paying my debt. Cooking dinner.

Checking homework. Tucking my kids into bed.

By the time the dust settled, I had more than a transcript and a handful of grades. I had proof. Proof that persistence could carve a path where none seemed to exist.

I graduated cum laude with a Bachelor of Science in Legal Studies.

CHAPTER 90

Third Time's a Charm

"Our greatest glory is not in never falling, but in rising every time we fall."

— Confucius

I went in there all willy nilly, like it was just another exam. No studying. No research. I hadn't done anything except sign up.

I showed up with a number two pencil and confidence.

The second I opened that booklet, I realized I should have stayed home, made myself a sandwich, and took a nap. I sat there like, *what in the fresh hell is this?* This was not the kind of exam you could wing.

See, the LSAT is not a normal test. It is not about what you know, it is about how your brain works under pressure. It came with four main parts.

First there's logical reasoning. which consists of reading short arguments and finding the flaw or figuring out what strengthens or weakens the argument.

Then there's analytical reasoning, better known as logic games. That's where they're like, "Six people are sitting in five chairs. Bob can't sit next to Sarah. Sarah refuses to sit on Tuesday. Who's sitting where?" And you're supposed to figure that out like you're Sherlock Holmes.

Next is reading comprehension. They'll give you four pages about the mating rituals of moths in Eastern Europe, and then hit you with fifteen questions like, "What was the author's tone in paragraph three?" reading comprehension was likely trying to cure insomnia.

And for a little razzle dazzle, they throw in a writing sample. Nobody even grades it, but you still gotta sit there like, "Yes, let me write an essay on why we should build a parking garage or a playground." Sir, I am fighting for my future. Why am I arguing about swing sets?

Everybody always said the logic games were the hardest part, but I actually liked them. My brain has never been great at the obvious stuff. You want me to balance a checkbook? Nah, that's gonna take me all day. But you want me to figure out who sits in chair number four if Greg refuses to sit next to Susan? Oh, I got that.

Still, enjoying the games was not enough to carry the whole test. I walked out that exam knowing two things. One, I was not getting into law school with the 144 I received. And two, if I wanted a higher score, I was going to have to study like my life depended on it.

This wasn't just a hoop to jump through. It was the whole obstacle course, and I had shown up in flip-flops.

So, I went home and did what I should have done the first time. I studied the exam inside and out. I read everything I could find. I made a plan. I signed up for a tutor. I built study blocks that coincided with the kid's schedules.

When I took the LSAT the second time, I expected more. I had worked with a tutor, done practice sets, and put in effort I thought would carry me. But when the score came back, it was a 146.

Only two points higher.

That 146 was enough to get me a conditional admission into the TAP program. TAP, or the Trial Admissions Program, was basically a back door into law school. You were admitted, but only on the condition that you took summer courses and proved you could handle the work before they let you all the way in. That was not good enough for me. I was not operating under conditions anymore. I wanted in, fully.

If a tutor only got me two points higher, that service wasn't serving me. I let it go and trusted myself to figure it out.

By then I was deep into my master's program in criminal justice, and that gave me a new kind of discipline. Graduate school forced me to think critically, write faster, and analyze systems instead of reacting to them. I started applying those same skills to LSAT prep.

I studied differently, weaving prep into the daily routine of cooking, checking homework, and tucking kids into bed. But when the house was quiet, I tore into that prep.

I drilled the questions that gave me trouble instead of the ones I liked. Reading comprehension was my weakest section. Those passages were written like they were designed to put me to sleep.

So, I made them interesting.

If the passage was about clouds, I turned it into a storyline. Cirrus was the high and mighty one, always floating above everybody else, acting all stuck up. Cumulus was the show-off, big and loud, always trying to make an entrance like, "Look at me." And then here come Nimbostratus, dark and heavy, storming in with drama, ruining the whole vibe.

I treated every passage like it was an urban book with characters I could see and hear. Once I did that, the section I dreaded most became the one that made me laugh my way through.

I also sought accommodations. Extra time. A quiet room. Space to show what I knew without the panic.

When I sat for the LSAT the third time, it felt different. I was calmer. I could see the arguments more clearly. I finished sections with focus.

The score came back a 152. Modest, maybe, but enough to turn a locked gate into an open one. With it, Delaware Law said yes, and they backed it with a Dean's Scholarship.

Law school was more than education, more than a degree, more than becoming a lawyer. It was one step closer to changing a system that had once tried to bury me.

CHAPTER 91

An Uphill Battle

"It is not the mountain we conquer but ourselves."

— Sir Edmund Hillary

The work hit like a wave. Casebooks as thick as bricks. Reading that never seemed to end. One cold call could split your chest open if you weren't ready. In law school, one exam usually decided your entire grade. No makeup. No extra credit. No second shot. Learn it or pay for it.

My first year was rough. My GPA barely stayed above the 2.0 threshold. I had looked forward to criminal law more than any other class, and somehow, I walked out with a D. The disappointment cut deep. But at the end of the day, D stood for Degree, and it was enough to keep me from academic dismissal.

I took Professional Responsibility that summer determined to raise my GPA and give myself some breathing room. I earned an A, and it felt like a breakthrough. By the following semesters I had found my rhythm, and my grades began to climb. I even started to enjoy classes like Constitutional Law and Criminal Procedure.

They had once seemed intimidating, but the deeper I dug into them, the more they became my favorites.

One professor noticed the anxiety hidden in my rushed writing and encouraged me to seek accommodations for extra time. I had never asked for accommodations in college before, but once I did, everything shifted. My grades began to reflect my true ability, not the ticking of a clock.

Still, it wasn't all smooth sailing. My Legal Writing professor seemed to have it out for me. She called on me relentlessly, her critiques sharper with me than with anyone else. At first, I was convinced it was personal. She reminded me too much of my mother, from the golden hair to the hardworking hands, and it rattled me. Tough, unyielding, impossible to please, she made every class feel like an uphill battle.

When I finally vented to my mom, she surprised me with a different perspective. She reminded me that women like my professor had probably fought three times as hard to earn their place in academia, and maybe she was pushing me to rise to the same standard.

I couldn't say for sure if that was true, but it changed the way I carried myself in her class.

By the end, I respected her toughness, even if it stung in the moment. And truthfully, her class was just one more weight added to the load I was already carrying.

Law school alone was relentless, but balancing it with raising five children made every day feel like a test of endurance. I briefed cases in the bleachers at basketball games, outlined arguments in the school parking lot, and prepped for cold calls while stirring dinner on the stove.

My kids did not always understand why I was buried in books long after they had gone to bed, but they knew enough to be proud of what I was doing.

CHAPTER 92

Surviving a Princess

"Though she be but little, she is fierce."

— William Shakespeare

From the moment she was born, Lilly carried both light and shadow. She was loved, but the instability of her childhood made that love feel fragile, as if it could vanish overnight. Foster care, night terrors, and being torn from everything familiar left scars that never quite faded.

By the time Lilly started school, the damage was already done. She carried the weight of her early years into the classroom, even if no one else could see it. At first, her struggles were the kind no one could point to. There was fear in her eyes when routines changed. She clung to me at drop-off. Panic rose up over small things most children brushed aside. Those were the scars no one really noticed.

Then came the scars everyone noticed. Strange discolorations appeared on her skin, faint at first, then spreading until they could not be ignored. We went from doctor to doctor searching for an explanation, but none came. Each appointment ended the same way, with more questions than answers. While the adults puzzled over causes, the children around her needed none. They saw something different, and in the unforgiving world of a schoolyard, different was enough. They pointed. They whispered. They were cruel.

She would come home quiet, shoulders tense, her head low. When I asked her what was wrong, she whispered that the kids at school called her ugly, that they laughed at her skin. Those words clung to her and chipped away at her self-esteem.

505

It shattered me. She had already been through so much, torn from her family, shuffled between strangers, and now this? How much could one little girl carry?

I couldn't let those children be louder than the truth. I needed to remind her of who she was.

One evening, after yet another day of watching her crumble under their cruelty, I pulled her close and looked into her eyes. "If they're going to call you names," I told her, "Let them call you Princess."

For a second, she just blinked, as if she wasn't sure she heard me right.

"What do you mean?" she asked, intrigued.

"I'm changing your name to Princess," I said, a smile tugging at the corner of my mouth. "Now, every single person who wants to talk to you has no choice but to call you Princess. Whether they like it or not."

She laughed then. Not just any laugh, but a soft, unexpected sound that seemed to surprise even her. And in that moment, it was beautiful.

And it was true. I had always called her my Perfect Princess, saying it so often, it had practically become her name already. Now it was official. It was supposed to be a shield, a name to protect her, to remind her of who she was in a world trying to convince her otherwise.

But behind the name was still a little girl quietly weathering storms no one else could feel.

As Princess grew older, it became painfully clear that her struggles stretched far beyond the teasing she endured at school.

By six or seven, there were already signs that something deeper was unraveling inside her. What began as typical childhood tantrums evolved into violent, unpredictable outbursts.

The smallest things could set her off. Losing a game. Someone brushing past her while she colored. Being told no. In a blink she would reach for whatever was close, knives, scissors, a broom, and swing at whoever was near.

It was terrifying.

There was no warning, no buildup. One second, she was quiet, and the next, we were scrambling to keep everyone safe. It was rage too big for such a small body.

Her eyes would darken, distant yet fixed on whoever had set her off. We learned not to trust her face alone. We scanned the room, measuring what could be used, what could be broken, what could be turned into a weapon. We knew the sounds that meant danger and how fast we had to move when they came. Most times it was mere seconds.

Our home turned into a fortress. Locks were installed on every bedroom door, alarms placed on door frames. Cabinets secured. Not to protect us from the outside world but to protect us from what was already inside it. Princess.

We tried everything. Princess was put on countless medications, each one promising relief but delivering none. Therapy became a part of our daily lives. Therapists cycled in and out of our home, sometimes even on weekends, each one offering new strategies that never seemed to stick. Despite all these efforts, nothing changed. If anything, things got worse.

No matter how hard I tried, the help we desperately needed never came.

I reached out to the county for support, pleading for resources, for guidance, for anything. I explained everything. The erratic behavior. The violent outbursts. The fear that settled in my chest every time my children had to lock their bedroom door at night. I told them I was doing everything I could to get her help, but it wasn't enough. I was met with cold indifference. They told me they only help kids who are abused.

I struggled to process their words. So, the only way you will help is if I hurt my daughter? I was pleading for protection, trying to keep us safe, trying to keep her safe, and once again the very system designed to help was refusing to act.

The state that was supposed to help only showed up when it was too late, after the damage was done and after the headlines forced them to. Then they would have the audacity to act outraged, as if they had not ignored every warning, every report, and every call for help along the way.

I couldn't wait for that.

I hated this system, suffered under it, lost *everything* to it. And yet, here I was, standing at its doors, begging it for help.

I was drowning, desperate, and out of options. Even a broken system had to be better than no help at all.

My daughter was losing herself to something I couldn't help her with. She believed she had a direct connection with the Devil. She thought she and the Devil's daughter, whom she called Genie, were best friends. She heard voices that told her to kill her family and she listened.

One night she slipped into her brother's room with a knife. He had fallen asleep across the bed without locking his door. I caught her at the doorway and wrestled the knife from her hands as I begged her to come back.

In those moments she was not my little girl. She was someone else. She had the kind of *superhuman* strength that only ever seemed to exist in movies. And no matter how hard I fought to pull her back, to bring her *home*, it was like the thing inside her kept winning.

She spoke to people no one else could see. She reacted to things no one else could feel. The room could be calm and still and she would flinch as if something had just struck her. Eventually the doctors put a name to it, adjustment disorder.

But even that felt incomplete.

We kept trying. Medications. Therapy. In home sessions. The storms didn't ease.

In sheer desperation, I faced a choice that tore at my heart. The state would not step in without grounds of abuse. Without that, every plea for help was ignored.

I lived with the fear that one day I would not be fast enough, that one night one of my children would not make it through the storm. The weight of that truth left me with no way out.

So, I did the unthinkable. I filled out the paperwork to give up custody of her to the state. With every line I wrote, I felt I was betraying her and protecting her at the same time. My hand shook as I signed my name. It was not a request. It was surrender.

I was terrified, not only of losing her, but of what would happen to all of us if I did nothing.

Their response?

"If you submit the paperwork to give custody of your daughter to the state, you will be charged with abandonment."

Not we will help you. Not let us get her the care she needs.

They threatened to criminalize me as if I were a heartless mother discarding her child. As if I was not on my knees, begging for someone, anyone, to step in before it was too late.

I could not risk criminal charges, not with four other children depending on me, not with our lives already unraveling. So, we did what we always did. We kept surviving.

This time, we were surviving a Princess.

CHAPTER 93

The Breaking Point

"The truth is still the truth, even if no one believes it."

— David Stevens

Abigail with tears streaming down her face. Her shoulders shaking as she spoke, "Mommy, I'm sad most of the time. The only time I feel at peace is when I'm in the shower or asleep because those are the only two places Princess can't bother me."

My heart shattered.

No child should ever feel that way in their own home.

Abigail, though older, had always been gentle and childlike. She was the kind of soul who would not hurt a fly, literally. Yet Princess targeted her constantly, feeding on her vulnerability.

I would not let Abigail keep living in turmoil. I refused to be the mother who found her daughter hurt, or worse, because I hadn't done enough to protect her.

I thought separating them would help. Give them both space to breathe.

But of course, life had other plans.

Abigail had been pouring her heart into cosmetology, something that gave her joy. She was so proud of her work, carefully styling her mannequin head, her face glowing with accomplishment.

Then Princess destroyed it. She took scissors and cut the hair off. Abigail came to me devastated, sobbing over what Princess had done. And I was livid.

I stormed into Princess's room, blood boiling.

"Why would you do that?" I demanded, my voice shaking with fury.

Princess just stared at me. Cold. Emotionless. Like I wasn't even standing there.

She sat there smug, daring me to react. And in that moment, after years of watching her torment this house, especially Abigail, my sweet, gentle girl who wouldn't even step on an ant, I snapped.

Her room was museum clean. Absolutely spotless. Clothes neatly folded, everything in perfect order.

I grabbed those folded clothes and threw them in the air.

Then I yanked open her drawers and hurled every piece of clothing across the room. I ripped the drawer out and slammed it onto her bed.

I seized her favorite Barbie and drove it into the footboard until my arms ached. The plastic clicked and the wood thudded.

I tore open the closet. Ripped shirts off hangers and threw them too. Clothes lifted and drifted like snow while hangers clacked against the floor.

In that instant I had lost my own mind. I stormed out of her room and yelled for her to clean it up.

It wasn't my proudest moment. Parenting isn't always graceful. But I wanted her to feel at least a fraction of what Abigail had felt. To know what it was like to be antagonized.

Princess didn't say a word. I heard her slam the door but I didn't care.

I thought it was over.

It wasn't.

Hours later, there was a hard knock at the door.

I opened it to find two police officers standing there.

"What's going on, Officers?" I asked, confused.

One of them, a tall, stone-faced man, with a blue lives matter face mask on, sneered down at me. His tone was cold, condescending.

"We received a report that you struck your daughter with a Barbie doll, a belt, and threw a dresser on her."

I froze.

"Wait, I did WHAT?" My voice shot up in disbelief.

Princess had called the police. She had fabricated an entire story.

I was stunned.

The officer didn't care about the truth. He wasn't interested in hearing my side. I was guilty the second he stepped onto my porch.

All that mattered was that they had a report, and suddenly I was the problem. The danger. The villain in my home.

One of the officers stepped forward, looking around, his eyes sharp and judgmental.

"Where is your daughter?" he asked coldly.

"She's upstairs," I said, my voice tight but steady.

Princess came down the stairs slowly, like she was putting on a show. Her face was carefully blank, void of emotion, yet I knew better. This was calculated.

The officer knelt down slightly to meet her eye level. "Sweetheart, can you tell me what happened?"

Without missing a beat, Princess repeated the story she gave 911.

"She hit me with a doll. And a belt. And she threw a dresser on me."

Her voice was small, fragile, perfectly rehearsed.

I stood there in disbelief.

I wanted to scream, to demand that they see through this act.

"She's lying," I said, forcing my voice to stay calm. "That didn't happen. Nothing like that happened."

The officer's eyes narrowed slightly. "Ma'am, we're going to need you to be quiet, this is an active investigation and you're impeding on it."

Princess stood there quietly, a flicker of delight dancing in her eyes, hidden in plain sight.

She knew what she had done.

They called in Child Protective Services. Again.

Frustrated and exhausted, I said, "If you think something is wrong with her, then take her with you!" It wasn't a challenge. It was a plea.

The officer's cold stare didn't waver. His response cut through the air like a knife.

"The only person we're going to be taking anywhere is you."

My breath caught in my throat.

I tried to steady my voice as I explained again about Princess's long history of mental health struggles. I told them about the diagnoses, the therapists, the endless sessions, the medications that never seemed to work. I told them about the in-home counselors who came by almost daily, even on weekends, trying to reach her.

I told them how every door in my house had locks and alarms to protect my other children, how I had done everything humanly possible to keep my family safe.

But it didn't matter.

Their faces remained expressionless, cold, and unbothered. It was like talking to statues. No understanding. No compassion. Just judgment.

To them, I wasn't a mother on the edge trying to protect her family.

I was dramatic. Defensive. A woman making excuses to cover her own wrongdoing.

One look at Princess's soft, sweet face and they had already decided who was telling the truth.

Her apparent innocence made her believable. My desperation made me guilty.

They didn't see her diagnosis, her history, or the help I had begged for.

They saw a child with big eyes and a trembling voice, and a mother who must be lying.

There was no female officer on scene to check her, so I asked for a supervisor. When he arrived, he told them to stand down.

That there was no evidence of a crime.

I thought that would be the end of it.

I was wrong. Blue Lives Matter mask couldn't let it go.

He came back, again and again, knocking on my door like I owed him something. Calling from blocked numbers. Leaving voicemails. Coming over throughout the day and night. Each attempt louder than the last, like my silence was some kind of defiance he couldn't tolerate.

He acted like I was obligated to explain myself, to open the door and hand him a confession.

I didn't care if he knocked on that door all day. He could camp on my porch. I still wasn't answering.

By then, I was in my third year of law school. I knew exactly what my rights were, and I had every intention of exercising them. I wasn't about to hand over anything he could twist into something it wasn't.

When he realized I wasn't going to play his game, he issued a warrant for my arrest.

Child Abuse.

That's what he came up with. The police report filled with outright lies. He claimed I had confessed to hitting my daughter.

A complete fabrication. It stated details that were not only false but impossible to reconcile with reality.

I wasn't worried. I knew the truth. And more importantly, I knew the law.

I wasn't about to let him drag me out of my house in front of my children especially not in front of Princess. He wasn't going to have that power over me and neither was she. I turned myself in on my own terms, head held high.

At booking, the officer glanced at the charge, then back at me. A flicker of disbelief crossed his face.

He shook his head slightly. "I'm sorry you're going through this."

This charge was the least of my worries. I had one of the best criminal defense attorneys in the state in my corner, my evidence professor. The case barely made it past the first appearance before he shut it down.

Dismissed. Expunged.

The system had put my life under review again, twisting my motherhood into a crime. They tried to punish me for refusing to be quiet, for daring to stand up. They thought I would roll over and accept the story they forced on me, but they were wrong.

All they did was add another obstacle.

A little derailment wasn't going to stop me.

I graduated law school.

CHAPTER 94

So Be It

"I am the master of my fate, I am the captain of my soul."

— William Ernest Henley

The first time I sat for the bar exam, in my home state, the experience was nothing short of a nightmare. I had been granted accommodations, a separate room and extended time to level the playing field because of my ADHD, PTSD, and other diagnoses. But instead of fairness, I was met with mayhem.

Two proctors were assigned to me, and it was as if they had been instructed to make the experience unbearable. One coughed nonstop, an unsettling sound during the height of COVID-19. The other typed incessantly, each keyboard click slicing through my concentration. The interviewer's phone rang, breaking the already tense atmosphere. As if that weren't enough, my computer crashed three separate times during the exam, forcing me to restart and fight to stay focused despite the mounting frustration.

And then there was the smell.

One of the proctors shamelessly passed gas, the stench filling the room, thick and revolting. It lingered, heavy and foul, like rotten eggs or garbage truck juice baking under the summer sun. It turned an already difficult situation into a nearly impossible one.

This was the most important exam of my life, and instead, it felt like I was set up to fail. I had studied relentlessly, juggling motherhood and coursework, pushing myself harder than I ever had. Failing that exam hit me like a brick. I was devastated. For two weeks, I sank into a fog of disappointment, convinced I would never take that exam again.

But I didn't stay there. I picked myself up and pivoted toward the Uniform Bar Exam. I threw myself into studying, harder, smarter, with a fire that failure had ignited. This time, I was determined not just to survive the process, but to win.

And then came the day that everything changed.

I remember exactly where I was when the email came through. Rayna and I were sitting in the living room, chatting about something I can't even recall now because that moment eclipsed everything. My phone buzzed, and I casually glanced down, expecting just another notification. But it wasn't just any alert. It was from the State Board of Bar Examiners.

Scores had been released.

My heart jumped into my throat. My hands trembled as I scrambled to log in, each second dragging on for what felt like hours. I was fumbling, fingers shaking over the keyboard, holding my breath as I clicked through the portal. And then it appeared.

"Congratulations "

I didn't read another word. I didn't need to. I screamed, loud and raw, and Rayna screamed with me, even before knowing why. After everything, I had done it. I had passed the Bar.

For the first time, it felt like my dream was within reach. I could breathe again. The relief did not just wash over me. It soaked in. It settled my bones. It made the years of strain feel worth it.

Then came the part no class prepares you for.

Character and Fitness.

While most people barely think twice about it, for me it became a mountain I never saw coming. I believed honesty, transparency, and hard work would be enough. Instead, the very system I had worked so hard to join, the one sworn to uphold justice, turned everything I had lived, every page you have just read, into the reason I didn't belong.

I had rebuilt my whole life. I had worked. I had learned. I had changed. I had believed the system would see me as I am now, not as a collection of headlines and rumors and old wounds.

Instead, I watched them turn my life into exhibits.

The first hearing was for the Uniform Bar Jurisdiction. The panel sat in a neat line, pens ready. They asked about everything. My relationships. My history with Child Protective Services. The day my children were removed when I was begging for help. They asked about the freezer incident even though the case had been expunged. They asked about my daughter's false police report and how it twisted the truth. They asked about people I had known who had criminal records.

They lifted the hardest pieces of my life and held them up to the light as if pain itself were evidence.

Despite the intensity, I answered every question with honesty and integrity. I didn't shy away from my past. I owned it, because those experiences had shaped me into the person sitting before them. They sharpened my determination and gave me the strength to keep going when everything seemed stacked against me.

I was not ashamed of my story. It is the foundation of who I became. My struggles made me kind, empathetic, and fiercely protective of justice. They taught me to advocate not only for myself but for others. They also gave me a depth of understanding no textbook could provide and a compassion that can't be faked.

Eight witnesses waited to speak for me. They never took the stand. The panel said my testimony had covered what they needed to hear. I had also submitted more than ten letters from judges, professors, and colleagues. People who had watched me grind. People who had seen the work, not just the wreckage.

My attorney was full of assurance when the hearing concluded.

He said we were in a good place. He said a decision would come soon.

Soon never came.

Days turned to weeks. The silence grew loud.

Then I was told the Uniform Bar Jurisdiction would not move forward until my home state admitted me. It made no sense.

When I sat for that hearing I had not even taken the home state exam again. I wasn't even required to take it. I didn't even want to retake it. And even if I did take it, there was no guarantee I would pass.

None of that mattered. Another door closed, and nobody would say why.

When I asked my attorney to push for an answer, he told me it was improper to question a tribunal.

That response was frustrating, illogical, and inexcusable. I wasn't challenging authority. I just wanted clarity.

Why did that state get to hold the power to decide my future? This was my dream, and I wasn't going to let anyone take it from me.

So, I did the only thing I could do.

I turned toward the next mountain. Since the Uniform Bar Jurisdiction insisted I wait for my home state's decision, I made it my mission to conquer that exam.

If that's what it was going to take, then so be it. I would take the exam again.

I built a new study plan. I set quiet alarms on my phone. I cleared my schedule of anything that didn't matter. I threw myself into studying with everything I had.

I didn't have the luxury of study breaks or quiet time. If I wasn't eating or using the bathroom, I was studying.

The only way to make time for my kids was to pull them into it with me. I gave each of them an hour a day, one by one, where they would sit with me, quiz me, and hold me accountable.

They thought I was slow sometimes, and they didn't hide it. They rolled their eyes, sighed, and complained when I missed something. But they kept showing up for me anyway.

Somewhere in that process, they started to understand. They caught a glimpse of what it had felt like all those years when I suffered with them through their homework, late nights, tears, and frustration, refusing to give up on them. Now the roles were reversed. They were the ones pushing me forward, keeping me in the fight, making sure I did not give up on myself.

With their support wrapped around me, I could not afford to fail. Not after everything we had endured. Not with everything on the line.

Still, part of me carried the scars of my first attempt. That experience had been a nightmare. For a while I was not even sure I wanted to put myself through it again. But then I watched LeBron James break the NBA all-time scoring record, and something inside me clicked.

If he could commit to greatness, so could I.

I decided I was gonna be the LeBron James of bar exams. I was gonna outwork every obstacle, rise above every challenge, and make sure nothing stood in my way, not people, not proctors, not even myself.

CHAPTER 95

Surviving Character and Fitness

"Be more concerned with your character than your reputation, because your character is what you really are, while your reputation is merely what others think you are."

— John Wooden

Not only did I pass my home state's bar exam, but I also crushed it. My Contracts essay, the very subject that had been my second lowest score before, was selected as a model answer. Something I once struggled with was now the gold standard.

You'd think that would be the end of the road. My home state exam was complete, and the Uniform Bar Jurisdiction had been waiting for that result. It should have been a simple next step.

But nothing about this journey had been simple.

My home state wasn't done with me yet.

When they couldn't stop me from passing, it felt like they weaponized the Character and Fitness process.

Walking into my first interview with the Board of Bar Examiners was like stepping into an ambush. No greeting, no courtesy, just a cold question hurled at me the moment I sat down.

"Did you put your son in the freezer?"

The words stunned me. Were they serious? A decade old expunged event, something I wasn't even required to disclose to them, was dragged out and thrown at me as their opening shot.

Unlike the UBE, my home state doesn't require disclosure of expunged matters. They weren't supposed to bring it up at all, yet here they were.

It felt calculated, like they wanted to break me before the interview even began.

That was only the start.

They asked about a worthless check from twenty years ago, demanding to know if I had been on a payment plan.

They pressed me about the Section 8 investigation from fifteen years earlier, when Wilma used my address, questioning why I described the outcome as "unfounded."

I had to explain the word's definition to attorneys who seemed more interested in catching me on a technicality than in hearing the truth.

Then came questions about my daughter Princess, another expunged matter they had no right to raise. The Uniform Jurisdiction had asked fair questions. This jurisdiction came armed with disdain in their voices and judgment in their eyes.

They accused me of lying.

It didn't matter what I said. I could have pointed to the sky and called it blue, and they would have labeled it a lie.

What made it worse was that they only had this information because I gave it to them. I had voluntarily provided every document I could find, even records no longer publicly accessible.

I wanted to show transparency. Instead, the more I gave, the more they demanded. They asked for the retention policy on a two-decade old check, and for proof I had contacted an attorney about the false police report filed against me. None of it was relevant, but I complied anyway.

526

Months passed in silence. I wrote a detailed four-page letter addressing every supposed inconsistency.

Still, nothing.

When I finally pressed for an update, they demanded more. This time the custody petition I had filed years earlier when I needed to obtain my children's passports.

A clerical error in that document, where a judge mistakenly wrote that Noah and I were never married, became their new fixation. Even though my petition itself clearly stated "ex-husband," they treated the error as if it were proof of deceit.

I understood the purpose of the Character and Fitness process, but this wasn't that. This was psychological warfare. I realized then that they weren't looking for truth. They were looking for something, anything, they could twist.

While my home state stalled, I focused on what I could control. I hired an attorney with deep experience in the Uniform Jurisdiction. Her fee was steep, but she knew the process inside out. Within weeks, she secured my admission there.

For the first time, I felt a measure of victory.

But my home state continued to drag its feet. Suddenly, after one of the law school deans reached out on my behalf, I was summoned for a second interview with different interviewers, they claimed.

By then, my father was dying. Junior, the man who raised me and loved me unconditionally, was fading before my eyes. My daughter was undergoing chemotherapy. My world was collapsing, and the bar's games felt trivial in comparison.

I wasn't interested in jumping through hoops for these people. As far as I was concerned, they could kick rocks. I'd take the fight straight to the highest court. If they wanted to play games, they'd have to do it without me.

I had no desire to go. The two people closest to me begged me to attend, hoping new interviewers might mean a fresh perspective. Against my better judgment, I agreed.

When I walked in, I saw the truth immediately. Two new faces, yes, but three of the same as before. Five in total. This was no interview. It was an inquisition. Their sheer number was suffocating, a deliberate tactic to make me feel small, overwhelmed, and outnumbered.

I took a slow breath and told myself to stay steady. I knew my limits that day. My father was slipping away. My daughter was fighting through chemo. I was there in body. My mind was scattered and my focus was shattered. I had started recording before I walked in. My state allows one party consent, and I knew I wouldn't absorb everything in real time.

As soon as I sat down, they began.

They opened with my credit report. Why are there so many variations of your name? I asked if they had read the first page.

The report explains that bureaus pull names from creditors, courts, and public records. Misspellings happen. Old married names linger. Middle initials get dropped or added.

If they had bothered to read the whole report, they would have seen that, but they chose accusation instead.

That set the tone. They moved from the credit report to whether I had paid the decade-old check on a plan, to Princess, to the earlier charge with Enrique.

They even questioned the significance of my work, one organization supporting survivors of domestic violence and another helping those who were incarcerated. They dissected my contributions as though they didn't matter, as though helping others wasn't significant enough for them.

But even if my contributions weren't significant to them, they were significant to me, and to the people I helped. To the survivors who found hope in moments of despair. To the individuals who felt seen, valued, and human, even in the darkest corners of their lives. That work wasn't just meaningful, it was transformative.

And then, as if all of that wasn't enough, they crossed a line I'll never forget. One of them, with smug certainty, started saying she'd been appointed to child protective cases several times.

She insisted there was no way on the planet they would take children without cause, treating the very idea as absurd, as if I were pathetic, delusional, or dishonest for even saying it out loud.

I looked at her and said, "Well, they took mine. Domestic violence isn't a reason to take someone's children. They could have helped me get away from that situation."

She looked straight through me, her voice like ice, as she said, "It's your own damn responsibility to remove yourself from that dangerous situation."

She knew nothing about me. Nothing about the impossible choices I'd made to stay alive, for my children to stay alive.

She didn't know the terror of running barefoot in the night, clutching your babies to your chest. She didn't know the humiliation of standing in court with a no contact order you knew couldn't stop a bullet. She didn't know what it meant to survive hell and still wake up every morning to make breakfast, tie shoes, and hold yourself together so your children didn't see you falling apart.

She'd never smiled through cracked ribs or cradled a crying child with fingers still swollen from the last time you tried to fight back. She'd never watched the news and seen another woman's face flash across the screen, murdered, missing, silenced, and wondered if she'd be next.

She didn't know what it was like to live in fear more than a decade later, checking over your shoulder, googling yourself every few months just to make sure your address hadn't leaked online. Because if he ever found you, your life could end.

So, when she sat across from me with her cold, rehearsed judgment, daring to suggest that the violence in my past was my fault, I knew she hadn't lived a single ounce of what I'd survived. She wasn't qualified to question me. And she sure as hell wasn't qualified to judge me.

Her cruelty was staggering. As a professional, as a woman, as a mother, her words were inexcusable.

I refused to react. That was what they wanted. For me to snap. For me to prove their story right. But I didn't give them the satisfaction.

To them, this was a game. They put my entire life under review, all to see how much they could throw at me before I broke.

But by that point….. I was unfuckingbreakable.

CHAPTER 96

The Petition

"Power concedes nothing without a demand. It never did and it never will."

— Frederick Douglass

Weeks later, as I grieved my father's death, their decision arrived: **DENIED**. They claimed I lacked the requisite fitness to practice law.

They had no idea what they had just ignited.

That denial was the beginning of a fight I looked forward to. It gave me exactly what I wanted, a path to the State Supreme Court. I poured every ounce of grief, frustration, and determination into a thirty-page petition that laid bare every violation, every injustice, every abuse they had inflicted on me.

With every page, I made it clear I was not backing down. I documented their relentless questioning about expunged records they were forbidden to use. I recorded the fishing expeditions into decades-old matters and their cruel remarks about my children and my past. I exposed their blatant disregard for their own rules and their refusal to engage with the truth I had placed in front of them.

I also called out what felt like retaliation. Retaliation for holding them accountable when they denied me the accommodations I needed during my first attempt at their bar exam. I had forced them to confront their failures, and now they were using the Character and Fitness process to make sure I paid for it with mine.

I raised another issue they couldn't ignore. Out of sixty-six board members, only one was African American. How could a board entrusted with evaluating the character and fitness of future attorneys be so unrepresentative of the profession and the

531

communities it serves? That imbalance was not cosmetic. It shaped outcomes.

For nearly a year they had dragged me through the mud, demanding irrelevant documents, interrogating me over my past, and wasting months in delay. But the moment I filed my petition, suddenly they could move at lightning speed. Almost as if they had been waiting for me to challenge them, they scheduled a hearing within two weeks.

When the hearing date was announced, they sent me an email listing the panel members. As I reviewed it, something immediately stood out. They had scrambled to stack the panel with diverse faces, no doubt to counter the lack of diversity I had highlighted. But their attempt to appear inclusive was careless, and worse, it was insulting.

They hadn't even performed a basic conflicts check. One of the panelists worked at the same firm as my attorney, the same counsel who had represented me in my earlier battle with them. They knew who he was. They knew where he worked. The conflict was not subtle. It was undeniable.

I raised it immediately, letting them know I intended to have that same attorney represent me again.

Their response arrived in clipped language: "Please accept this email as notice that the October 30, 2024 hearing and October 15, 2024 pre-hearing conference are vacated. Once your attorney enters his appearance we will reschedule."

It was outrageous. There was no valid reason to vacate the hearing. Replacing the compromised panelist would have solved the problem. Instead, they canceled the entire hearing and pointed to my decision to hire counsel as the reason, as though exercising my rights was the issue rather than their own incompetence.

I wrote back immediately: "Vacating the hearing without any further communication appears to perpetuate unnecessary delays, and I am unequivocally not in agreement with vacating the actual hearing date. I have not and would not make that request regardless of whether I hire the attorney."

Their reply was just as hollow: "Given the issues raised in your email below (including that you intend to hire counsel to represent you at the hearing), the Board is vacating the notice of the October 30 hearing and will circulate an amended notice. The fact that one of the current panel members works at the attorney's firm triggered the Board to reconsider her appointment, and the October 30 hearing date is no longer viable."

And with that, they fell silent, as if I were to blame for their failure to conduct the conflicts check.

Two weeks later, my attorney formally entered his appearance.

That same day, the Board contacted him directly to say they were withdrawing their denial.

There would be no hearing.

According to my attorney, they admitted they had made mistakes. They conceded they were not permitted to use my expunged record and offered an apology. But not to me. Their apology was quietly funneled through him.

That was all. After everything I had endured, their response was a brief apology delivered secondhand.

They hadn't just tried to humiliate me. They had tried to dismantle me. For almost a year they trapped me in a cycle of re-traumatization, dragging me back through chapters of my life I had fought to survive and spent years trying to heal from. They tore through my past with surgical cruelty, twisting every hardship I had overcome, every scar I carried, into a mark against me.

Their focus was never on my ability to practice law or the work I had done to rebuild my life. It was on the wreckage, the pain, the parts of my story I had already fought to overcome.

And all they could offer was a secondhand apology?!

They were never interested in the person I had become. They were fixated on whether they could stomach the idea of someone like me, someone who had endured the worst, standing beside them as an equal.

They probably couldn't, but in the voice of DMX …

Bring it.

I'm right here.

I'm not going anywhere.

This is mine and I don't share.

I'm right here.

CONCLUSION: THE TRUTH OF CHARACTER

"Character is the result of two things: mental attitude and the way we spend our time."

— Elbert Hubbard

Almost two months later, I stood in court for the swearing-in. It was not joy that filled me, it was obligation. My children sat in the gallery, their faces glowing with pride. That part mattered. For them, this day was not just about watching me take an oath.

It was the closing of a chapter they had written with me.

They carried this journey on their shoulders too. My son cooked for me every day, making sure I ate when I was too consumed by study to notice the time. My daughters sat with me, quizzing me on case law and reading through outlines, their laughter breaking through the heaviness. Even my daughter who was away found her way back into the fight, FaceTiming me late into the night so I would not have to study alone. They gave me strength when I had none left. This oath belonged to them as much as it belonged to me.

As I stood there, I knew this moment was not mine alone. It carried the echoes of women who had stood before me, women who faced walls higher than mine and still pressed forward.

Charlotte E. Ray hid her gender under the initials "C.E." just to study law. She passed the bar in 1872, only to be locked out by firms and clients who refused to see her worth. She was not erased though. Her presence left cracks in the walls that were meant to keep her out, cracks wide enough for women like me to push through.

Belva Lockwood wrote, petitioned, fought, and finally forced Congress to admit her to the Supreme Court bar. They called her defiant. They told her no. She answered with persistence until the no turned into silence. And when silence was not enough, she ran for President of the United States. She stepped into rooms never meant for her and refused to leave.

That is what this oath meant to me. Not approval. Not celebration. It was something that already belonged to me. Something I had earned. Something that was mine, just as Charlotte Ray's law degree was hers even when they refused to hire her, just as Belva Lockwood's place before the Supreme Court was hers even when they tried to deny it.

There was no more denying me. As I raised my hand and repeated after the Justices, I felt a surge of pride. Not just for myself, but for my children who had walked every step of this journey with me, and for the people I would stand beside in the fight for justice.

If you have ever felt shut out, unheard, overlooked, silenced, accused, dismissed, doubted, abused, or reduced to your past, let this be your reminder: You do not need their permission. You do not need their approval. You did not come this far to only come this far. Keep walking forward. Keep stepping into the spaces they said were not for you. Keep claiming what is already yours.

The world does not get to decide if you belong. You do.

ABOUT THE AUTHOR

Marla Matrice Murphy is an attorney, writer, and mother of five. She also proudly identifies as Tee Tee to her daughter's six-year-old son, Tiny Tot, a title she considers just as important as any other. She knows people sometimes make choices they believe are right, whether out of love, desperation, inexperience, or survival. Those choices may shape a moment, but they do not tell the whole story. Her own choices, with their risks and consequences, became the foundation for the work she does today.

Marla Matrice founded Surviving Character and Fitness, a consulting practice that guides aspiring attorneys through the bar admissions process with honesty and hard-earned insight. She also founded No Promises Incorporated, a nonprofit that provides resources to families facing the foster care system, work rooted in her belief that no family should have to face that fight alone.

Beyond law and advocacy, Marla Matrice is determined to pursue her dream of becoming an actress. For her, no single decision marks the end of a story. Some choices close doors, some leave you trapped longer than you ever planned, but none of them stop the story from moving forward.

This memoir is Marla Matrice's first published book. It will not be her last.

To learn more about the author, visit:

www.SurvivingCharacterAndFitness.com
or
www.NoPromisesIncorporated.com